PERL TO PYTHON MIGRATION

PERL TO PYTHON MIGRATION
MARTIN C. BROWN

Addison-Wesley

An imprint of PEARSON EDUCATION
Boston ■ San Francisco ■ New York ■ Toronto ■ Montreal ■
London ■ Munich ■ Paris ■ Madrid ■ Cape Town ■ Sydney ■
Tokyo ■ Singapore ■ Mexico City

PEARSON EDUCATION LIMITED

Head Office:
Edinburgh Gate
Harlow CM20 2JE
Tel: +44 (0)1279 623623
Fax: +44 (0)1279 431059

London Office:
128 Long Acre
London WC2E 9AN
Tel: +44 (0)20 7447 2000
Fax: +44 (0)20 7240 5771

Websites: www.informit.com and www.aw.com/cseng

First published in Great Britain in 2002

© Martin Brown 2002

The right of Martin Brown to be identified as Author of this Work has been
asserted by him in accordance with the Copyright, Designs and Patents Act 1988.

ISBN 0 201 73488 5

British Library Cataloguing in Publication Data
A CIP catalogue record for this book can be obtained from the British Library

Library of Congress Cataloging-in-Publication Data
Applied for.

The programs in this book have been included for their instuctional value. The Publisher does not offer
any warranties or representations in respect of their fitness for a particular purpose, nor does the
Publisher accept any liability for any loss or damage arising from their use.

Many of the designations used by manufacturers and sellers to distinguish their products are
claimed as trademarks. Pearson Education Limited has made every attempt to supply trademark
information about manufacturers and their products mentioned in this book.

10 9 8 7 6 5 4 3 2 1

Typeset by Pantek Arts Ltd, Maidstone, Kent
Printed and bound in Great Britain by Biddles Ltd of Guildford and King's Lynn

The publishers' policy is to use paper manufactured from sustainable forests.

To Darcy and Leon, two kittens who still can't type, but do find work in the office as over-efficient paper shredders.

CONTENTS

ACKNOWLEDGMENTS

First of all, as always, I'd like to thank my wife. Despite all my rants and complaints, she still stands by me and tells me that what I'm doing is worthwhile, and keeps poking me to get those chapters written!

Next, I'd like to thank the people at Pearson Education for making this book possible. Special thanks should go to Viki Williams, who offered the book in the first place and continued to believe in me even when things weren't going according to plan. Thanks also to Karen Sellwood and Katherin Ekstrom.

For technical input, thanks to my tech editor, (Matthias Neeracher), the guys on Cix (especially Nik, DJ, and Paul) and a myriad of people on the Internet.com sites who gave me info, encouragement and corrections when working on the articles that preceded this book.

Finally, thanks to, the inventor of Python for his continued work on a language that just begs to get used more.

If there's anybody I've forgotten to acknowledge, I apologize unreservedly in advance now. I have done my best to check and verify all sources and contact all parties involved, but it's perfectly possible I made a mistake.

INTRODUCTION

As a long time Perl and Python programmer, I'm constantly finding myself using Perl constructs in Python or Python constructs in Perl. Worse, I can suddenly find myself trying to use a feature or system in a Python program that just doesn't exist, or does and works differently. What I needed was some sort of cross reference.

After talking to other programmers and developers it became apparent that a number of people were "jumping ship" from Perl to Python. Some with varying levels of success. The reasons for using Python in preference to Perl were different for each person, but there were some common themes:

▶ **Python is object-oriented**. Although Perl has object orientation facilities they are not integrated into the system. In Python everything is an object or class – even the base data types are objects and have their own methods and attributes. This makes Python a great language to use in situations where you are working on applications that use object orientation as a core technology.

▶ **Python is easy to use**. Python has a very clean and structured layout, and it's very easy to follow what's going on. Perl can frequently look like line noise, and particularly for new programmers this becomes a problem as they try to understand why their program works.

▶ **Python does what you tell it to**. Perl suffers from a severe case of semi-intelligence. Statements and expressions in Perl have all sorts of rules, exceptions to those rules, and other artefacts that can make it difficult to follow what is going on. Just think about what happens when you call a function, was it called in list or scalar context?, what arguments did it have?, how do I get them back? These are regular questions when programming with Perl.

▶ **Python is cross-platform compatible**. Perl is also cross-platform compatible, for certain values of compatible. Because of Perl's Unix roots – it is very much a Unix language – use Perl under Windows or MacOS and a large proportion of the built-in functions become obsolete. Python's functionality is supported by external modules, many of which use the correct version according to their platform whilst retaining the same API.

These aren't really hard and fast reasons for why you should make the jump to Python, but they are compelling reasons for why Python is at least worth a look.

In this book that's exactly what we try to do – show you how you can make the move from Perl to Python. Many of the basics are the same, and despite a change of language, you're unlikely to need to change the algorithms you are already using.

For the more advanced programmer, or, like me, the programmer who has to use both languages most days, the book should also work as a handy cross reference to allow you to look up Perl and Python statements and functions, and find out what you should use in both languages.

WHO IS THE BOOK FOR?

Anybody who has used Perl and who wants or needs to learn Python will find this book useful. The book gives a full guide on the basics of programming in Python from the perspective of a Perl programmer. Right from the basics of line and program structure all the way up to object-orientation and using external modules.

You don't need to be an expert Perl programmer , you just need to be able to understand the basics. I've tried to make the text as easy to read and follow as possible. However, on occasion things get technical, and to get the best out of the book you should at least know how to use and create your own functions, extension modules and classes and objects.

Without trying to give you the plot before you've read the book, if you know how to work with references, classes and objects in Perl, then your migration to Python is already 50% there!

HOW TO USE THIS BOOK

The book is split into three main sections. The first section gives you an introduction to Python, including information on the basic mechanics of the language and information on who and where it is used.

Section 2 concentrates on the fundamentals of the language from the basics of expressions and statements through to comparing Python's object types with Perl variables. We'll also look at creating functions, error handling, and extending Python with modules and classes.

The last section concentrates on applying Python in real situations compared to the equivalent Perl process, function or module. For example, Chapter 8 looks at Python's built-in functions and their Perl equivalents, whilst Chapter 10 looks at manipulating data and regular expressions.

There are also two appendices at the back of the book. Appendix A provides a handy guide to getting more information about Python, including other books, websites, newsgroups, mailing lists and details on how to get the Python documentation to help you with your programming. Appendix B is a quick reference – it lists every Perl token, variable or function and provides you with the Python alternative. Where possible, it will also direct you straight to the page elsewhere in the book where you can find more information on the Python alternative.

If you are completely new to Python but know Perl then read Sections 1 and 2 first. If you've played with Python but never used it in anger, then start with Section 2. Finally if you know Python and just want quick reference information then use Appendix B to look up the Perl fragment you are looking for, or go straight to the suitable chapters in sections 2 and 3.

If you don't know Perl, then this book will not be a lot of help. Try reading Perl: The Complete Reference 2nd Edition (Osborne/McGraw-Hill, 2001) or Learning Perl, 2nd Edition (O'Reilly, 1997).

CHAPTER BREAKDOWN

There are fourteen chapters and two appendices in the book. Throughout the book examples of a Perl expression or statement are given, along with the equivalent Python version and information on why the changes and modifications are required. The rough content of each chapter is as follows:

Chapter 1, Introduction – An overview of Python covering information on it's history and who uses the language.

Chapter 2, Executing Python Programs – Python is much more of an interactive language, so before we look at the specifics of Perl and Python programs, we'll look at how to use and execute Python programs.

Chapter 3, Python Overview – Our first look at how Perl and Python differ from an overall structure and approach perspective.

Chapter 4, Components of a Python Program – Details the statements, data types and operators supported by Python and how they relate to their Perl equivalents.

Chapter 5, Functions – How to create and use Python functions and to migrate your Perl functions and argument handling into Python.

Chapter 6, Exceptions and Error Trapping – The mechanics of Python's exception system which is used throughout the language as a method for highlighting errors, right from parsing the source code through to creating and raising your own exceptions to indicate errors.

Chapter 7, Modules, Classes, and Object Orientation – Information on how to extend your Python applications with modules and classes, and how these relate to the Perl module and class structure.

Chapter 8, Built-in Functions – Quick guide to the functions that Python supports in the native interpreter.

Chapter 9, Interfacing with the Operating System – Details on how to communicate with the operating system, including information on getting command-line arguments, determining your environment and communicating with and starting new processes.

Chapter 10, Data Manipulation – How to manipulate numbers, strings, and work with regular expressions in Python.

Chapter 11, File Manipulation – File processing and management, from reading and writing to files through to managing directories, file permissions and controlling access.

Chapter 12, Communicating Over a Network – Details the processes behind communicating with network services, both from the perspective of a client and a server.

Chapter 13, Web Development – A quick guide to programming for the web under Python.

Chapter 14, GUI Development with Tk – Information on how to migrate your user interfaces from Perl/Tk to Python's Tkinter system.

Appendix A, Python Resources – A guide to the books, mailing lists, websites and online documentation available for information on Python.

Appendix B, Perl to Python Quick Reference – A cross reference that lists all the Perl tokens, variables and functions used in Perl and the corresponding Python equivalent.

CONVENTIONS USED IN THIS BOOK

All Perl keywords are highlighted in **bold**, but functions are listed without parentheses. This is because the C functions on which the Perl versions may be based are shown like **this**().

```
Examples and code are displayed using a fixed-width
font.
```

Function descriptions are formatted using the same fixed-width font.

Note: notes are formatted like this and include additional information about a particular topic. You'll also find similarly formatted "Warnings," which highlight possible dangerous tools or tricks to watch out for when programming.

CONTACTING THE AUTHOR

I always welcome comments and suggestions on my work. The best way to contact me is via e-mail. You can use either books@mcwords.com. Alternatively, visit my website, http://www.mcwords.com, which contains resources and updated information about the scripts and contents of this book. You can find the homepage for this book at http://www.mcwords.com/projects/books/p2py/.

>> SECTION 1
INTRODUCTION TO PYTHON

1 INTRODUCTION

Perl is probably one of the best known languages on the web. Although to many it takes second place to Visual Basic or C/C++, Perl still has a place in history as one of the most prolific languages on the web.

The reason for its popularity is that it's very quick to program and execute, easy to use, and generally easy to learn. It can even be a lot of fun. However, Perl owes a lot of its abilities and its functionality to older programs like **sed** and **awk** and as such has a number of quirks; sometimes they work in your favor, and sometimes they don't.

Python, on the other hand, is a relatively new language (in fact it's only a few years younger than Perl, but in computing terms that's almost a lifetime!). Developed almost exclusively by Guido van Rossum, Python takes a slightly different approach to the problems of program development.

Python is completely object-oriented, almost every item you use in Python is either an object (even the base variable types), or a method that operates on those objects. Also in comparison to Perl, which relies heavily on a suite of built-in functions with the occasional dip into an external library, Python, on its own, is almost completely dumb. Although Python supports basic operations on the base data types, and some statements and utility functions such as **print**, all of the main functionality used in Perl is supported in an external module. Python uses external modules covering everything from the basics of accessing the environment and cooperating with the operating system through to the complexities of network and web programming.

Rather than listing the specific differences between the two languages, we'll instead start with a quick look at Perl, its history, and working methods. Then we'll take a closer look at Python, what it can do, who uses it, and how this relates to some of the systems in Perl.

Before we go any further, we should probably explain about names. Perl stands for Practical Extraction and Reporting Language (or one of a number of similar alternatives, including my favorite Pathalogically Eclectic Rubbish Lister). Python is not an acronym, it is named after the comedy group Monty Python, best known for the talents of John Cleese, Eric Idle, *et al,* and such films as *Life of Brian* and *The Holy Grail.*

PERL BACKGROUND

Perl was originally developed by Larry Wall as the Practical Extraction and Reporting Language, a system design to read, extract, process, collate, and summarize information from the logs and other data files. As such, Perl has become known as an excellent general tool for processing data – from the simple collection and formatting of information from text files, to the generation and processing of HTML and web forms.

Originally developed on the Unix platform, Perl borrows much of its abilities from some of the standard Unix tools developed for Unix, including **sed**, **gawk**, **split**, and the Bourne, Korn and C shells. The semantics of the language therefore allow you to take in data, split it up, execute regular expressions, and reconstitute the information without the need of any external modules. By supporting such a large set of internal functions it makes the base language very powerful.

Perl is in fact one of the most functionally rich languages available. Although there has been a move to replace the built-in functions with external, mostly object based, modules, Perl still includes those built-in functions for file access, networking, interprocess communication, and interfacing to some of the core Unix systems.

Although it was not originally part of Perl's core language, Perl does support object-oriented programming. The object system is an optional rather than compulsory part of the language. However, large portions of the internal function set and the standard Perl library have been modified to use objects and classes over the traditional function and variable system. Although only the DBM functions have been formally replaced with an external module, many other systems including IPC (Inter Process Communication), networking, and file handling now have a module alternative to the internal systems.

Over the years, Perl has also gained a dedicated and significant amount of support from the Internet community, largely driven by Perl's use in the world of web forms and dynamic content. Amongst other things, this has led to an enormous library of modules on CPAN (the Comprehensive Perl Archive Network) and extensions providing everything from XML parsing to sound generation.

With this complex mix of built-in function support and additional modules Perl is now considered much more of a general purpose programming language and is therefore used for everything from database and systems management, to network and application development. Despite its general-purpose outlook, Perl has played its own small part in both the development and continued existence of the Internet and the current crop of dynamic websites and it's now hard to imagine a Web without Perl.

Despite its Unix roots, Perl is now a strong force on Windows systems, and has a dedicated following amongst Mac users. At the beginning of 2001 Apple released Mac OS X and Perl is a standard component of the new operating system. Mac OS X is Unix-based, but that doesn't mean that development of the MacPerl versions has halted. The reverse has happened – at the beginning of 2001 MacPerl used a four-year-old version of the core Perl language, but by March MacPerl had been updated to use the core Perl 5.6 sources.

Despite these changes, support across the three main platforms is not completely compatible. Ignoring OS differences – neither Windows nor Mac OS support many of the Unix-specific functions in Perl – support for certain extension modules is also limited. For example, the Tk interface library, libnet and LWP modules are supported across Unix and Windows. But Tk, despite being available for Mac OS, is not supported under MacPerl.

PYTHON BACKGROUND

Python's original development was somewhat different. From its inception Python was designed as an object-oriented language. The basic data types, which closely mirror Perl's in most respects, are all objects. The reliance on objects means that mentally, even for basic operations, you need to think not in terms of functions and operators, but methods instead. As a quick example, to get the keys from a hash in Perl you use:

```
@keys = keys %hash;
```

but in Python (where hashes are called dictionaries) we do:

```
keys = dict.keys
```

Aside from talking to files (which Python treats as objects, and therefore has its own sequence of methods), all other operations, including regular expressions, network access, and communication with the operating system, are provided through a series of external modules. These all come as part of the standard Python library – you don't need to separately download these elements. In addition to the "basic" modules others in the standard library include modules for parsing XML, CGI, and network programming.

This reliance on modules also requires a slight change in the way you program. To perform a regular expression match – something we can do inline in Perl – you need to load an external module. On the face of it, this seems like a backwards step, but in reality it makes Python much more powerful in many ways. For example, we can choose which modules we need, making the Python interpreter very lightweight, and the facilities offered by Python can be updated without requiring changes to the interpreter itself.

Although Python has been a relatively low-key language, it still has its fans. Python supports arbitrarily long integers (there is no practical limit to the number of digits) and complex numbers natively which makes it a great alternative to Fortran for complex mathematical programming. Python therefore has a long history of being used by universities and research establishments to help with their computations – even NASA use it!

However, don't think that Python is in any way limited or pigeonholed in terms of what it can be used to develop. Python has a strong following in the web and Internet arenas, where products like Zope (Z-Objects Publishing Environment), Mailman (an integrated mailing list manager), and Jython (formerly JPython, a Python interpreter written entirely in Java) demonstrate its flexibility. More recently Python has become a strong contender for XML development, as Python 2.0 contained a completely rewritten set of XML modules.

One final point worth noting is that Python is cross-platform and develop ment is controlled and developed for all the major platforms by the core Python team. You can take a script from Unix, give it to Python on a Mac and have the script execute without any changes. You can even run Tk-based GUI applications on all three platforms with very few differences between each implementation. Much of the cross platform flexibility comes from the use of external, rather than internal functions for supporting a particular feature. Rather than having to modify the internal code to introduce a platform-specific facility, they can just modify the module supporting the facility.

MORE ABOUT PYTHON

Now we know about the basics of Perl and Python, and some of the differences between the two, it's worth taking a closer look at some of the specifics of the Python language.

Python is portable

Python is supported on a huge range of platforms and like Perl is open source so you can read the source and compile it for yourself. Python comes in both source and precompiled formats for Unix, Windows, and MacOS and the latter platforms include the Tk libraries as standard. For all other platforms Python is available as source code which you compile yourself.

In addition to the native cross-platform ability, Python also supports some platform native extensions to help ease the process or bridge gaps with other languages and environments. For example, the SunOS/Solaris implementation includes a driver for Sun audio devices, and the SGI version comes with tools for interfacing to the audio and video capabilities (including OpenGL) built into SGI workstations. The Windows Python interpreter comes with toolkits to interface to the Visual C++ libraries and the Windows audio drivers. You can even communicate with COM (Common Object Method) objects to allow you to control Windows application such as Word and Outlook.

Python is powerful

There is very little you cannot do with Python. The core of the language is very small, but it provides enough of the basic building blocks to allow you to design most applications. Furthermore, because the language can be extended using C, C++, and even Java in certain circumstances, you should be able to develop any kind of program. The Python interpreter comes with a substantial library of additional modules that extend the abilities of the language to allow network communication, text processing, and regular expression matching.

Although Python's main push is in hiding much of the low level complexity from the programmer, it also supports the necessary hooks, extensions, and functions to allow low level access to certain areas of the operating system. By supporting both the high-level and low-level functionality Python can sit at the same level as C, or the same level as Visual Basic, as well as all the other levels inbetween.

Making a comparison with Perl is more difficult. Under Unix, Perl can sit at a lower level, closer to the operating system than Python, but if you look across all of the platforms then Python probably sits slightly higher than Perl. Python does its best to protect you from, rather than provide access to, the underlying operating system.

Python is extensible

Python and Perl are both written in C (with some extensions written in C++) and both provide the necessary conduits for extending and embedding the languages with more C/C++ code. Python also enables us, through Jython, to communicate and use Java objects, and for Java to use Python objects, making Python a great tool for browser-based UI development.

Python's main focus is a tool for rapid application development. It's not uncommon for people to test an idea in Python and migrate to C or C++. For most people though, Python handles and supports everything they need.

Python is easy

Although there are some mental changes to be made when programming with Python compared to Perl, on the whole Python is easier read. Perl has a habit of looking like line noise even to experienced programmers, whereas Python has a much simpler look. There are also lots of "quick tricks" in Perl that can ultimately confuse some programmers, and Perl often makes assumptions about what you want to do, rather than just failing because it doesn't understand what you are trying to do.

Python, on the other hand, has a correct way for everything, and will tell you if something is not right. Also, because of its object-based development, once you understand the principles for one object or class, you can apply the same rules and systems to a related object. For example, strings in Python are actually sequences of individual characters – once you understand how to access, slice and interpolate information into a string, the same rules apply to other sequence objects, including lists, tuples, and dictionaries (hashes).

WHAT IS IT GOOD FOR?

Unsurprisingly, with such wide support and extensive features, Python is very effective for a large number of tasks. Here's a quick list of the some of the more common uses of the Python language.

Mathematics

Python supports an extension called NumPy that provides interfaces to many standard mathematical libraries. The Python language also supports unlimited precision. If you want to add two 100-digit numbers together, you can do so without requiring an external or third party extension.

Text processing

Python can split, separate, summarize, and report on any data. It comes with modules that separate out the elements of a log file line, you can then use the built-in data types to record and summarize the information before writing it all out again. In addition, Python comes with regular expression libraries that allow you to use the same expressions as **emacs**, Perl, and many other utilities. This means that Python can do all of the things that other languages can do – one programmer even produced a complex SGML processing tool using Python to handle a large documentation project.

Rapid application development

Because Python is so straightforward to program, we can use Python to develop applications very quickly. The extensive module library that comes with Python provides direct interfaces into many of the protocols, tools, and libraries that you would otherwise have to develop.

Also, because Python natively supports Tk you can do more than just an interface example. It is not uncommon for many people to develop the entire application in Python in hours instead of the days it would take using C/C++. I've written a cross platform, Tk-based database query tool in less than a day, something that would have taken me two or three days with Perl, and a week or more in C.

Cross-platform development

We already know that Python supports a wide range of platforms in a completely neutral format. You can use Python to develop an application to be deployed across a network that uses a variety of different platforms. You can also use Python where you want to be sure that future implementations of your system are going to work. Many companies start with a specific platform and then move to a different platform as the performance starts to suffer. Using Python you will never need to re-write your software as you move between platforms.

Of course, you can also look at Python as an alternative when supplying software to end-users. Instead of developing three separate applications you only have to develop it once, saving significant time and money.

System utilities

Although much of the ethos with Python is to hide you from the low-level parts of the operating system, the tools and extensions are there if you do want to access the lowest levels. Because Python has access to the same set of functions as the operating system you can use it to duplicate and extend the functionality of the operating system, whilst still retaining all of the compatibility and interface issues that we already know Python supports.

Internet programming

Python comes with a standard set of modules to allow you to communicate over the standard network sockets both at a basic level, and at a protocol level. If you want to read e-mail from a POP server, for example, Python already comes with the library module to enable you to do that. In addition, Python also supports XML, HTML and CGI libraries so you can parse user input and produce top-quality formatted output via a web server.

You can even compile a module for Apache, the Unix and Windows web server that embeds the Python interpreter (in a similar fashion to mod_perl). This means that when you want to execute a Python script, it does not need to be loaded separately each time, providing the maximum possible performance from your CGI scripts.

Also Zope, which provides a content management and web publishing environment, and mailman, which provides mailing list functionality, show just how far you can go with Python programs.

Database programming

There are a myriad of extension modules that interface to all of the common database systems, from Oracle to Informix and free systems such as mySQL and PostgreSQL. If you don't have access to one of the free or commercial database systems, you can use Gadfly which provides a complete SQL environment written entirely in Python – no external modules or extensions are required. Because Python has strong text and data handling abilities we can use Python to interface between databases, and to act as a better summary and report tool than many of the interfaces that come with the database systems themselves. Furthermore, because Python supports a number of different systems instead of only one, we can use the same interface with any database. We can even use Tk to build the front end, and then put it on any of the supported platforms – you get an instant cross-platform, database-independent query tool!

Everything else

Python can be used for anything – there are literally no limits to what the language can do. By supporting a small core set of functions, data types and abilities Python provides an excellent base on which to build. Because we can extend the functionality with C and C++ we get the best of both worlds – unlimited and unfettered expansion to do whatever we want, but in a structured and manageable format.

WHAT ISN'T IT GOOD FOR?

It is very difficult to give a precise list of the problems that Python is unable to solve. Python provides most of its functionality in the extension modules that are supplied, and this shows how easy it is to add functionality to the language. If you can't do what you want to within Python, then it's just as easy to write a C or C++ extension to the job for you instead.

Some people criticize Python, not because it's not capable of doing a particular task, but because they don't understand *how* to do a particular task. One of the most common complaints is related to Python's apparent lack of regular expression support – when in fact there are two modules (**re** and the older **regex**) that enable you to handle regular expressions – the former even supports the same syntax as that used in Perl. Regular expression handling may not be built into the language, but it is still possible.

One area that neither Perl nor Python are good at is real-time or high performance graphics programming, for example that used in computer games.

The advantage of Python over a language such as Perl or Rebol is that the core of the language is very small. Python actually operates at a level closer to Java than one of the more traditional scripting languages. This improves the execution time – there's less code to be loaded each time the script is run – and also helps make the rest of the language more flexible.

Once you are familiar with the minimalist style of programming that Python supports, you'll find that you still have all the power, but without a lot of the extra baggage. And your code is easy to read whenever you look at it.

WHO USES IT?

Python is used by a large number of people for solving all sorts of tasks. Most of these are not known about, or at least not publicised, purely because the companies concerned do not normally divulge this sort of information. However, there are some larger companies that use Python within a commercial environment, and who are proud to announce and even celebrate the fact.

▶ Red Hat (www.redhat.com) uses Python in combination with Tk to provide a visual interface for configuring and managing the operating system called **linuxconf**. The system gives you complete control over all aspects of the Linux operating system, and automatically updates the configuration for you.

▶ Infoseek (www.infoseek.com) uses Python within certain parts of its public search engines. Python is also used for customizing the Infoseek software that can be downloaded from the site for use on end-users' machines.

▶ NASA (www.nasa.gov) uses Python in a number of different areas. The most significant is probably within the mission control center where Python is used in certain parts of the system for planning missions. Other uses relate to the strong numerical abilities of Python that make it ideal for calculating the location of celestial objects and also for plotting the paths taken by satellites.

▶ Industrial Light and Magic (www.ilm.com) famous for doing the special effects on films such as Star Wars, The Abyss, Star Trek, and Indiana Jones uses Python in the sequence and production management of commercial-grade animation. In fact, if you visit the web site you'll see that they have a number of vacancies for Python programmers!

2

EXECUTING PYTHON PROGRAMS

Python supports the same basic modes of script execution as Perl, from running the script explicitly through the Python interpreter to putting the script into a file and having the operating system automatically run the interpreter for us. We can also embed the Python interpreter into other programs – this is not something that we'll be covering in detail in this book, but be aware that there is no channel supported by Perl that isn't also available in Python.

Python does however offer one mode that isn't naturally within Perl – interactive mode. Within interactive mode you execute arbitrary Python statements and even start to write and execute a Python script, and it makes a great way both of demonstrating Python's abilities, and as a quick way for testing a particular statement or sequence. The closest equivalent in Perl is the interactive component of the Perl debugger.

The Perl debugger uses the **eval** function to evaluate each line and return the result. In comparison, the Python interactive mode is a single instance of the interpreter – you are effectively supplying new source lines direct to a single interpreter instead of individually executing each line. In practice this makes little difference to the execution of the lines that you type, but the interactive interface to the Python interpreter is a useful tool that can be used to check statements quickly.

We'll look at all the execution methods, including any platform peculiarities in this chapter.

INTERACTIVELY

The Python interpreter works slightly differently to many other interpreters in that you can enter Python statements directly into the interpreter, rather than having to create a file and then execute. Interactive mode is very useful when you want to quickly try a particular statement or for very short applications – it's possible for example to import a module and check your e-mail from within Python's interactive mode.

To start interactive mode, just load the Python interpreter. Under Unix, you do this by supplying the name of the Python interpreter at the command line:

```
$ python
Python 2.0 (#4, Dec 16 2000, 07:30:29)
[GCC 2.95.2 19991024 (release)] on sunos5
Type "copyright", "credits" or "license" for more
information.
>>>
```

When you enter a statement, the interpreter automatically compiles and executes the statement – you don't have to go through the separate compile stage first. Think of the interactive mode as the equivalent of the shell or command prompt used by **sh**, **ksh** or a DOS window under Windows.

The statements that you enter could just as easily be placed into a file (and for scripts that work with five or more lines it's recommended that you use a file!). Similarly, like the shell, once a statement has been executed you cannot "undo" the statement or it's effects. Unlike many shells, however, you cannot go back to a previous statement and edit it before trying again, there is no command history or editing functionality – although you can edit a line before you press Return.

For example, to assign a value to a variable and then perform a calculation:

```
>>> bytes = 65536
>>> kilobytes = bytes/1023
```

On the second line, I've made a mistake – I meant to divide by 1024. To perform the calculation I'll have to type it all in again:

```
>>> kilobytes = bytes/1024
```

For most situations the chances are that the test statements you'll be entering won't be complex enough for it be a problem – but be aware of both the limitations and the usefulness.

Here's a more complex example, this time using Python to calculate the area of a circle:

```
Python 2.0 (#4, Dec 16 2000, 07:30:29)
[GCC 2.95.2 19991024 (release)] on sunos5
Type "copyright", "credits" or "license" for more
information.
>>> pi = 3.141592654
>>> radius = 4
>>> area = pi*(radius^2)
>>> print 'Area of circle is:',area
Area of circle is: 18.849555924
>>>
```

Don't worry too much about the syntax used in the example above. Chapter 3 should give you a good idea of the main differences before we launch into the specific semantics that Python uses. Just remember that the interactive interface is exactly that, an interactive way of executing Python statements and a way of trying out statements or expressions you are unsure of.

If you want to exit the interactive interpreter press the end-of-file key combination. For most Unix terminals this is Ctrl-D; Windows uses Ctrl-Z. Alternatively, you can import the **sys** module which contains the system **exit** function:

```
$ python
Python 2.0 (#4, Dec 16 2000, 07:30:29)
[GCC 2.95.2 19991024 (release)] on sunos5
Type "copyright", "credits" or "license" for more
information.
>>> import sys
>>> sys.exit()
$
```

Python under Windows

Python is available under Windows both as a package from the PythonLabs team, or as an installer package from ActiveState under the

ActivePython banner. Personally, I use the ActivePython system which you can download from the ActiveState website (see Appendix A).

Once you have installed the Python interpreter you can load and execute Python statements interactively just as you can under Unix:

```
C:\> python
Python 2.0 (#8, Oct 16 2000, 17:27:58) [MSC 32 bit
(Intel)] on win32
Type "copyright", "credits" or "license" for more
information.
>>>
```

You may need to add the directory that contains the Python interpreter to your **%PATH%**. Within Windows 95/98 you will need to add the directory to your **AUTOEXEC.BAT** file, under Windows NT/2000 you need to modify the PATH setting in the System control panel. If you prefer, select the "Command Line" Python interpreter in the Start Menu.

Once you are in the interactive interpreter it works identically to the Unix version, but to exit you need to use the Windows end-of-file key combination, Ctrl-Z.

MacOS

Under MacOS you will need to start the Python IDE application. This opens a simple terminal style window – which is the interactive interface to the Python interpreter. You can see the Python application in action in Fig 2.1.

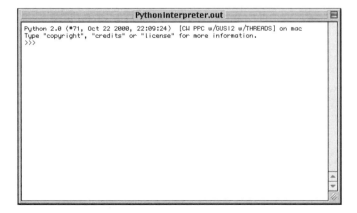

FIG 2.1 Python in action under MacOS

Again, because the same core Python interpreter is used in each case, you can try and execute statements just as you would with the Unix version.

EXECUTION FROM A FILE

Most Python scripts will be executed from a file. Python scripts are written just like Perl with a standard editor – we don't need a special environment or application to create the files. Line termination is significant, since Python relies on the line termination to identify the end of a statement, but Python is flexible enough to support Windows, MacOS, or Unix line endings under the corresponding platforms. However, if you want to exchange the script between platforms you must convert the line endings – you cannot use a Windows text script under MacOS for example.

Unlike Perl, Python doesn't distinguish quite so clearly between a "script" and a "module." All Python source can potentially be used as a module and imported directly into another script. Because of this, Python "scripts" are usually called "modules," just to add to the confusion! In this book we'll try and differentiate between scripts – those files that we write to execute a series of statements – and modules – those files that contain objects, classes, and other entities that we may want to import into a script. We'll look at modules and the reasons for these differences in Chapter 3 and in more detail in Chapter 7.

All Python scripts, modules and source code have the extension of .py. Like .pl, .pm, and other extensions under Perl, these have no significance except as a method of identity for programmers.

As a Unix script

Execution under Unix of an existing Python script requires us to specify the name (and path) to the script as an argument to the Python interpreter:

```
$ python myscript.py
```

Further arguments supplied on the command line are then supplied as arguments to the script itself. For example, we can print out a message using the first argument with this script:

```
import sys
print 'Hello', sys.argv[1]
```

If you save the above into a file called test.py, and then supply the filename as the first argument to the Python interpreter:

```
$ python test.py Martin
Hello Martin
```

we get the name printed out. The **sys** module contains all of the objects required to access system specific information, including as you see here the command line arguments, information about the current instance of the Python interpreter and system limits (integer and float maximum values). We'll be looking at the **sys** module in more detail in Chapter 9.

Because a Python script is just a text file, we can also rely on the operating system and shell to honor the "shebang" line, here showing the default install location:

```
#!/usr/local/bin/python
```

You will also need to change the mode of the file so that it is executable – this will make the Unix shell examine the shebang line to determine what application to use to execute the text script. We can now run the script directly:

```
$ test.py Martin
Hello Martin
```

The initial line tells Unix what application to use to execute the file. In this case, we've specified the location of the Python interpreter directly. A more compatible method, which causes the script to search the value of the **PATH** environment variable is to use the following line instead:

```
#!/usr/bin/env python
```

Make sure you check where the **env** utility is located, otherwise the shell will raise an error. You might find **env** in **/bin**, **/usr/bin**, **/usr/local/bin**, or **/usr/sbin**.

Command-line Options

Whichever method you decide to use when executing a Python script, there may be times when you want to supply additional command line switches to the Python interpreter. All of the command line arguments supported by Python control the execution of the script, rather than supporting extended functionality such as that offered by Perl.

For scripts manually executed by the Python interpreter you must supply those options before you supply the script name. For example, to cause the interpreter to go into interactive mode after the script has been executed you would need to specify:

```
$ python -i sample.py
```

Or, within the "shebang" line:

```
#!/usr/local/bin/python -i
```

The full list of command line options and environment variables is shown in Table 2.1.

Where a variable is available for configuring an option, its existence and value are used to determine whether the option is set. You'll need to both set the variable and export it. For example, in the Bourne shell you would do the following:

```
$ set PYTHONINSPECT = 0
$ export PYTHONINSPECT
$ sample.py
Hello World!
```

To enable a particular option you will need to assign the variable a value:

```
$ export set PYTHONINSPECT = 1
$ sample.py
Hello World!
>>>
```

Under the C shell, use:

```
$ setenv PYTHONINSPECT 1
$ sample.py
```

Or under all shells, use **env** for a portable way to set the value:

```
$ env PYTHONINSPECT = 1 sample.py
```

In addition, Python supports the environment variables shown in Table 2.2.

TABLE 2.1 Python command line options

Option	Environment variable	Description
D	PYTHONDEBUG	Generates debug information from the interpreter after the script has been compiled
-I	PYTHONINSPECT	Causes the interpreter to go into interactive mode after the script has been executed
-O	PYTHONOPTIMIZE	Optimize the bytecode generated by the interpreter before it is executed
-OO		Optimize the bytecode and also remove the embedded document strings from the optimized code before it is executed
-S		Does not automatically import the **site.py** module, which contains site specific Python statements, when the interpreter starts
-t		Give warnings when tab-based indentation of the script is inconsistent. See Chapter 3 for details on Python blocks
-tt		Give errors (and stop parsing) when the indentation of the script using tabs is inconsistent
-u	PYTHONUNBUFFERED	Force the standard output and error filehandles to operate unbuffered. If not specified then buffered output is used
-v	PYTHONVERBOSE	Generate information about modules imported by the script when executed
-x		Skip the first line of the source file. Useful when executing a script on a different platform to the source when you want to skip the "shebang" line
-X		Disable the class-based exceptions that are built into the interpreter (see Chapter 6)
-c cmd		**cmd** is used as the script source, instead of a source file
-		Read the source file from the standard input

TABLE 2.2 Python environment variables

Variable	Description
PYTHONSTARTUP	The name of a file to be executed when starting the interpreter in interactive mode
PYTHONPATH	A colon (under Unix) or semicolon (under Windows) separated list of directories to be searched when importing modules. The resulting list is available internally as **sys.path**
PYTHONHOME	The directory in which the core Python libraries can be found. Defaults to **/usr/local/lib/python2.0**. You can also specify an alternative executable prefix by separating the prefix and executable prefix by a colon, i.e.: /usr/local/lib:/usr/local/bin. Under Windows use a semicolon to separate the list

On a Windows host

Within Windows we have two options available – if you want to execute a Python script from the DOS prompt then just supply the name of the file to the application:

```
C:\> python test.py
```

The other alternative is to define the ".py" extension as a file type within Windows Explorer (the *File Types* tab under *Folder Options*). The Python installer does this for you when the interpreter is installed. When you double click on the file within an Explorer window, the Python interpreter is opened and then supplies the file, just as if you'd typed the instruction on the command line.

The only problem with this double-click method is that you cannot supply any arguments on the command line to the script – the script is only interactive if you add the necessary code to request information from the user when the script is started.

One final option eliminates the need to open the command-line prompt at all. If you name the file with a ".pyw" extension then a DOS command prompt is not opened when the script is run, allowing the script to appear just like a normal Windows application. However, in this mode there is no form of interaction unless defined within the script – you'll need to open a console window, or more likely develop a Tk-based interface within the script to allow interaction from the user. We'll look at using Tk to develop interfaces within Python in Chapter 14.

Python under Windows does not support the "shebang" line that is used under Unix to define which options are to be used when running the interpreter. This means that if you want to supply specific options to the interpreter when you run a script, then you will need to embed the call within a batch file. This is actually a limitation of the OS, rather than Python. All of the command line options available under Windows are identical to those under Unix. See Table 2.1 for details.

On a MacOS host

Under MacOS you can drag and drop a text file written using SimpleText or BBEdit on to the Python application in order for the application to execute the script. Double-clicking on the file at this stage will only open the file again within the editor. Note that when the file is executed, the Python application is opened, the script is run, and then the application exits. If you want to display some information to the user you will need to either pause the output by waiting for some input, or delay the normal exit procedure of the program. See the next section, *Configuring Python under MacOS*, for details on how to handle other execution options.

If you want to create a Python application that can just be double-clicked to be executed you need to use the **BuildApplet** application. Drag and drop your Python script onto this application and a new Python "applet" will be built. When you double click on the applet, the Python library will be loaded by the application and then the script will be executed, just as if you had dropped the script onto the Python interpreter.

However, the new applet is not self-contained, and you can't distribute the applet as a Python program to other users – they will only be able to use the applet if they already have Python installed on their machines. Unfortunately another side-effect of this procedure is that if you modify the source script you will need to rebuild the applet to incorporate the changes – the modifications are not automatically applied to the applet as well.

Configuring Python under MacOS

The MacOS does not support environment variables, or command line options. To modify the operation of the interpreter, or a Python Applet you must use the **EditPythonPrefs** application. If you want to modify the main Python application, and thereby any scripts dragged and dropped onto the interpreter, just double click on the application. The first window, as seen in Fig 2.2 enables you to specify the library search path for the Interpreter. You can also specify the "HOME" location for the execution of the interpreter – this information is used when looking for modules to be imported. Modifying this information is analogous to modifying the **PYTHONPATH** and **PYTHONHOME** environment variables under Windows and Unix.

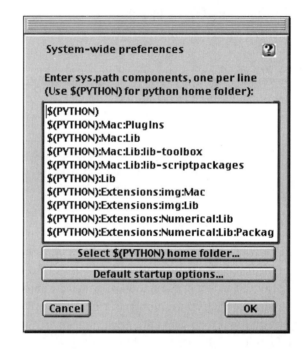

FIG 2.2 Editing the **PATH** options for Python under MacOS

If you click on *Default startup options* you can additionally configure many of the options available to Unix and Windows users, as well as some options specific to the Mac platform. You can see the option window in Fig 2.3.

The options which are identical to the command line versions are shown in Table 2.3.

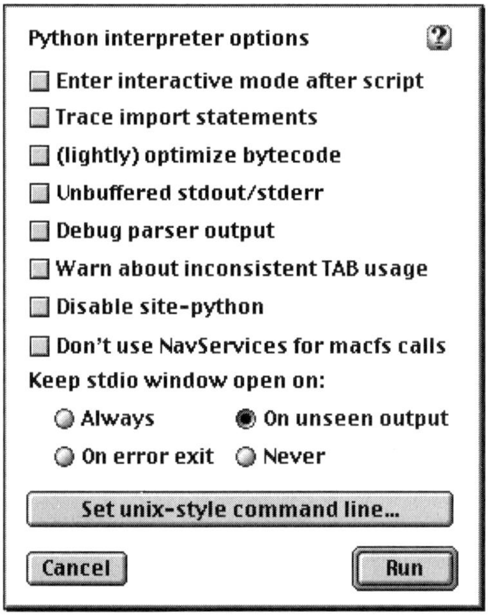

FIG 2.3 Editing other MacOS options

TABLE 2.3 MacOS/command line equivalents

MacOS option	Command line equivalent
Enter Interactive mode after script	-i
Trace import statements	-v
Optimize bytecode	-O
Unbuffered stdout/stderr	-u
Debug parser output	-d
Old-style standard exceptions	-X

Other options under the MacOS version are described in Table 2.4.

TABLE 2.4 MacOS specific options

MacOs option	Description
Keep stdio window open on normal exit	Keeps the "console" window created by the Python application open after the script exits, even if the execution was successful
Keep stdio window open on error exit (default)	Keeps the "console" window created by the Pythonapplication open after the script exits only if there was an error/exception
Default file creator	The four-letter code used as the file creator type when files are generated by a Python script. The creator code is used to define which application opens the file when it is double-clicked. The code "ttxt" refers to TeachText/SimpleText, "MSWD" to Microsoft Word, "R*ch" for BBedit. Note that if you want to use your own code you will need to register the code with Apple before supplying a public application
Default file type	The four-letter code to be used as the file type code for files created by Python scripts. "TEXT" is a normal text file, "bina" is a binary. Others are application/operating system specific
Disable interactive option-setting	If you hold down **Option** when starting the interpreter you are allowed to specify some of these options when Python is first loaded. Setting this option disables this feature
Disable argc/argv emulation	Disable the parsing of AppleEvents
Delay console window until needed	If the application does not require a console window, or does not use one until later in the application, you can avoid displaying an empty window by setting this option

Note that you can also specify these options on individual Python applets (but not scripts) by dragging and dropping the applet onto the **EditPythonPrefs** application.

OTHER METHODS

There are of course methods for executing Python statements. Like the **eval** function within Perl we can execute another Python script from within an existing script using the **execfile** function:

```
>>> script = 'hello.py'
>>> execfile(script)
Hello!!
```

The Python language was written as much more than just a simple interpreter. We can embed the Python interpreter into a C or C++ application, and therefore execute Python statements and even entire modules within the confines of another application. This is too advanced for this manual, so we won't into any detail, but it is another practical and indeed very useful way of executing Python applications.

If you want to embed Python into an application, see the standard documentation set which includes the manual *Extending and embedding the python interpreter* which should contain all the information you need.

3 PYTHON OVERVIEW

Migrating from Perl to Python is not actually as difficult as it first appears. Despite a distinctly different focus on the development of the two languages, they both have similar features and use similar methods and procedures to achieve their goals as all-round scripting languages.

But how can we gain the most benefit form our experience of Perl so that it can be used when we program in Python?

At a very basic level, there are few differences between the general execution and layout of a Python script compared to a Perl one. Statements are executed sequentially using a very similar precedence model to that employed by Perl. We also have access to a very similar set of basic data types – the familiar scalar, array, and hash are all available to us, albeit under different names in some cases.

Python also supports many of the other features used by many Perl programmers like functions (named and anonymous), regular expressions, and a large standard library from which you can pick and choose networking, string handling, and many other extensions.

Aside therefore from understanding the mechanics of Python, most of the tricks that you have learned and used when programming in Perl are still applicable in Python.

So why use Python over Perl?

The answer to that question is less clear cut, but the strongest reasons are probably:

▶ **Object support** – although Perl has support for objects and classes, it's a bolt-on, rather than embedded, part of the language. With Python, every variable you use is an object (all the base data types are object based) and many inherit features from other classes, helping to retain consistency.

▶ **Reduced complexity** – Perl has a huge army of operators, some of which are data type specific, and a similarly large built-in function arsenal. Python uses the same operators for all data types, and relies on external modules for the majority of its functionality.

▶ **Easier code reuse** – in Perl you should create a special module (using the **Exporter** module) to define and export your functions and variables to the outside world, and you must do this if you want to create dynamically loadable classes. In Python any script can be imported and its functions made available to the caller without any special modification of the source.

In this chapter we're going to look at some of the fundamental principles of the two languages starting with Perl's approach to a particular problem and then a brief overview of Python's approach. The aim is to give you a better understanding of the Python language without going into specifics. This should help you to approach the problem of writing Python scripts by thinking of the approach, rather than the specifics.

More detailed information is contained within the rest of the book and will focus on the ways in which you can use and in many cases convert your existing Perl knowledge and scripts to Python.

BASIC STRUCTURE

Both Perl and Python share the same basic rules and layout, although there are some specific differences you need to be aware of. To recap on the major points of operation for Perl:

▶ Scripts are executed sequentially, on a statement by statement basis.

▶ Statements must be terminated by a semicolon, statements can be separated by new lines.

▶ Blocks are delimited by braces.

▶ Functions can be defined before or after you use them.

▶ External modules are imported during the initial stages of execution to allow syntax and error checking (see *The execution model* on p. 34 for more information on the precise execution sequence).

Python's approach

Python follows a similar approach, although it will appear to many Perl programmers as being somewhat ambiguous:

▶ Scripts are executed sequentially, on a statement by statement basis.

▶ Statements are terminated by a new line, statements can be spread over multiple lines but you have to use the \ backslash character to logically join them together into a single statement.

▶ Blocks are started with a colon, and statements in a block share the same indentation.

▶ Functions can be defined before or after you use them.

▶ External modules are imported during the initial stages of execution to allow syntax and error checking (see *The execution model* on p. 34 for more information on the precise execution sequence).

More specific information on the layout and treatment of statements and blocks in comparison to Perl can be found in Chapter 4.

VARIABLES, DATA, AND OBJECTS

Within Perl we have a number of distinct variable types, starting with the basic scalar and moving up through the array of scalars (or just simply an array) to the hash (or associative array of scalars). There are some other basic types such as the filehandle (which has now largely been replaced by **IO::Handle**) and the all encompassing typeglob.

Objects are created by using a reference to one of the base data types and then using the **bless** function to associate the reference with a particular package (and therefore by association into a particular class).

Perl uses a large number of operators and functions in order to support the base data types. Many of these are compatible with the different base types, but operations are duplicated because Perl automatically converts between different types. This can lead to some confusion and occasional oddities when working with different values. Some examples of these differences are:

▶ To extract individual characters or sequences from a string we have to use **substr** or regular expressions. To extract information from an array we can name elements by number or use slices.

▶ Because Perl automatically converts between numbers and strings (when appropriate) we need two different operators to tell Perl when to compare numerical values and when to compare strings. For example, when we expect to compare numerical data we use the symbolic operators such as > and <=>, but for strings we use **gt** and **cmp**.

▶ Functions react and work differently according to the "context" in which they are used.

There are also other minor annoyances, such as the inability to use **sort** on scalars (without splitting and recombining with **split** and **join**).

Python's approach

Python is very different. All of Python's data types are objects themselves, so they have a set of methods with which you can modify or manipulate the objects, as well as a series of common operators which can be used with all of the objects to perform comparisons and modifications (addition, concatenation, and so forth).

Python sticks to some very basic principles:

▶ Objects share common attributes and abilities, so you can use the same methods and syntax on different object types. We can, for example, access individual characters within a string in the same manner as we can extract individual elements from an array, tuple, or hash.

▶ Objects use the same operators – we can add numbers, strings, and arrays together using the + operator, eliminating about half of the operators supported in Perl, and removing the need to make specific.

▶ Strings, arrays, and tuples (an immutable array) belong to the same group, the sequences, and share many of the same methods. For example, we can sort elements in a string or array using the same method and syntax.

▶ Comparison operators compare objects so we can compare numbers, strings, arrays, tuples, and hashes without having to predetermine the data they contain, or use loops to compare items individually.

See Chapter 4 for more information on the Python data types and operators and how to translate typical Perl statements into their Python equivalents.

STATEMENTS AND EXPRESSIONS

There's not really much to compare between the two languages. Most expressions rely on the use of operators, a topic we've already covered, and most of the semantics surrounding the evaluation of expressions remains the same. We also have access to the same loops and control statements.

We'll be covering statements in more detail in Chapter 4.

BUILT-IN FUNCTIONS

Perl has one of the largest sets of built-in functions of any language. Although this means that you can do a lot internally with Perl without ever requiring an external module. Because the modules provide the functionality it makes changing these internal interfaces or disabling them according to the current platform significantly easier. Many of the functions are Unix-specific and in recent years moves have been made to support the built-in operations with an alternative class-based module from the standard Perl library. For example, many people now use **IO::Socket** over the built-in network socket handling functions, and **IO::Handle** provides a much better interface for communicating with external data sources, including files and network sockets. The only functions on which the move has been actively enforced is the **dbmopen()** and **dbmclose()** functions which are now deprecated in favor of the **tie** function and supporting **DBM_File**, **GDBM_File**, and other classes.

Python's approach

Python has very few built-in functions, and most of those that do exist are there for the programmer to use to control or determine the state of the script or module during execution, rather than used within the script for performing a specific task. For example, it's impossible within Python to communicate over a network without first importing a module to support the operation.

At an even simpler level, you can't even access the system environment variables (available within the **%ENV** variable in Perl) without importing the **os** module.

The reasons behind these apparent limitations are simple:

▶ Reduces the role of the Python executable to interpretation, compilation, and execution. This results in a more highly optimized and debugged compiler code, a smaller overall footprint for the interpreter, and better management of resources.

▶ Places the compatibility of functions and abilities on multiple operating systems into the hands of the modules, which can be easily controlled and modified on a per OS basis. In Perl a significant proportion of the built-in functions are Unix specific which has meant that non-Unix OS-specific functions are supported by external modules. In Python, everything OS-specific, Unix or otherwise, is handled by an external module.

▶ Reduces complexity of the core language. In Perl 5.6 there are 213 functions or function-like operators in the core language, many of which are Unix-specific and have been replaced or usurped by a module/class-based alternative in the standard Perl library. With Python, you only need to load in the modules and functionality that you need for the program you are writing – if you never accept any command line arguments or access the environment then you can save both execution and parsing time by not importing those modules.

MODULES

In Perl, modules have been the main way to extend code and make the code reusable. They have also become the primary way of supporting object classes and inheritance. However, to create a proper Perl module that supports both entire and selective export of functions and variables you must place the functions or class definitions into a special file and add suitable header information. Without this information it's impossible for Perl to explicitly export entities correctly, or to support the class inheritance system.

Python's approach

In theory every Python script you create has the potential to be a module – unlike Perl, you do not need to explicitly create a Python module, you can import the contents from a file automatically into its namespace ready for you to use. This eliminates the need to create a special file, or include special header information.

THE EXECUTION MODEL

Although not a vital part of your understanding of the differences between Perl and Python, understanding the similarities and differences between the two models of execution is a useful side note.

Perl

Perl's execution model, follows a very simple path. The model assumes you've just run a Perl script from a text file, which with some minor differences applies equally to the methods used for executing embedded scripts (from C/C++), in-line evaluations (through **eval**), and the one line scripts supplied on the command line.

Following the figure the basic execution process for Perl goes like this:

1 Read the source code.

2 Immediately execute any **BEGIN** blocks in the source.

3 Import (and if necessary evaluate and execute) the text from an external module (imported using **use** or **require**) so that it becomes part of the text of the script. Execution only occurs for modules that define **BEGIN** blocks. Modules which export symbols into the caller's namespace create the necessary aliases and symbol table entries at this point.

4 Once all the code required to execute the script has been imported, compile the script into the internal opcode format used by the Perl "virtual machine."

5 Optimize the opcode tree generated in stage 5, reducing statements using a combination of lookahead and constant folding.

6 Follow the opcode tree generated in stage 5 to actually execute the code.

Unfortunately, this execution model implies an overhead during the execution process because the "import," compilation, and execution sequence occurs each time you execute a Perl script. There are of course solutions to this in specific environments – for example the **mod_perl** and PerlEx web server extensions which improve the performance of CGI scripts – but there is no standard method for all scripts.

Python

As already stated, Python is an object-oriented language that relies not on the manipulation of a number of internal data types using built-in functions, but works using a series of external classes and methods in combination with other classes, objects, and methods that you define within your Python script.

Because Python modules are treated as classes, and because of the strict naming system employed to support it, Python can import compiled versions of the modules and classes, rather than import the text used to describe them. This makes the Python execution process:

1 Read the source code.

2 Once all the code required to execute the script has been imported, compile the source script into the machine code format used by the Python virtual machine.

3 Optimize the machine code generated in stage 5, reducing statements using a combination of lookahead and constant folding.

4 Follow the opcode tree generated in stage 5 to actually execute the code.

5 Any **import** statements or class inheritance requirements are handled during the execution process – only those **import** statements which are actually required to be executed are ever honored.

The critical difference is stage 5, which is roughly equivalent to stage 3 in the Perl execution sequence. Python imports modules only when they are requested to be imported. Furthermore, by the time the **import** statements are executed the source script has already been compiled into bytecode. In order to avoid importing and recompiling the entire script Python imports pre-compiled versions of the modules requested. If the modules are not already compiled then they are compiled and imported.

The compiled version is saved, so that next time the module is requested the compiled version can be imported directly.

By using pre-compiled modules we eliminate the slowdown experienced by a complex Perl script. In Perl, if we import 10 or 20 modules their contents will be re-parsed and compiled every time the script is called, even though it's unlikely that the module source code has changed since the last time it was executed. Although this seems insignificant, it can increase the execution time considerably, especially on scripts that may be run many times – for example on a web server. The **mod_perl** extension for Apache, or ActiveState's PerlEx extension for Microsoft's IIS web server get round this by retaining the byte compiled versions of an entire script in memory. These are, however, web-only solutions.

Perl does come with a byte compiler (it's part of the Perl compiler system), but it's not used and the system is not enabled or enforced by the interpreter.

>> SECTION 2
LANGUAGE FUNDAMENTALS

4 COMPONENTS OF A PYTHON PROGRAM

There are three basic components to any language – the statement, the variable and the operator. When migrating from Perl to Python many of the operators and principles are actually the same: we can add two numbers together using +, compare two numbers using ==, and print out information to the screen using **print**.

However, there are also some differences – we can also concatenate (add) two strings together using the + operator, compare two objects – irrespective of type – using ==, and **print** is a statement, not a function.

In this chapter we're going to go through the basics of all three elements comparing the Perl versions to their Python equivalents where possible. We'll also look at some of the additional functionality offered by Python and how to convert some aspects of your Perl scripts to Python.

THE BASICS

There are some basic rules that apply to all programming languages, such as how lines are formed, how we introduce comments, and how the core of the language such as statements and expressions are organized.

Line format

Python uses a very simple structure for the individual lines which make up your script. Semicolons, used in Perl to terminate each line, are optional. Instead, Python uses the normal line termination, linefeed and or carriage return to indicate the end of each statement:

```
print "Hello World!"
print "I am a test program"
```

The Python interpreter expects to see the correct line termination according to the platform you are working on – using a Unix-sourced script on a Mac without first translating the carriage returns into linefeed characters will cause the interpreter to fail.

For extra long lines, such as the one below, you have a number of options, depending on the line contents. For strings and quoted text we can simply continue and let the line wrap, but if you introduce a manual line break then the quoted text will also contain a linebreak:

```
print "Hello, I am a test program and I am printing an
extra long line so I can demonstrate how to split me up"
```

For most lines, the easier method is to append a backslash to the end of the line where you want to split it, for example:

```
print "Hello, I am a test program and I am printing \
an extra  long line so I can demonstrate how to split \
me up"
```

For statements that incorporate a matching pair of parentheses you do not have to use the backslash technique – Python automatically searches the following lines looking for the terminating parenthesis. We can modify our print statement above to **print** a tuple of our message, which requires parentheses and therefore implies a termination character:

```
print ("Hello, I am a test program",
"and I am printing an extra",
"long line so I can demonstrate",
"how to split me up")
```

Comments

Like Perl, Python allows you to incorporate comments by inserting the hash symbol into code. For example:

```
version = 1.0 # This is the current version number
```

Everything after the hash sign is taken to be a comment and is therefore ignored by the Python interpreter. Note that, as you would expect, this does not affect hash signs embedded within quotes.

Contexts

There are no contexts in Python. Within Perl you constantly have to make allowances for how you treat certain expressions. Evaluating an entire array in scalar context for example returns the array's length in Perl. In Python there are no such intricacies. Objects and variables are evaluated in exactly the form you specify. For example, if you return a list of items from a function and assign the return value to a variable, then the variable becomes a list, irrespective of what the variable was before the assignment.

Remember as well that we are always dealing with objects, which are the same as references to objects within Perl. This means that we never have to worry about how we supply arguments to functions and we never have to dereference either.

Using print

In Python **print** is a statement, not a function, and its behavior is somewhat different to Perl's. First and foremost because it's a statement parentheses are *always* optional. You don't have to make an exception for those situations when you might inadvertently evaluate something in the wrong context – Python doesn't support contexts.

The **print** statement follows these basic rules:

▶ Objects and constants separated by commas will be separated by spaces when printed. Use string concatenation or the % formatting operator to avoid this.

▶ Objects cannot be interpolated into any constant – see *Formatting operator* on p. 68 for information on how to format information before it is output.

▶ Objects are converted, where possible, to a format suitable for printing. For example when printing a list, the variable is actually printed in the same format as if it had been created manually within the script. For example:

```
a = [1,2,3,4,'Five']
print a
```

produces:

```
[1,2,3,4,'Five']
```

▶ A linefeed is appended to every output line. To avoid this, append a comma to the end of the line.

Here are some examples of all the different facilities available for printing variables and information:

```
print 'Hello','World'
print 'This is a' + 'concatenated', string
print 'The first line',
print 'Plus some continuation'
print 'I ordered %d dozen %s today' % (6, 'eggs')
contacts = [{'Name' : 'Martin',
             'Email' : 'mc@mcwords.com'},
            {'Name' : 'Bob',
             'Email' : 'bob@bob.com'}]
print contacts
```

The script produces the following output:

```
Hello World
This is a concatenated string
The first line Plus some continuation
I ordered 6 dozen eggs today
[{'Email': 'mc@mcwords.com', 'Name': 'Martin'},
{'Email': 'bob@bob.com', 'Name': 'Bob'}]
```

PYTHON VARIABLES

Python is entirely object-based, this means that many Perl programmers will have to get used to working with a combination of objects, compatible operators, and the class-specific methods which can be used to manipulate them.

For example, consider the Perl code fragment below which creates an array and then sorts the results into a new array:

```
my @array = qw/fred bob alice/;
my @sorted = sort @array;
```

Within Python we can create the new list (the Python array type) and then use the **sort()** method on the new object to create an ordered version.

```
array = ['fred','bob','alice']
array.sort()
```

Although the process still takes two lines, we've created only one list and haven't had to exchange any data with an additional function, everything was done within the confines of the object that we created.

The other significant difference between Perl and Python variables is that Python does not use special characters to identify the variable type. Instead, Python automatically creates the correct type of object according to the type of information that you try to assign to the variable you are creating. For example, here are some of the objects you can create:

```
number = 3.141592654
string = 'This is a string'
list = ['a',1,'string',pi]
dictionary = {'one':1, 'two':2, 'three':3}
tuple = (1, 'Two', 3)
```

You'll notice in each case that the format of the information being assigned is what drives the object type that is created.

It's probably best to think of this process as identical to the process for creating anonymous references to particular data types within Perl. However, unlike Perl, we don't have to dereference the variable to get the information back:

```
a = 45
b = 67
print a + b
```

If you try to use a method that doesn't exist in the objects class, or try to mix incompatible variable types, Python will raise an exception (see Chapter 6, Exceptions). Although this lack of indication can be frustrating, it ultimately makes the code easier to read!

Python itself supports a number of different built-in object types, but there are six primary types: Numbers, Strings, Lists, Dictionaries, Tuples, and Files. The file object is treated as a data type because we can associate a file with an object within Python and then use a series of methods to access the information in the file.

You can see a list of the supported objects and their Perl equivalents in Table 4.1.

The only object that doesn't have a Perl equivalent is the tuple. We'll be having a look at the tuple more specifically later in this chapter, but for the moment think of a tuple as an immutable (non-modifiable) list.

TABLE 4.1 Perl and Python data types

Equivalent Perl variable type	Python object
scalar	Number
scalar	String
array	List
hash (associative array)	Dictionary
See main text	Tuple
FILE or **IO::Handle**	File

Because the different variable types are objects, many of the methods and operators that you use are identical, and are also supported across all the object types. For example, to add two numbers together you use the familiar + operator, but to do the same in Perl with strings (without explicitly overloading the same operator) we use a period. The reason for this is that in Perl, variables are silently converted between numerical and string formats where appropriate, so we have to explicitly join the values together as strings, rather than numeric values, using a different operator.

With Python you can use the + operator to "add" together numbers, strings, lists (arrays), and tuples. But in Python, variables are not automatically converted between numerical and string forms. Therefore **number + number** in Python adds two numbers together whilst **string + string** concatenates two strings. The expression **number + string** will fail – Python does not know how to add a string and a number together.

Variable name rules

Python follows very basic rules for naming variables:

▶ Variables must begin with an underscore or letter, followed by any combination of letters, digits, or underscores. You cannot use any other punctuation characters.

▶ Variables are case sensitive – **string** and **String** are two different variable names.

▶ Reserved words cannot be superceded by variables. The full list of reserved words are as follows:

and	assert	break	class	continue
def	del	elif	else	except
exec	finally	for	from	global
if	import	in	is	lambda
not	or	pass	print	raise
return	try	while		

Because Python is case sensitive, there is no reason why you cannot have variables called **Return** or **RETURN**, except that this will affect the script's readability!

Numbers

There are no restrictions on what type of number can be stored within a Number object, unlike C, where you need to use a different data type to store integer and floating point numbers. In addition to these basic types, Python also supports complex numbers and arbitrarily large integers.

As we already know, Python creates an object using the type as determined from information that is assigned to the object when it is created. With number objects it is the format of the number that determines the method in which the information is stored. We therefore need to know how to introduce numerical constants into our Python programs. Details on the different types of constants, and how Python stores them internally are outlined below.

Integer numbers

You can create normal integer Number object by supplying a sequence of numbers. For example:

```
number = 1234
number = -1234
```

The objects created are integers, and are actually stored internally as a C **long**, which should be at least 32 bits long, and may be longer depending on the C compiler and processor being used. Also note that zero is considered to be a number:

```
zero = 0
```

Also note that Python uses integer values when determining the logical value of an expression. As with other languages, zero equates to a false value, and any other number equates to true. This allows you to use integers for simple boolean values without the need for an additional data type.

Hexadecimal and octal numbers

You can specify hexadecimal (base 16) and octal (base 8) constants using the same notation available in Perl and C/C++. That is, **0x** or **0X** prefixed to a number forces Python to interpret it as a hexadecimal number, whilst a single leading **0** (zero) indicates an octal number. For example, to set the value of an integer to 255 we could use any one of the following statements:

```
decimal = 255
hexadecimal = 0xff
octal = 0377
```

Since these are simply integers, Python stores them in the same way as normal decimal integers. If you actually want to print an integer in octal or hexadecimal format then see the interpolation method shown for formatting String objects later in this chapter or use the **hex**() or **oct**() functions shown in Chapter 9.

Long integers

The built-in basic integer type is limited to a storage width of at least 32 bits. This means that the maximum number that we could represent would be $2^{31}-1$ (since we must use one bit to allow for negative numbers). Python also supports arbitrarily long integers – you can literally create an integer a thousand digits long and used it within Python as you would any other number.

To create a long integer you must append an **l** or **L** to the end of the number constant, for example:

```
long =
123456789123456789123456789123456789123456789123456789L
```

Once you have created a long integer you can execute expressions as if it were a normal number – the Python interpreter handles the complexities of dealing with the super-sized number. For example, the statements:

```
long =
123456789123456789123456789123456789123456789123456789L
print long+1
```

Outputs:

```
123456789123456789123456789123456789123456789123456790L
```

Or you can continue to do long integer math:

```
long =
123456789123456789123456789123456789123456789123456789L
print
long+876543219876543219876543219876543219876543219876543
21L
```

which generates:

```
2111111111111111111111111111111111111111111111111111110L
```

Although Python uses these long integers as if they were normal integer values, the interpreter has to do a significant amount of extra work to support the option, even though the support for such large numbers is written in C. If you can, use the built-in integer or floating point types in preference to using long integer math.

Floating point numbers

Python supports the normal decimal point and scientific notation formats for accepting floating point numbers. For example, the following constants are valid:

```
number = 1234.5678
number = 12.34E10
number = -12.34E-56
```

Internally, Python stores floating point values as C **doubles** – exactly the same way as Perl.

Like Perl, mixing floating point and integer values results in a floating point result. But, unlike Perl, supplying only integers results in integer results. This is the same behavior as exhibited by Perl when the **integer** pragma is in effect. For example:

```
Python 2.0 (#4, Dec 16 2000, 07:30:29)
[GCC 2.95.2 19991024 (release)] on sunos5
Type "copyright", "credits" or "license" for more
information.
>>> print 5/12
0
>>> print 5.0/12
0.416666666667
```

You can coerce any numeric object into its integer or floating-point equivalent during an expression by using the **int**() or **float**() functions, or you can use the **coerce**() function to change a Numeric object in place. For example:

```
a=1
b=2.0
coerce(a,b)
```

Changes **a** to be a floating point rather than integer value. See Chapter 9 for more information.

Complex numbers

Python allows you to create complex numbers using the normal mathematical notation – the real and imaginary numbers are separated by a plus and the imaginary uses a single **j** or **J** suffix. For example, the following are examples of complex number constants:

```
cplx = 1+2j
cplx = 1.2+3.4j
```

Python uses two floating point numbers to store the complex number, irrespective of the precision of the original. Because complex numbers are a separate entity within Python, the interpreter will automatically perform complex math on expressions that include complex numbers.

Strings

Strings in Python work in a similar fashion to Perl. We can create a string object by assigning a string value:

```
string = 'This is a string!'
```

However, Python strings are not the same as strings stored in Perl scalars for two basic reasons:

▶ A Python string is a sequence of individual characters, and we can address each character within a string in the same way as you would address an element of a list.

▶ Python strings are not automatically converted to numerical values when used in numerical expressions.

String constants

Python supports three different operators for introducing string constants into a Python module. You can use single or double quotes, for example:

```
single = 'single quotes'
double = "double quotes"
```

There is technically no difference between using single or double quotes to introduce a string constant. As we'll see later, Python does not support interpolation of variables in strings instead you need to use the formatted string operator (%) which works in a similar fashion to the **printf**() function in Perl (see *Formatting operator* on p. 68). The only reason to use one set of quotes over another is support the embedding of the other type, i.e.:

```
single = 'So I said "Get away!"'
```

The last format is identical to the "here" document supported by Perl. This uses a triple quote to start and end a long string constant. For example the Perl fragment:

```
print <<EOF;
This is a long paragraph, especially designed so that we
can see exactly how embedding large text blocks into
Python scripts works.
EOF
```

Can be rewritten in Python as:

```
print """This is a long paragraph, especially designed
so that we can see exactly how embedding large text
blocks into Python scripts works."""
```

First and foremost, you can see from the above example that the string is terminated, start and end position, using the triple quote. Python is not limited to using double quotes, the single quote has the same effect, but the double quote is the accepted default. Second, you'll note that we don't have to explicitly tell Python to identify an end marker, and we don't have to place the termination sequence on it's own line (although we could if we wanted).

In all other respects the two methods are identical. Remember though that Python does not support variable interpolation, even in triple quoted blocks.

Strings are lists of characters

As I've already mentioned, Python strings are not the same as a scalar string in Perl. In Perl, to extract the first character of a string you'd normally use **substr()**:

```
$string = 'I am the walrus';
$first = substr($string,0,1)
```

With Python, because a string is one of the sequence objects we can instead access the first character using the familiar array notation we've used before in Perl:

```
string = 'I am the walrus'
first = string[0]
```

You can also extract slices, in the same way as **substr()**, using the notation:

```
string[start:end]
```

Slice extractions are slightly different to those in Perl and follow these rules:

▶ The returned string contains all of the characters starting from **start** up until, but not including, **end**.

▶ If **start** is specified but **end** is not then the slice continues until the end of the string.

▶ If **end** is specified but **start** is not then the slice starts from zero up to, but not including, **end**.

▶ If either **start** or **end** are specified as a negative numbers then the index specification is taken from the end, rather than the start of the string where −1 is the last character.

For example:

```
print string[0]     #Prints the first character
print string[2:10] #Prints characters 3 to 9
print string[-1]    #Prints the last character
print string[13:]   #Prints all of the characters after
                     the 14th
print string[-9:]   #Prints the last 9 characters
print string[:-9]   #Prints everything except the last
                     nine characters
```

These methods for slicing sequences and accessing their contents is shared by all of the sequence types supported in Python. Once you get to know slices on strings, you'll equally be able to access elements and slices on the other sequence objects in exactly the same fashion.

String manipulation

To get the length of a string you need to use the **len()** function:

```
length = len(string)
```

To concatenate two strings together you use the + operator which is a direct replacement for the . operator in Perl:

```
a = 'Hello'
b = 'World!'
message = a+b
```

It works in the same way as you would expect the + operator to work on two numerical values. We can also multiply strings using the * operator:

```
>>> z = 'z'
>>> sleep = z*25
zzzzzzzzzzzzzzzzzzzzzzzzz
```

See the section *Sequence operators* on p. 67.

Strings are immutable

Despite the similarities to the **substr()** function in Perl, the Python string cannot be modified "in place," the following statement will fail:

```
string[2:10] = 'new text'
```

Instead you must get used to extracting the components from a string that you need and recombining them into a new string object, or you'll need to use an external module such as **string** or **re** (for regular expressions). The recombining method is the most straightforward. For example, to replace "cat" with "dog:"

```
string = 'the cat sat on the mat'
newstring = string[0:4] + 'dog' + string[7:]
```

Escape sequences

Python supports most of the accepted escape sequences used in Perl. But remember that we can use these escape sequences within any Python string constant, they are not limited to those delimited to double quotes as they are in Perl. The supported escape sequences are shown in Table 4.2.

TABLE 4.2 Python's supported escape character sequences

Escape character	Description
\ (at end of line)	Continuation (appends next line before parsing)
\\	Backslash
\'	Single quote
\"	Double quote
\a	Bell
\b	Backspace
\e	Escape
\000	Null (Python strings are not null terminated)
\n	Newline or linefeed
\v	Vertical tab
\t	Horizontal tab
\r	Carriage return
\f	Formfeed
\0yy	Character represented by the octal number **yy** (i.e. \012 is equivalent to a newline)
\xyy number	Character represented by the hexadecimal **yy** (i.e. \x0a is equivalent to a newline)
\y	Any other character "y" not listed above is output as normal

Raw strings

For raw strings – i.e. those situations where you do not want any escape character processing you can use the **r**'' and **R**"" raw strings. For example:

```
print r'\a\n\x99'
```

This outputs "\a\n\x99" without any form of interpretation and escape sequence translation. Raw strings are used primarily for regular expressions, where the backslash character is required for escaping regular expression operations.

Lists

The Python list type is equivalent to Perl's array type. You use square brackets to define a list object:

```
list = [1, 2, 3, 4]
songs = ['I should be allowed to think',
'Birdhouse in your Soul']
```

Don't be tempted to use normal parentheses, as parentheses create a tuple – see the next section in this chapter, *Tuples*, for more information.

Nested or multidimensional lists are created by placing lists within lists, i.e.:

```
hex = [[0,1,2,3,4,5,6,7,8,9],
['A', 'B', 'C', 'D', 'E', 'F' ]]
```

Lists are another type of sequence, just like strings, so to pull out the third element of the **list** list above:

```
print list[3]
```

To get an entire nested list:

```
characters = hex[1]
```

Or for a specific element within a multidimensional list:

```
last = hex[1][5]
```

Finally, slice operations work too:

```
morethanfive = hex[0][5:]
```

Manipulating lists

You use the **len()** function to get the length of a list, so the Perl fragment:

```
$length = scalar @array;
```

is the same as the Python fragment:

```
length = len(array)
```

We can also combine lists using the + operator:

```
>>> numbers = [0,1,2,3,4,5,6,7,8,9]
>>> letters = ['A', 'B', 'C', 'D', 'E', 'F' ]
>>> hex = numbers+letters
[0,1,2,3,4,5,6,7,8,9,'A','B','C','D','E','F']
```

The augmented assignment also works for the += operator:

```
>>> list = [1,2,3,4]
>>> list += [5,6,7,8]
[1,2,3,4,5,6,7,8]
```

Additionally we can multiply lists by a numeric value:

```
>>> numbers = [1,2,3,4]
>>> numbers*2
[1,2,3,4,1,2,3,4]
```

But you cannot multiply a list by another list.

Building lists programmatically

Python 2.0 allows the creation of a new list based on a simple expression. For example, starting with the list:

```
>>> list = [1,2,3,4]
```

We could use the **map()** function (which is identical to Perl's **map()** function):

```
>>> cubes = map(lambda(x): x**3, list)
```

With Python 2.0 onwards the method is much easier. You can simply rewrite the above as:

```
>>> cubes = [x**3 for x in list]
```

The nested loop within the square brackets tells Python to create a new list based on the contents of **list**.

Lists are mutable

The String type seen earlier in this chapter was a type of sequence that could not be modified. The List type is also a sequence but you can modify its contents just as you can in Perl. For example to change the fourth element of the list below:

```
>>> list = [0, 1, 2, 4, 16]
>>> list[3:4] = [4, 8]
>>> list
[0,1,2,4,8,16]
```

Note that we've had to use a single-element slice because we are replacing a single value with two new values. Using a single-element reference we get an embedded two-element list:

```
>>> list = [0, 1, 2, 4, 16]
>>> list[3] = [4, 8]
>>> list
[0,1,2,[4,8],16]
```

Providing we use the correct notation the list will automatically shrink or grow to accommodate the additional list elements.

To delete items from the list you need to use the **del** function which accepts an element or slice from a list to be deleted, such that:

```
del list[3]
```

which deletes the fourth element and

```
del list[1:4]
```

deletes the middle three elements from our list.

List methods

The List is the first of the built-in object types which has a number of class methods which can be used to modify and manipulate the elements of the list. For example, to sort the contents of a list object we use the **sort()** method:

```
numbers = [3, 5, 2, 0, 4]
numbers.sort()
```

The list is actually sorted "in place" – nothing is returned by the method call. When migrating from Perl this often causes confusion. In Perl, we can print a copy of a sorted array or list using:

```
print sort @array;
```

In Python we have to do it in two lines:

```
numbers.sort()
print numbers
```

Conversely, to sort an array in Perl it's common to first put it into a temporary variable:

```
@sorted = sort @array;
@array = @sorted;
```

In Python we can do it in one simple statement:

```
list.sort()
```

Other methods for lists allow us to append, insert and otherwise modify the elements and list as a whole. The methods supported for lists are shown in Table 4.3.

Some examples (and their results) are shown below for the methods shown in Table 4.3.

```
list = [1,2,3]
more = [11,12,13]
list.append(4)           # [1,2,3,4]
list.append(('5a','5b')) # [1,2,3,4,(5a,5b)]
list.extend(more)        # [1,2,3,4,(5a,5b),11,12,13]
list.index(11)           # Returns 5
list.insert(5,'Six')     # [1,2,3,('5a','5b'),
                         # 'Six',11,12,13]
list.pop()               # Returns (and removes) 13
list.pop(4)              # Returns the tuple ('5a','5b')
list.remove('Six')       # [1,2,3,11,12]
list.reverse()           # [12,11,3,2,1]
list.sort()              # [1,2,3,11,12]
```

TABLE 4.3 Methods supported by list objects

Python method	Perl equivalent	Description
append(x)	push @array, x	Appends the single object **x** to the end of the list.Supplying multiple arguments will raise an exception. To append a tuple, explicitly supply a tuple, i.e. **list.append((1,2,3))** Returns **None**
count(x)	scalar @array	Returns a count of the number of times the object **x** appears in the list
extend(list)	push @array, @list	Add the items in the list **list** to the list. Returns **None**
index(x)	None	Returns the index for the first item in the list matching the object **x**. Raises an exception if there is no matching element
insert(i, x)	None, but @array = @array[0..i-1], x, @array[i..scalar @array] will work for i > 0	Inserts the object **x** before the element pointed to by **i**. Thus **list.insert(0,x)** inserts the object before the first item. Returns **None**
pop(i)	delete $array[i]	Remove the item at point **x** within the list, and return its value. If no index is specified then **pop** returns the last item in the list
remove(x)	None	Delete the first element from the list that matches the object **x**. Raises an exception if there is no matching element. Returns **None**
reverse()	@array = reverse @array	Reverses the order of the elements in the list, in place. Returns **None**
sort()	@array = sort @array	Sorts the list in place. Returns **None**

Tuples

Tuples are probably the hardest concept for most Perl programmers to grasp as there is no direct equivalent in Perl. To put it very simply, a tuple is identical to the list type, except that the tuple, once created, cannot be modified (it's immutable). Although at first it seems odd to have a built-in object type that we can create but not modify, in practice the object comes in very handy.

Tuples are created using commas to separate individual elements, for example to create a list of days of the week:

```
daytuple = 'Mon', 'Tue', 'Wed', 'Thu', 'Fri', 'Sat', Sun'
```

It's better, however, to use parentheses to indicate that you are explicitly creating a tuple:

```
daytuple = ('Mon', 'Tue', 'Wed', 'Thu', 'Fri', 'Sat', 'Sun')
```

The parentheses form should always be used in an expression to ensure Python is creating a tuple. To create a one element tuple you must append a comma, i.e.:

```
onetuple = (1,)
```

Python would otherwise interpret the single element as an expression.

The benefit of the tuple is that we cannot modify the information once it is created. That means that no matter what you try within a Python script, you will be unable to change the order or content of the days of the week. In Perl, on the other hand, it's quite easy to accidentally change the order or contents of a variable that you wanted to keep static. Re-ordering, as in this case the days of the week, could have all sorts of ramifications within a program that used index numbers to access the information.

Aside from the inability to change the data, tuples otherwise work like lists. For example, to get the third day of the week:

```
daytuple[2]
```

Note the use of square brackets. Python uses square brackets to access any piece of embedded information in a sequence (as we've seen with strings and lists) or sequence-like (dictionary) objects.

Slices also work as with lists, so we can obtain a list of work days using:

```
daytuple[0:5]
```

We can also concatenate tuples (using +) and multiply them (using *), while the **len**() function returns the length of a tuple. However, be aware that slices, concatenation, and multiplication operations on tuples return tuples. For example:

```
a = (1,2,3,4)
b = a * 2
```

Makes **b** a tuple, not a list. You also cannot automatically convert between a list and a tuple, the following will fail because the two types do not match:

```
a = (1,2,3,4) + [5,6,7,8]
```

To convert between tuples and lists use the **tuple**() or **list**() functions. See Chapter 8, for more details.

Trying to modify a tuple in any way raises an exception:

```
>>> daytuple = 'Mon', 'Tue', 'Wed', 'Thu', 'Fri', 'Sat',
              'Sun'
>>> daytuple
('Mon', 'Tue', 'Wed', 'Thu', 'Fri', 'Sat', 'Sun')
>>> daytuple[0] = 'Monday'
Traceback (most recent call last):
  File "<stdin>", line 1, in ?
TypeError: object doesn't support item assignment
```

Dictionaries

Dictionaries are the Python equivalent to Perl hashes. They operate in exactly the same way and use the same key/value pair structure. The major differences are in the way in which we create the dictionary and the format we use to get it back. For example, using Perl to create a dictionary containing month names and the number of days in each we'd probably type:

```
%monthdays = ('Jan' => 31, 'Feb' => 28, 'Mar' => 31,
              'Apr' => 30, 'May' => 31, 'Jun' => 30,
              'Jul' => 31, 'Aug' => 31, 'Sep' => 30,
              'Oct' => 31, 'Nov' => 30, 'Dec' => 31);
```

The => operator is an alias for , and is really only used to help clarify the process on screen. With Python we create a dictionary using the curly braces and use a colon to separate each key and value:

```
monthdays = {'Jan' : 31, 'Feb' : 28, 'Mar' : 31,
             'Apr' : 30, 'May' : 31, 'Jun' : 30,
             'Jul' : 31, 'Aug' : 31, 'Sep' : 30,
             'Oct' : 31, 'Nov' : 30, 'Dec' : 31}
```

When retrieving information, however, we use square brackets:

```
print "Days in March: ",monthdays['Mar']
```

Similarly when assigning information to a specific key:

```
monthdays['Feb'] = 29
```

To get the length of a dictionary in Perl we use:

```
$length = scalar keys %hash;
```

In Python we use the **len()** function:

```
length = len(dict)
```

For deleting keys use the **del()** function:

```
del(monthdays['Feb'])
```

Dictionary methods

For all other operations that you would apply to a Perl hash, such as getting the list of keys, values, checking for membership, and sorting, you need to use one of the dictionary class methods. See Table 4.4 for a list of all the methods and the equivalent Perl statement.

TABLE 4.4 Methods for dictionaries

Method	Perl equivalent	Description
has_key(x)	exists($hash{x})	Returns true if the dictionary has the key **x**
keys()	keys %hash	Returns a list of keys
values()	values (%hash)	Returns a list of values
items()	each %hash	Returns a list of tuples, each tuple consists of a key and it's corresponding value from the dictionary "dict"
clear()	%hash = ()	Removes all the items from the dictionary
copy()	None	Returns a copy of the top-level of the dictionary, but does not copy nested structures, only copies the references to those structures. See *Nesting* on p. 64

TABLE 4.4 *cont*

Method	Perl equivalent	Description
update(x)	None	Updates the contents of the dictionary with the key/value pairs from the dictionary **x**. Note that the dictionaries are merged, not concatenated, since you can't have duplicate keys in a dictionary
get(x [, y])	$hash{x}, which returns **undef**	Returns the key **x** or **None** if the key cannot be found, and can therefore be used in place of **dict[x]**. If **y** is supplied then returns that value if **x** is not found

Sorting dictionaries

From first viewing the **keys()** and **values()** methods operate in the same way as the **keys()** and **values()** functions within Perl. But there is no **sort()** method and Python does not support a **sort()** function. This makes the typical Perl fragment

```
foreach my $key (sort keys %hash)
```

impossible to reproduce. The **keys()** method does return a list, but you cannot nest calls; the Python fragment

```
for key in monthdays.keys().sort()
```

will not work. The reason is that the **sort()** list method sorts the list in place, but doesn't return any values. It does, however, create a sorted list of the keys from **monthdays**, we just have no way of accessing the list that was created.

Instead, the solution is to use a two stage process to first get the list of keys, and then to sort it:

```
keys = monthdays.keys()
keys.sort()
for key in keys:
    ...
```

If you want to sort the list based on the values, rather than the keys, the process gets even more complicated. You can't access the information in a dictionary by using the values as a reference. What you need to do is sort a list of tuple pairs by supplying a custom compare function to the **sort** method of a list.

We can get a list of tuple pairs using the **items** method. The process looks something like this:

```
monthdays = {'Jan' : 31, 'Feb' : 28, 'Mar' : 31,
             'Apr' : 30, 'May' : 31, 'Jun' : 30,
             'Jul' : 31, 'Aug' : 31, 'Sep' : 30,
             'Oct' : 31, 'Nov' : 30, 'Dec' : 31}
months = monthdays.items()
months.sort(lambda f, s: cmp(f[1], s[1]))
for month, days in months:
print 'There are',days,'days in',month
```

The **months** list is actually a list of tuples, with each tuple containing the key and value from the dictionary, i.e.:

```
[('Jan',31), ('Feb',28), ('Mar', 31), ... ]
```

The **sort()** method uses an anonymous function to compare the values from each tuple pair. The **f** and **s** arguments to the function are the two tuple pairs passed to the anonymous function, operating just like the **$a** and **$b** references we use in a Perl **sort** block or function.

The **for** loop then selects both items from each tuple in **months**. The way it works is that the **for...in...** statement works through each element of the **months** list – in this case each element is a tuple. Then **month, days** takes each element from the tuple extracted from **months**. This is the quicker method of doing so:

```
for pair in months:
    month, days = pair
```

When executed, the script output looks like this:

```
There are 28 days in Feb
There are 30 days in Jun
There are 30 days in Nov
There are 30 days in Apr
There are 30 days in Sep
There are 31 days in Aug
There are 31 days in May
There are 31 days in Oct
There are 31 days in Jul
There are 31 days in Jan
There are 31 days in Dec
There are 31 days in Mar
```

There are other tricks and traps with using and sorting lists and dictionaries. We'll be looking in more detail at these in Chapter 11.

Files

The Python file object is similar to the filehandle as returned when using **IO::Handle**. Once a file has been opened it operates just like any other object – we use methods to read and write information to and from the file and to control how we use and buffer the information within it.

We'll be looking at file manipulation in more detail in Chapter 10, but for the moment be aware that the Perl fragment:

```
open(DATA, 'myfile.txt')
while(<DATA>)
{
    print $_;
}
close(DATA);
```

can be rewritten in Python as:

```
input = open('myfile.txt')
for line in input.readlines():
    print line
input.close()
```

OBJECT ODDITIES

Although Python always creates objects when you create a variable, it's important to understand the association between the name, the object, and the variable. In truth, Python stores references or pointers to the internal structures used to store the information for a specific object type. This is the equivalent of the Perl reference – a Python object is merely the address of a structure stored in memory, in the same way that a scalar reference in Perl is merely a reference to the real variable type stored in memory.

With Perl, the programmer also has to make a conscious effort to use a reference as a specific data type. You must dereference a Perl reference before you can access the information. If you don't dereference, or you dereference to the wrong type (i.e. try to access a hash as a scalar) you get either the physical address of the variable, or an error during compilation.

Easy to spot, but it adds extra complication to the programming process that frankly we could do without.

Because of this difference in the way objects and variable names are linked there are some oddities that you need to be aware of when migrating from Perl.

Python copies references, not data

When you refer to a Python object by name when assigning information to an object, Python stores the reference, not the data. For example, the code below appears to create two objects:

```
objecta = [1,2,3]
objectb = objecta
```

In fact, we have only created one object – but we have created two names (pointers) to that object, as demonstrated by trying the statements interactively:

```
>>> objecta = [1,2,3]
>>> objectb=objecta
>>> objecta[1] = 4
>>> print objectb
[1, 4, 3]
```

If you want to create a copy of an object, you must force Python to explicitly return either the value of the object or by using one of the type converters we'll see shortly. The former method is often the easiest with lists and tuples:

```
objectb = objecta[:]
```

The effects of copying the pointer to the object rather than copying the contents of the object pose some interesting possibilities. Most useful of all is the fact that because this is Python's normal behavior, building complex structures becomes a natural rather than a forced process. For example, you can use objects to specify the keys used for dictionaries. We could build a list of tables for our contacts database like this:

```
contacts = ['Tom', 'Dick', 'Harry']
addresses = ['Flat 1', 'Flat 20', 'Flat 30']
tables = {contacts : 'A list of contacts',
          addresses : 'A list of addresses'}
```

Even though we've used objects as the keys of the **addressbook** hash, it won't affect how we access the information. For example if we change the **contacts** array and add a new person to our list, we can still get a description of our table:

```
contacts.append('Fred')
print 'Contacts is ',tables[contacts]
```

Although in essence this is no different to the way Perl handles references and objects in most instances, it is important to remember that at all times we are dealing with references – there is no such thing as an array variable in Python, only a reference to a list object.

Nesting

Because Python copies object pointers, we can use objects anywhere – we are not limited to the normal boundaries and restrictions placed on variables in other languages. For example, we have already seen that a list can contain a mixture of strings and numbers, and even other lists. For example, the structure below describes a list of contacts, using a combination of lists and dictionaries to describe the information:

```
contacts = [{'Name' : 'Martin',
             'Email' : 'mc@mcwords.com'},
            {'Name' : 'Bob',
             'Email' : 'bob@bob.com'}]
```

If you nest objects by name – for example by adding **contacts** above to another list or dictionary, then all you are doing is adding a reference to the full variable to the list, we're not adding the list itself. This is the same treatment used by Perl.

Variables dereference automatically

In Python a variable is a pointer to an object in memory, and that object automatically knows how to "dereference" itself – it knows what type of object it is, what its methods are, and what you can do with it. It is impossible to dereference a variable in Python to anything other than the object's true type.

PYTHON OPERATORS

Python supports a very similar set of operators to those supported by Perl. The major difference is that operators in Python tend to be consistent across all the different object types. We've already seen examples of this with the + and * operators. The other place where this has an effect are the comparison operators – Python uses only one set of operators which can be used for comparing numbers and strings, Perl uses different operator sets.

Also, the different parentheses and braces are used to define the object type, rather than being used to access information from different objects. For example, the [] brackets are used to create a list, and also to extract the information from any sequence type and dictionaries.

The operators and their precedence are shown in Table 4.5 – operators at the bottom of the table have the highest precedence. Separate tables are listed later in this chapter for use with specific data types and we'll look at the Perl equivalents then.

TABLE 4.5 Python operator and expression precedence

Python operator	Description
x or y	Logical **or** (**y** is evaluated only if **x** is false)
lambda args: expression	Anonymous function
x and y	Logical and (**y** is evaluated only if **x** is true)
not x	Logical negation
<, <=, >, >=, ==, <>, !=	Comparison tests
is, is not	Identity tests
in, not in	Membership tests
x|y	Bitwise or
x^y	Bitwise exclusive or
x&y	Bitwise and
x<<y, x>>y	Shift **x** left or right by **y** bits
x+y, x-y	Addition/concatenation, subtraction
x*y, x/y, x%y	Multiplication/repetition, division remainder/format
-x, +x, ~x	Unary negation, identity, bitwise compliment
x[i], x[i:j], x.y, x(...)	Indexing, slicing, qualification, function call
(...), [...], {...}, `...`	Tuple, list, dictionary, conversion to string

Numeric operators

Most of the operators that we saw in Table 4.5 apply to numbers, see Table 4.6 for a more explicit list of numeric operators used for calculations – these are all the familiar mathematical operations.

TABLE 4.6 Numeric operators for all number types

Operation	Perl equivalent	Description
x+y	x+y	Add **x** to **y**
x-y	x-y	Subtract **y** from **x**
x*y	x*y	Multiply **x** by **y**
x/y	x/y	Divide **x** by **y**
x**y	x**y	Raise **x** to the power of **y**
x%y	x%y	Modulo (returns the remainder of **x/y**)
-x	-x	Unary minus
+x	+x	Unary plus

There are also a series of shift and bitwise operators that can be used for binary and bit math which are listed in Table 4.7. Note that these can only be applied to integers – trying the operations on a floating point number will raise an exception.

TABLE 4.7 Bitwise/shift operators for Integer numbers

Operation	Perl equivalent	Description
x << y	x << y	Left shift (moves the binary form of **x**, **y** digits to the left), i.e. 1 << 2 = 4
x >> y	x >> y	Right shift (moves the binary form of **x**, **y** digits to the right), i.e. 16 >> 2 = 4
x & y	x & y	Bitwise and
x | y	x | y	Bitwise or
x ^ y	x ^ y	Bitwise exclusive or (xor)
~x	~x	Bitwise negation

Finally, there is a set of augmented assignment operators which work identically to the Perl versions. Python supports a slightly reduced list compared to Perl. The operators supported by Python are:

```
+=  -=  *=  /=  %=  **=  <<=  >>=  &=  ^=  |=
```

Sequence operators

All sequences (strings, lists and tuples) share the same basic set of operations as shown in Table 4.8.

TABLE 4.8 Sequence operators and functions

Operation	Perl equivalent	Description
a + b	$a . $b (scalars) (@a,@b) (arrays)	Concatenates **a** and **b**
a * n, n * a	$a x n (scalars) (@a) x n (arrays)	Creates **n** copies of the sequence **a**, where **n** is an integer
string % list	**sprintf()**	Formats **string** using the values of the objects in **list**. (only works on strings)
sequence[i]	$array[index]	Accesses element **i** of **sequence**
sequence[i:j]	$array[i..j]	Access the slice of **sequence** starting with element **i** up to, but not including, element **j**
x in s, x not in s	**grep()** or regular expression	Returns true if **x** is, or is not, a member of **s**
len(s)	**length()**	Returns the length of the sequence **s**
min(s)	None	Returns the smallest element of **s**
max(s)	None	Returns the largest element of **s**

In addition the list object also supports assignment and element deletion, as listed here in Table 4.9.

TABLE 4.9 List-specific operators and functions

Operation	Perl equivalent	Description
list[i] = x	$list[i] = x	Assigns the object **x** to the element **i** of **list**
list[i:j] = x	@list[i..j] = x	Assigns the object **x** to the slice **list[i:j]**
del list[i]	None (need to use a slice)	Deletes the element at index **i** of **list**
del list[i:j]	delete @list[i..j]	Deletes the elements within the slice **list[i:j]**

Formatting operator

The % operator in Python allows you to format strings and other objects using the same basic notation as supported by the **sprintf()** function in Perl. The % operator works as a formatting tool only when it's been supplied a string object or constant on the left-hand side, when supplied a number it works like the modulus operator in Perl.

The operator uses the format:

```
format % tuple
```

Where **format** is a **sprintf**-like string containing formatting sequences and **tuple** is a list of the values which you want to apply to each format specifier.

For example:

```
'And the sum was $%d, %s' % (1, 'which wasn't nice')
```

returns

```
And the sum was $1, which wasn't nice
```

The return value is always a string and can therefore be used as a direct replacement for both **sprintf()** and **printf()**, when combined with the **print** statement. The operator itself accepts the same list of options as the C **sprintf** function, see Table 4.10 for a complete list.

TABLE 4.10 Conversion formats for the % operator

Format	Result
%%	A percent sign
%c	A character with the given ASCII code
%s	A string – Python in fact converts the corresponding object to a string before printing, so **%s** can be used for any object (see *Type conversion* on p. 72 for more details)
%d	A signed integer (decimal)
%u	An unsigned integer (decimal)
%o	An unsigned integer (octal)
%x	An unsigned integer (hexadecimal)
%X	An unsigned integer (hexadecimal using uppercase characters)
%e	A floating point number (scientific notation)
%E	A floating point number (scientific notation using "E" in place of "e")
%f	A floating point number (fixed decimal notation)
%g	A floating point number (%e or %f notation according to value size)
%G	A floating point number (as %g, but using "E" in place of "e" when appropriate)
%p	A pointer (prints the memory address of the value in hexa-decimal)
%n	Stores the number of characters output so far into the next variable in the parameter list

Like C and Perl, Python also supports flags that optionally adjust the output format. These are specified between the % and conversion letter, as shown in Table 4.11.

TABLE 4.11 Optional formatting flags

Flag	Result
space	Prefix positive number with a space
+	Prefix positive number with a plus sign
-	Left-justify within field
0	Use zeros, not spaces, to right-justify
#	Prefix non-zero octal with "0" and hexadecimal with "0x"
number	Minimum field width
.number	Specify precision (number of digits after decimal point) for floating point numbers

The **%** operator also works with dictionaries by quoting the name of the dictionary element to be extracted using the format **%(NAME)** followed by the formatting codes shown in Tables 4.10 and 4.11. For example, the statements:

```
album = {'title':'Flood', 'id':56}
print "Catalog Number %(id)05d is %(title)s" % album
```

produces "Catalog Number 00056 is Flood."

Assignments

The assignment operators in Python work in the same fashion as they do in Perl. Python also supports list (and tuple) assignment. Python supports four different methods of assignment: basic, tuple assignment, list assignment, and multiple assignment.

Note that all variables are created within the scope of the current block – there are no equivalents to the Perl **my** or **local** statements in Python. There is however an equivalent to the Perl 5.6 and later **our** statement, called **global**. We'll be looking at the scoping rules applied by Python in Chapter 5.

Basic assignment

The basic assignment is the one we have seen most examples of. It creates a new object, using the correct type according to the value assigned to the object, and then points the specified name to the new object:

```
number = 45
message = 'Hello World'
mylist = ['I Palindrome I', 'Mammal']
mytuple = ('Mon', 'Tue', 'Wed', 'Thu', 'Fri')
mydict = {'Twisting':Flood, 'Mammal':'Apollo 18'}
```

Tuple and list assignments

In Perl it is common to want to extract two or more elements from a function call or list to separate them into individual variables. For example:

```
my ($arga, $options) = @_;
($sec,$min,$hour,$mday,$mon,$year,$wday,$yday) =
gmtime($diff);
```

Python supports the same basic process, allowing you to extract individual elements from a tuple or list into individual objects:

```
title, name = 'Mr', 'Martin'
album = ('TMBG', 'Flood', 'Theme from Flood', 'Birdhouse
in your Soul')
artist, title = album[0:2]
track1, track2 = album[-2:]
```

In essence we've just created a new tuple on the left-hand side of the assignment operator, but we don't store a reference to the whole tuple. Also note that we don't need to use parentheses – whereas in Perl it's a requirement as we have to tell the interpreter to identify the items as a list. In Python, the use of commas to separate values automatically implies the creation of a tuple, whether it's embedded in parentheses or not. This is one of the reasons tuples exist, they are the equivalent of the Perl list, except that we can store the entire list in its own object.

When extracting values from a list we can use square brackets to imply a list:

```
album = ['TMBG', 'Lincoln', 'Ana Ng', 'Cowtown']
[artist, title] = album[0:2]
```

Or we can assign to a tuple, as the assignation works on an element by element basis so it doesn't give a **TypeError** exception.

The tuple and list assignments have another trick up their sleeve. Because names are merely pointers, we can "swap" two object/name combinations by performing a tuple or list assignment like this:

```
artist, title = title, artist
```

Multiple-target assignments

You can create a single object with multiple pointers using the multiple-target assignment statement:

```
group = title = 'They Might Be Giants'
```

Here, we have created a single string object, with two different pointers called **group** and **title**. Remember that because the two pointers point at the same object modifying the object contents using one name also modifies the information available via the other. This is effectively the same as:

```
group = 'They Might Be Giants'
title = group
```

Type converison

Unlike Perl, Python does not automatically convert between types so it's impossible to mix and match numbers and strings, for example, in the same statement. To counter this, Python does not provide a series of built-in functions that convert between the different data types. See Table 4.12.

There is also a special operator supported by Python that works in the same way as the **str**() built-in function. The " (back ticks) operator evaluates the enclosed statement and then returns a string representation, as in the following example:

```
>>> print `(34*56.0)`
1904
>>> album = ('TMBG', 'Flood', 'Theme from Flood',
'Birdhouse in your Soul')
>>> album
('TMBG', 'Flood', 'Theme from Flood', 'Birdhouse in your
Soul')
>>> `album[:2]`
"('TMBG', 'Flood')"
```

TABLE 4.12 Built-in type conversion

Function	Description
str(x)	Translates the object **x** into a string.
list(x)	Returns the sequence object x as a list. For example, the string "hello" is returned as ['h', 'e', 'l', 'l', 'o']. Converts tuples and lists to lists
tuple(x)	Returns the sequence object **x** as a tuple
int(x)	Converts a string or number to an integer. Note that floating-point numbers are truncated, not rounded; **int(3.6)** becomes 3
long(x)	Converts a string or number to a long integer. Conversion as for **int**
float(x)	Converts a string or number to a floating-point object
complex(x,y)	Creates a complex number with real part of **x** and imaginery part of **y**
hex(x)	Converts an integer or long to a hexadecimal string
oct(x)	Converts an integer or long to an octal string
ord(x)	Returns the ASCII value for the character **x**
chr(x)	Returns the character (as a string) for the ASCII code **x**

```
>>> str(album[:2])
"('TMBG', 'Flood')"
>>> `list(album)`
"['TMBG', 'Flood', 'Theme from Flood', 'Birdhouse in
your Soul']"
```

Note that the format used by both **str** and `` ` `` when returning the information is the same as would be required to build the object. Therefore, to display the Python statements required to build the earlier album list, use the following statements:

```
contacts = [{'Name' : 'Martin',
            'Email' : 'mc@mcwords.com'},
           {'Name' : 'Bob',
            'Email' : 'bob@bob.com'}]
>>> >>> `contacts`
"[{'Email': 'mc@mcwords.com', 'Name': 'Martin'},
{'Email': 'bob@bob.com', 'Name': 'Bob'}]"
```

Comparing objects

Python supports only one set of comparison operators and these compare the values of two objects explicitly. That is, when you compare two lists they are compared on an element by element and order basis to determine if they are the same:

```
>>> a = [1,2,3]
>>> b = [3,2,1]
>>> a == b
0
```

The lists **a** and **b** are not identical because the order of the individual objects is not the same. If we sort b however:

```
>>> b.sort()
>>> a == b
1
```

The two are identical. If you think this through logically then you can see why we only need one set of operators with Python – a string is a list of individual characters, so the comparison just has to check each string on a character by character basis. Lists and tuples follow the same logic. Dictionaries are slightly different as the comparison doesn't worry about the order, since there is no order, but it still compares the individual key/value pairs:

```
>>> a = {'one':1, 'two':2, 'three':3}
>>> b = {'one':1, 'two':2, 'three':3}
>>> a == b
1
>>> b = {'three':3,'two':2,'one':1}
>>> a == b
1
>>> b = {'three':1, 'two':1, 'one':3}
>>> a == b
0
```

The list of supported comparison operators and their Perl equivalents, are shown in Table 4.13.

In addition to the basic Perl equivalent tests there are also object specific tests. The **is** comparison operator returns true only if the two names point to the same object:

TABLE 4.13 Comparison operators

Operator	Perl equivalent	Description
x < y	x < y, x lt y	Less than
x <= y	x <= y, x le y	Less than or equal to
x > y	x > y, x gt y	Greater than
x >= y	x >= y, x ge y	Greater than or equal to
x == y	x == y, x eq y	Have equal value
x != y, x <> y	x != y, x ne y	Do not have equal value
x is y	x == y	Pointers to same object
x is not y	x != y	Different objects
not x	!x	Inverse – returns true if x is false/ false if x is true
x or y	x || y, x or y	Returns x if x is true, or y if x is false
x and y	x && y, x and y	Returns x if x is false, or y if x is true
x < y < z	None	Chained comparisons, returns true only if all operators return true.

```
>>> a = [1,2,3]
>>> b = [1,2,3]
>>> a is b
0
```

This is because there are two separate objects that contain the same information. Copying the object reference from **a** to **b** however:

```
>>> b = a
>>> a is b
1
```

Gives us the result we expect. The **is** operator is useful when you want to check the source and validity of a object against a source or control object.

Comparison values

Python bases its comparisons using the following rules:

▶ Numbers are compared by magnitude.

▶ Strings are compared character by character.

▶ Lists and tuples are compared by element, from the lowest to highest index.

▶ Dictionaries are compared by comparing sorted key/value pairs.

All comparisons within Python return **1** if the result is true, or **zero** if the comparison fails. In addition, Python treats any non-zero value as true, including a string. The only exceptions to this rule are **None**, which is false, and any empty object (list, tuple, dictionary). You can see a summary of the different true/false values in Table 4.14.

TABLE 4.14 True/false values of objects and constants

Object/constant	Value
' '	False
'string'	True
0	False
>1	True
<-1	True
() (empty tuple)	False
[] (empty list)	False
{} (empty dictionary)	False
None	False

The None value

The **None** value is the logical equivalent of the **undef** value within Perl. It's used as the same dummy/null value. It's automatically returned by functions that don't explicitly return a value and can also be used in function call arguments to indicate a null object or list.

Loops and control statements

Python supports only three control statements, the **if** test statement, and the **for** and **while** loops.

if

The Python **if** statement is identical to the Perl **if** statement – it supports the primary test, secondary tests (using **elif** as opposed to **elsif**), and the **else** option. The general format for the **if** statement is:

```
if EXPRESSION:
    BLOCK
elif EXPRESSION2:
    BLOCK2
else:
    BLOCK3
```

The big difference is the overall format of the statement itself. The initial test statement is terminated by a colon, and the indentation of the following block of code is significant. Python uses indentation to identify individual blocks, not the curly braces employed by Perl.

For example, the Perl fragment:

```
if ($today == $bday)
{
    print "Happy Birthday\n";
}
else
{
    print "Happy Unbirthday\n";
}
```

Although it's customary in Perl to use indentation to help signify individual blocks they are not actually required – the braces are used to delimit the start and end of each block.

By comparison, the same sequence in Python looks like this:

```
if (today == bday):
    print 'Happy Birthday'
else:
    print 'Happy Unbirthday!'
```

The colon signifies the start of the block to be used should the preceding statement evaluate to true. The indentation then signifies the block. If we expand on this example you can also see how statements blocks nest:

```
if (today == bday):
    print 'Good Morning!'
    if (time <= btime):
        print 'Happy Birthday!'
    else:
        print 'I'm sorry, I missed your birth time.'
        print 'Happy Birthday!'
else:
    print 'Happy Unbirthday!'
```

As soon as the indentation changes, Python assumes the end of the corresponding block, according to the indentation used.

Python does not support any of the shorter forms of **if** or conditional statement supported by Perl. For example, the following do not work:

```
print 'Happy Birthday!' if (today == bday)
print 'Happy ' (today == bday) ? 'Birthday' : 'Unbirthday'
```

However, we can shorten a single line **if** statement:

```
if (true): print 'Hello World'
```

while

The **while** loop is identical to the **while** loop in Perl in most situations. The basic format is:

```
while EXPRESSION:
    BLOCK
else:
    BLOCK
```

For example, to work through the characters in a string we might use:

```
string = 'Martin'
while(len(string)):
    char = string[0]
    string = string[1:]
    print 'Give me a',char
```

Which outputs:

```
Give me a M
Give me a a
...
Give me a n
```

The optional **else** block is only executed if the loop exits when **EXPRESSION** returns false, rather than the execution being broken by the **break** statement. Using **else** we can run a block of code when the loop exists normally – for example we might close a file at the end of processing it.

for

The **for** loop is identical to the list form of the **for** loop in Perl. The basic format for the loop is:

```
for TARGET in OBJECT:
    BLOCK
else:
    BLOCK
```

You specify the object to be used as the iterator within the loop, and then supply any form of sequence object to iterate through. For example:

```
for number in [1,2,3,4,5,6,7,8,9]:
    print 'I can count to',number
```

For each iteration of the loop, **number** is set to the next value within the list producing the output:

```
I can count to 1
I can count to 2
...
I can count to 9
```

The **OBJECT** can be any sequence, so we can also iterate over a string:

```
for letter in 'Martin':
    print 'Give me a', letter
```

which generates:

```
Give me a M
Give me a a
...
Give me a n
```

In addition, just like the **while** loop, the **else** statement block is executed when the loop exits normally:

```
for number in [1,3,5,7]:
    if number > 8:
        print "I can't work with numbers that are higher
        than 8!"
        break
    print '%d squared is %d' % (number, pow(number,2))
else:
    print 'Made it!'
```

Which outputs:

```
1 squared is 1
3 squared is 9
5 squared is 25
7 squared is 49
Made it!
```

Ranges

Because the **for** loop does not support the loop counter format offered by Perl and C we need to use a different method to iterate through a numerical range. There are two possible. Either use the **while** loop:

```
while(x <10):
    print x
    x = x+1
```

Alternatively, we can use the **range** function to generate a list of values:

```
for x in range(10):
...
```

The **range** function returns a list. The basic format for the function is:

```
range([start, ] stop [, step])
```

In its single argument form **range** returns a list consisting of each number up to, but not including, the number supplied:

```
>>> range(10)
[0, 1, 2, 3, 4, 5, 6, 7, 8, 9]
```

If the **range** function is supplied two arguments then it returns a list of numbers starting at the first argument, up to but not including the last:

```
>>> range(4,9)
[4, 5, 6, 7, 8]
```

The final form, with three arguments, allows you to define the intervening step:

```
>>> range(0,10,2)
[0, 2, 4, 6, 8]
```

Because the **range** function returns a list it can create, for very large ranges, very large lists that require vast amounts of memory to store. To get round this, you can use the **xrange** function. This has exactly the same format and indeed performs exactly the same operation as **range**, but it does not create an intervening list and therefore requires less memory for very large ranges.

Loop control statements

Python supports three loop control statements that modify the normal execution of a loop. They are **break**, **continue** and **pass**:

▶ **break** is equivalent to the Perl **last** control statement, terminating the current loop, ignoring any **else** statement, continuing execution after the last line in the loop's statement block.

▶ **continue** is equivalent to the Perl **next** control statement, immediately forcing the loop to proceed to the next iteration, ignoring any remaining statements in the current block. The loop statement expression is reevaluated.

▶ **pass** is a no-op – it does nothing when called. **pass** is useful in situations where you want to identify a particular event, but want to ignore it. Often used in Exceptions.

For example:

```
x=20
while (x):
    x = x-1
    if not x % 3: continue
    print x,'is not a multiple of 3'
```

Which generates the following output:

```
19 is not a multiple of 3
17 is not a multiple of 3
...
2 is not a multiple of 3
1 is not a multiple of 3
```

5

FUNCTIONS

Functions in Python borrow more from C rather than Perl. Perl's approach to functions is to allow you to supply a list of arguments to any function and the entire list, including the contents of arrays or hashes supplied, are placed into the @_ variable. It's up to the function definition to decide what to do with the list of arguments that has been supplied and how to interpret the supplied list into the information the function needs.

There are a few minor problems with this approach, some of which have been resolved over the years. For example, there is no way to identify the types of arguments you expect, unless you use prototypes. When calling a function we are also limited to accepting a list of arguments or supplying a list that will be interpreted by a hash, and the method by which we call the function is set by how the function interprets the list of arguments that are supplied.

When writing functions we have to decide how to retrieve the arguments (using assignment, **shift**, **pop**, or direct access) and how to interpret the different arguments for us within the function itself. There are also numerous ways in which we can decide to accept multiple arguments, default options and other function tricks.

Python is much more explicit, it uses named arguments and has explicit methods for getting default arguments.

BASIC FUNCTION DEFINITION

Functions in Perl are defined using the **sub** statement:

```
sub FUNC
{
}
```

The equivalent in Python is the **def** statement:

```
def FUNC():
    # Statements
```

Note that the parentheses in the Python statement are compulsory.

Arguments are passed to a function in Perl as part of the @_ array. For example, the **add()** function can be defined like this:

```
sub add
{
    my ($x, $y) = @_;
    my $result = $x+$y;
    return $result;
}
```

I've deliberately made this function definition quite long so as to help when comparing it against the Python version.

Within Python, the function definition defines the arguments that the function accepts. For example, we can rewrite the above statement as:

```
def add(x,y):
    result = x+y
    return result
```

The **x** and **y** arguments are extracted and populated in the same order as they are supplied when the function is called, so:

```
print add(1,2)
```

Should print out a value of three.

The number of arguments defined by the function *must* match the number of the arguments supplied when the function is called. Using the wrong number of arguments will raise an exception:

```
>>> add(1)
Traceback (most recent call last):
  File "<stdin>", line 1, in ?
TypeError: not enough arguments; expected 2, got 1
```

This method of operation is very different from Perl, which doesn't by default enforce any checking on the number of arguments supplied. If you are used to using prototypes however then you will be familiar with the requirement.

Default values

You can add an assignment within the function definition to set the default value of an argument if it hasn't been supplied. For example we could rewrite the **add()** function like this:

```
def add(x=0,y=0):
    return x+y
```

Now we can call the function in any of three ways:

```
add()    # Returns 0 (0+0)
add(1)   # Returns 1 (1+0)
add(1,2) # Returns 3 (1+2)
```

This is similar to the manual checks you might place within a Perl function to validate the information supplied:

```
sub add
{
    my ($x, $y) = @_;
    defined $x or $x = 0;
    defined $y or $y = 0;
    return $x+$y;
}
```

Note that default values apply at the time the function was defined, so in the fragment:

```
value = 20
def foo(x = value):
    return x+1
```

```
value = 10
foo()
```

the call to **foo()** would return 21, not 11.

However, with mutable sequences the same is not true:

```
list = ['Hello']
def foo(x = list):
    print x
list.append('World')
foo()
```

The call to **foo()** will now output ['Hello', 'World'].

Passing sequences and dictionaries

This is really a bit of a trick question – because Python always works with objects, the equivalent of Perl references, we no longer have to worry about how we supply multiple arrays, dictionaries or any other sequence. For example, the following is perfectly legal and will return exactly what we expect:

```
def output(x,y,z):
    for item in x: print 'X:',item
    for (key,value) in y.items():
        print '%s => %s' %      (key,value)
    print z

list = [1,2,3,4,5,6]
dictionary = {'Fred':'Wilma', 'Barney':'Betty'}
string = "That's it!"

output(list, dictionary, string)
```

Running the above produces:

```
X: 1
X: 2
X: 3
X: 4
X: 5
X: 6
Fred => Wilma
Barney => Betty
That's it!
```

Variable arguments

You can accept a variable list of arguments by prefixing the argument within the function definition with an asterisk. For example, we could emulate the **sprintf()** Perl function (which doesn't exist in Python) using:

```
def sprintf(format,*args):
    return format % (args)
```

Now we can call the function just as we would in Perl:

```
quote = sprintf("The value of %s is $%f", 'Widget', 17.95)
```

Keyword arguments

You can specify the arguments and their values by name in any function call without requiring any special definition. For example, we could call our original **add()** function like this:

```
add(y=56, x=99)
```

Also note that they can be mixed with arguments called normally, for example:

```
add(45, y=44)
```

but the positional arguments must be called first, followed by the keyword arguments.

Freeform arguments

As an extension of the keyword argument idea we can also set functions to accept a number of named arguments without explicitly giving the definition. For example, we could have a function for opening a window or other dialog box which we could call using the following statement:

```
window(topright=(89,1), bottomleft=(210,100),
        message="That file already exists")
```

The function definition might look like this:

```
def window(**args):
    ...
```

The double-asterisk tells python to place any arguments supplied as keyword arguments into a dictionary with the given name. Now we could access the message supplied to us in the arguments as **args['message']**.

This is especially useful in situations where you are building a front end to an existing function that supports such arguments – the Tk GUI system is a good case in point.

Prototypes

There is no such thing as a prototype in Python, the named argument definitions act as the only form of test during the execution stage to ensure that any supplied arguments match the definition.

Arguments are references

At all times Python arguments are references. For immutable objects such as numbers and strings the effect is identical to supplying a normal argument in Perl. However, when you supply a list or dictionary (or other mutable object) then modifying the argument also modifies the original. For example:

```
a = [1,2,3,4,5]
def thirdcube(x):
    x[3] = x[3]**3

thirdcube(a)
print a
```

Will output:

```
[1, 2, 3, 64, 5]
```

Return values

Perl automatically returns the result of the last expression to the caller, such that we can get away with:

```
sub add
{
    $_[0]+$_[1];
}
```

and still expect to get a result.

Python functions do not return any value unless you explicitly use the **return** statement. If you try to obtain a value from a function that does explicitly return a value then you will get the Python **None** value.

The **return** statement accepts multiple values, which are returned as a tuple to the caller. For example:

```
def sqtwo(one,two):
    return one**2,two**2
```

You can extract the values using the tuple assignment method we've already seen in Chapter 4 – the following statements are all valid:

```
resone,restwo = sqtwo(2,3)
(resone,restwo) = sqtwo(3,4)
```

Note that we don't have to worry about the return types again as we're dealing with objects, not variables as we do in Perl.

Scope

In Perl, technically, all variables are created within the scope of the package unless they are further qualified using **local**, **my**, or **our**. For example, the following fragment works correctly, printing the result of the calculation, even though it's embedded in the function definition:

```
sub subtract
{
    $result = $_[0]-$_[1];
}

subtract(10,1);
print $result;
```

In Python, all variables defined within a function definition are automatically defined within a namespace local to the function. In essence, Python implies the declaration of each variable as if using **my** within Perl. The equivalent of the code above fails in Python:

```
def subtract(x,y):
    result = x-y

subtract(10,1)
print result
```

Python will raise a **NameError** exception because it will be unable to find the variable **result** within the scope of the main script.

The actual sequence Python uses when looking for a variable is defined by the LGB rule, which defines that variables are searched for first within the local scope, then the global scope and finally the built-in scope. Local variables therefore have priority over global variables, and global variables have priority over any built-in variables.

Because of the LGB rule certain operations have peculiarities that Perl programmers will not be familiar with. The following code attempts to modify a global variable:

```
age = 29
def birthday():
    age += 1

birthday()
print age
```

The above actually outputs 29, not 30, because Python would create a new, locally-scoped variable called **age** that exists only within the name-space of the **birthday()** function. This is similar to the effect of declaring a variable using **my** with the same name as that of a global variable.

We can modify this behavior in Python by using the **global** statement. By using **global** you define the list of variables which belong to the global namespace, rather than the local namespace and is therefore only required when you want to modify the value of a global variable. The above script could be rewritten as:

```
age = 29
def birthday():
    global age
    age += 1

birthday()
print age
```

Also note that **global** will mark a variable within the global scope even if it doesn't yet exist, such that we can rewrite our original script as:

```
def subtract(x,y):
    global result
    result = x-y

subtract(10,1)
print result
```

Nested definitions

Unlike Perl, which limits function definitions to the base of a package or within another subroutine, functions in Python can be defined more or less anywhere – even within an **if** statement:

```
if (result == 'cube'):
    def calc(x):
        return x**3
else:
    def calc(x):
        return x**2
```

Functions can also be defined within another function, for example:

```
def count():
    x = list(10)
    def prvalue(a):
        print "Count:",a
    for y in x:
        prvalue(y)
```

In both cases the **prvalue()** and **calc()** functions are defined within the parent scope. In the former case the parent is the entire script, so **calc()** will be available to all other functions. But in the case of **prvalue()**, only statements within **count()** will be able to use the **prvalue()** function. Trying to use **prvalue()** outside of the **count()** function will raise a **NameError** exception.

However, the LGB rule still applies within the **prvalue()** function. Had we tried to access the **x** variable within **prvalue()** it would have failed. This is because Python will look first for a variable **x** within **prvalue()** and then within the global scope – the scope of the **count()** function will never be searched. In these situations either use **global** in both functions or make sure that you pass the value each time you need it, as we have done here.

ADVANCED FUNCTION CALLING

Beyond the basics of functions that we have already seen, Python also supports some more advanced function handling. The **apply** statement is a required feature if you want to be able to dynamically call a function without knowing its name or the arguments you will supply it beforehand. The

map statement provides the same functionality as the Perl **map** function – it allows you to apply the same function to an arbitrary list.

The last two features are connected. It should come as no surprise that functions are just Python objects. As such, we can assign functions to names and then call them dynamically and therefore indirectly. As an extension of this, we can also create a name that points to a function that has no real name – an anonymous function which is created within Python using the **lambda** statement.

Indirect function calls

Functions are just Python objects which means they can be assigned to names and passed to other functions just like any other object. This means that we can create an alias to a function simply by assigning the function to a variable:

```
def hello():
    print "Hello World"
x = hello
```

Now we can call **hello** using **hello()** or **x()**. This is identical to assigning a variable to the reference to a function in Perl:

```
sub myfunc { print "Hello World\n" }
$call = \&myfunc;
&$call();
```

Python naturally copies function references so we can supply a function object as an argument to a function:

```
def call(function, *args):
    function(args)

call(multiply,2,2)
```

which emulates the ability of Perl to use hard references for calling functions. In Perl we can call the function **myfunc** using its character string name like this:

```
$function = 'myfunc'
&{$function}(1,'Text');
```

The **apply()** built-in function accepts the name of the function to be called as a string in the first argument and a tuple of arguments to be supplied to the function when it is called. The above Perl fragment could be re-written as:

```
function = 'myfunc'
apply(function, (1, 'Text'))
```

Or for a more complex example:

```
obj_dict = { 'function' : multiply, 'args' : (2,2) }
apply(obj_dict['function'],obj_dict['args'])
```

Anonymous functions

Anonymous functions are used all over the place in Perl, from those implied when using the **map** and **sort** functions, to those we explicitly use when setting up signal handlers. For example, we can create a function directly within a variable using:

```
$function = sub { print 'Hello World' }
```

and we can call it using:

```
&$function();
```

In Python, the **lambda** statement works in the same way, albeit much more explicitly in situations where Perl implies it. For example, in Python we *must* use **lambda** within a **map** or **sort** function call, it's not implied at all. Also, because we can assign the code object generated by **lambda** to a variable, we can call it, just as we can with Perl:

```
f = lambda x: x*x*x
f(2)
```

We can therefore rewrite the Perl fragment:

```
@numbers = (1,2,3,4);
@cubes = map( { $_ = $_**3 } @numbers);
```

in Python as:

```
numbers = [1,2,3,4]
cubes = map( lambda x: x**3, numbers)
```

Note that we still have to accept one, or more, arguments within the definition – there is no equivalent to the **$_** variable used in Perl.

6

EXCEPTIONS AND ERROR TRAPPING

Error trapping and handling is a necessary part of all programming. There are many different specific reasons for trapping an error, but they basically come down to two basic reasons:

1 Avoiding doing something that would cause the program/application to fail at a later stage. For example, checking that we've opened a file correctly before we start writing to it.

2 Letting the user know when something has happened that either you didn't plan on or expect. For example, suddenly running out of disk space.

The model used by Perl is borrowed heavily from the C and shell script methods of checking the results of function calls. This presents some problems when dealing with certain errors, and also makes propagating errors within a script difficult. This is one of the reasons why we have the **Carp** module, it's there to facilitate error reporting that makes more sense to the programmer using the module, rather than the module programmer.

Python uses a different focus. Instead of having to check individual lines and function calls for problems, with Python we can "trap" an exception. The exception could be raised anywhere within a block of code, and we can trap and handle all of the different possible errors without having to explicitly check each line of the code.

In this chapter we'll start by looking at the Perl error system before having a quick overview of the Python exception system. Then we'll move on to looking at specific methods and systems that we can use within the Python exception system.

ERROR TRAPPING IN PERL

Error trapping in Perl is handled either by checking the return value of individual function calls using an **if** or **unless**, by using "short-circuit" logic operators (**and/or**) or, if you think the error is severe or normally untrappable, you can embed the statement into a call to **eval()** and check the return value of **$@**. For example, to check for errors when opening a file we can do:

```
if (open(DATA,$file))
{
    # Do something
}
else
{
    die "Error opening $file: $!\n";
}
```

or

```
open(DATA,$file) or die "Error opening $file: $!\n";
```

or when checking a calculation:

```
$calculation = "34/0";
$result = eval($calculation);
print "Error: $@\n" if ($@);
```

In essence there is nothing wrong with any of these methods in Perl, but in a larger program the amount of error checking required becomes prohibitive. It's quite possible to have a script which contains as much error checking code as it does active code for the application, just because we have to manually check and verify each function call and operation.

ERROR TRAPPING IN PYTHON

When migrating to Python it's important to basically forget everything you know about error trapping in Perl. Python functions don't as a rule return a value that indicates their success or failure. When opening a file for example we don't have to explicitly test the return value of the **open** function to determine whether the open has succeeded. Instead, Python supports a number of exceptions.

In principle, these appear to work in the same fashion as embedding Perl statements into **eval** blocks. Exceptions propagate up through the code and they can be trapped and located locally, or "remotely." For example, below is a function which accepts a single argument, the file name. The function opens the file, reads the lines from the file, and then returns the array to the caller. The whole script, including some code to print out what we've found, looks like this:

```
import sys

def getfile(filename):
    lines = []
    myfile=open(filename,'r')
    lines = myfile.readlines()
    return lines

mylines = getfile(sys.argv[1])
for line in mylines:
        print "line:",line
```

If we pick out the areas in Perl in which we'd normally place some checking, we can see how many lines of code are required to check for all the possible problems. In Perl, we'd probably do the following:

▶ Put a check before using the argument from the command line, **sys.argv[1]**, to make sure we received an argument.

▶ Check before the **for** loop that we'd got some lines from the function call, and therefore from the file itself.

▶ Check that we'd opened the file correctly, which would encompass whether the file existed and was readable.

Looking at the last item first, the normal way of handling an error during opening a file is to either trap the whole procedure using an **if** statement or use **warn** or **die** in combination with **or** to raise a warning or simply exit. The problem with all of these approaches is that we don't know why the error occurred – **$!** contains the error string or number, but the information contained within it is frequently used only to describe the problem to the user. The **$!** variable is often not used as a way of identifying the reason for the error and reacting differently according to the type of failure.

Furthermore, if the function had been defined in a module, simply calling the Python equivalent of **warn** or **die** from that function when an error occurred wouldn't be helpful to the programmer. We could set the function up so that it returned **None** (the Python equivalent of **undef**) or an empty list on error, but if we did that, the caller would just know that the function had failed, not why, and therefore would be unable to determine whether the error was recoverable from or whether the file was just empty.

Instead, what we need is a way of raising an error that doesn't rely on a return value, that doesn't require the module programmer to code any sort of error system, but that still allows us to identify the type of error that occurred and any additional information that goes with the error.

This is where Python's exception system fits in. Exceptions work a bit like a special function call, or a "super-goto" function. The basic operation is to install an exception handler, through the **try** statement, and then execute some code. If no error occurs then execution just continues. If however some sort of exception is raised whilst executing that block of code then execution immediately jumps back to that exception handler.

Let's look at a simple example that we know will raise a divide by zero error:

```
try:
    print 24/0
except:
    print "Calculation failed!"
```

The **try** block sets up the exception handler and the code immediately following the block is what will be executed with any errors being handled by the entire **try...except** statement. In this case, when any type of exception occurs, we print an error message. Note that execution hasn't stopped – any code after the **try...except** statement would have executed normally.

Now let's look at a more complex example that shows the propagation of exceptions through function calls, and also shows how we can trap more specific errors:

```
def divide(x,y):
    return x/y

def calc(x,y):
    return x*(divide(x,y))
```

```
try:
    print calc('Hello',1)
except ZeroDivisionError:
    print "Whoa!: You're trying to divide by zero and
you can't!"
except TypeError:
    print "Whoa!: That doesn't look like a number!"
except:
    print "Whoa!: Some other kind of error occurred!"
```

If you try running the script, you'll get the following output:

```
Whoa!: That doesn't look like a number!
```

In this example, we've got two functions, **calc()** and **divide()** which perform a calculation, but we've actually supplied a piece of incompatible data, the "**Hello**" string instead of a number.

The **try…except** statement has been designed to identify when there is a problem with the calculation, but we haven't modified the functions to either identify or handle what happens when a bad argument is supplied to them. In fact, the functions are completely dumb – it's the exception handler round the function call which is responsible for trapping any error. We can be as specific or as vague as we like in the exception process – in this example we've got both specific exceptions (**ZeroDivisionError** and **TypeError**) and a generalized **Exception** error – it doesn't matter what fails in the statements we are calling, we can trap it and act upon it.

THE EXCEPTION SYSTEM

We'll be looking at the specifics of the exception system shortly, but before we do that keep in mind the following:

▶ Exceptions are used throughout Python – during the parsing process of a Python script, any faults in the syntax are highlighted by raising a **SyntaxError** exception. Exceptions in Python are not a bolt-on feature, they are used by the interpreter itself as a way of highlighting problems.

▶ Exceptions are classes – all exceptions are based on the **Exception** class and follow a strict hierarchy. This allows you to trap a general exception such as **ArithmeticError**, or a more specific problem such as **ZeroDivisionError**.

▶ Exceptions are "dumb" – exceptions can pass objects and error information, they are simply a semaphore to say that an error has occurred.

With these points in mind, let's look at the specifics of the Python exception system.

EXCEPTION HANDLERS

The exception process uses the **try** statement in two different forms, the **try**...**except**...**else** statement and the **try**...**finally** statement. We've already seen a few examples of the first format; the second format provides a simplified operation sequence when you want to act upon an exception, but not actually handle the exception. We'll look at some examples to make it clearer.

try...except...else

The first form of the **try** statement acts a bit like an **if** statement in reverse – you embed a block of code which is executed, and then a number of **except** statements account for exceptions if they occur. The basic format for this first form is:

```
try:
    BLOCK
except [EXCEPTION [, DATA...]]:
    BLOCK
```

else:

```
    BLOCK
```

The **else** block is optional.

When the Python interpreter encounters a **try** statement it follows this basic procedure:

1 The **BLOCK** under the **try** statement is executed, if an exception is raised then execution returns immediately to the first **except** statement.

2 If the exception that was raised matches the **EXCEPTION** specified – or all exceptions if **EXCEPTION** is not defined – then the corresponding **BLOCK** is executed, with the objects defined in **DATA** being accessible to the handler.

3 If the exception does not match then execution jumps to the next **except** statement – you can have as many **except** statements as you like.

4 If no **except** statement matches, then the exception is passed to the next highest **try** block that called this block.

5 If no exception occurred then the **else** block is executed.

Out of this process there are a few core components that deserve extra mention.

except *statements support multiple formats*

Although it's not all that clear from the template above, you can trap errors and introduce a number of exception handlers in a number of different ways. The **except** statement accepts five different formats, as outlined in Table 6.1.

TABLE 6.1 Formats accepted by the **except** statement

Format	Description
except:	Catch all (or all other) exceptions
except name:	Catch the exception specified by name
except (name1, name2):	Catch all the exceptions listed
except name, data:	Catch the exception and any additional data returned
except (name1,name2),data:	Catch the exceptions listed and any addtional data returned

except *statements are checked in sequence*

In points 2 and 3 you can see that when the exception is raised, each **except** statement is examined to see if the specific exception matches the exception that occurs. The examination occurs in sequence, Python doesn't check all the **except** clauses in one go. This means that you can identify individual exceptions and classes until you reach the top. We saw an example of this earlier. In the script below we look for a **ZeroDivisionError** exception, and a **TypeError**, and finally trap everything else:

```
def divide(x,y):
    return x/y
```

```
def calc(x,y):
    return x*(divide(x,y))
try:
    print calc('Hello',1)
except ZeroDivisionError:
    print "Whoa!: You're trying to divide by zero and
    you can't!"
except TypeError:
    print "Whoa!: That doesn't look like a number!"
except:
    print "Whoa!: Some other kind of error occurred!"
```

The important thing to remember is to work from the most-specific exception to least-specific – if we'd placed **Exception** – the base class for all exception types – in the first **except** statement then the remaining handlers would never have been checked.

Handlers run once

If you've run the earlier script, you'll notice that it's the **TypeError** exception that is reported. Even though the general **Exception** would normally catch all exceptions where there has been a match – only one match by the **try...except...else** statement is allowed. As soon as the exception block has been executed control returns to the statements immediately after the entire **try** statement. Unless, of course, you've called another function, raised a new exception, or called one of the **exit** functions.

else only runs when there are no exceptions

According to point 5 of the exception handler execution sequence on p. 102, the **else** statement is only executed if no exceptions occur. Normally you use this in the same way as you might an **if** block:

```
try:
    file = open('file')
except EnvironmentError:
    print "Whoops: Can't seem to open the file"
else:
    lines = file.readlines()
    file.close()
```

The statements in the **else** block are not covered by the same exception handler as the block after **try** – if you want to run similar statements in an exception handler then you'll either need to duplicate the statements or create a function to handle them.

Catching data

Most exceptions will include additional information about the cause of an exception in addition to the information about the error itself. For example, consider the code below:

```
def parsefile(filename):
    file = open(filename,'rw')
    print file.readline()
    file.write('Hello World!')
    file.close()

try:
    parsefile('strings')
except EnvironmentError,(errno,msg):
    print "Error: %s (%d) whilst parsing the file"
    % (msg, errno)
```

Here we've got a single exception handler for **EnvironmentError**, this is the base class used for problems encountered by Python when using and accessing information outside of the Python interpreter, such as when accessing and using a file. Rather than trying to trap all of the different errors that might occur, such as a non-existent file, full file system, or an end of file condition we can instead just use the generic exception and additional information supplied by the exception to further describe the error to the user.

In the case of the **EnvironmentError** exception it automatically returns the C library error number and the associated message (if there is one) – identical to the error number or message contained in **$!** in Perl. For example, all of the following are perfectly valid error messages when calling the function:

```
Error: No such file or directory (2) whilst parsing the
        file
Error: Bad file descriptor (9) whilst parsing the file
Error: No space left on device (28) whilst parsing the
        file
```

If you specify a single object to catch the data then the built-in exceptions will convert the information into a string format and place that into the reference pointed to by the variable. If you want to catch specific information, as we have done here, you need to supply a tuple. The exact format for the returned information is defined by each exception – see *Built-in exceptions* on p. 108 for more information on the data returned by the standard exceptions.

try...finally

The other alternative to the **try**...**except**...**else** format is the **try**...**finally** format. The general format for this version of the **try** statement is:

```
try:
    BLOCK
finally:
    BLOCK
```

The rules are as follows:

1 The statements in the **try BLOCK** are executed.

2 If an exception occurs then the **finally BLOCK** is executed before the exception is propagated up to the next level.

3 If no exception occurs then the **finally BLOCK** is executed and control continues as normal until after the entire **try** statement.

The **try**...**finally** statement is useful in those situations where you want to run a piece of code irrespective of whether an exception occurs. For example, when communicating with a remote server over a network, you want to trap an error but still ensure that the communications channel is closed regardless of the error. With a **try**...**finally** statement you can do that:

```
try:
    remote.send_data(destination,datastream)
finally:
    remote.close_connection()
```

Of course, on it's own a **try**...**finally** statement will only propagate the error up to the next level, so you'll probably want to embed the call within another **try** statement:

```
try:
    try:
        remote.send_data(destination,datastream)
```

```
    finally:
        remote.close_connection()
except NetworkError,errorstr:
    print "Error: Couldn't send data,",errorstr
else:
    print "Data sent successfully"
```

Now the connection will be closed whether an exception occurs or not, whilst the outer **try** statement will trap and handle the actual exception raised during the process.

Exception propagation

It should be pretty clear by now that exceptions are always handled by the enclosing exception handler, but what happens if our exception handler doesn't explicitly handle all of the possible exceptions?

The answer is quite simple, the exception is raised to the next highest level exception handler. For example, in the second **try**...**finally** example earlier the exception raised by the **send_data** method was raised to the next exception handler, in this case a **try**...**except**...**else** statement.

Exceptions are logically stacked during the execution of the script such that exceptions will be removed from the stack if an exception handler catches them, or they will be propagated up to the next level if the local exception handler doesn't know what to do with them. Consider the following script, a modification of our earlier calculation script:

```
def divide(x,y):
    try:
        result = x/y
    except ZeroDivisionError:
        print "Whoa!: You're trying to divide by zero
        and you can't!"
        raise
    return result

def calc(x,y):
    return x*(divide(x,y))

try:
    print calc(1,0)
except TypeError:
    print "Whoa!: That doesn't look like a number!"
```

```
except:
    print "Whoa!: Couldn't complete the calculation"
```

If you run this you should get two error messages – one is from the exception handler within the **divide** function and identifies the attempt to divide by zero. The handler also raises its own exception which is then passed back to the main exception handler:

```
Whoa!: Your trying to divide by zero and you can't!
Whoa!: Couldn't complete the calculation
```

Alternatively, if you replace the main section with this version:

```
try:
    print calc('Hello',0)
except TypeError:
    print "Whoa!: That doesn't look like a number!"
except:
    print "Whoa!: Couldn't complete the calculation"
```

the local exception handler catches the error.

Raising exceptions

You can explicitly raise an exception using the **raise** statement. This has the same effect as if the exception had been raised by an internal error. The format for the **raise** statement is:

```
raise [EXCEPTION [, DATA]]
```

Where **EXCEPTION** is the name of the exception you want to raise and **DATA** is the additional data you want to supply back to the exception handler.

The **EXCEPTION** can either be one of the built-in exceptions or you can use an exception or exception class that you have already defined (see *Creating new exception classes* on p. 115 later in this chapter). The **DATA** will be passed to the exception handler as normal.

The assert statement

A shorthand for a **raise** statement is the **assert** statement which works in a similar fashion to the **ASSERT()** macro within C/C++. This works like a **raise** statement, but the exception will only be raised if the interpreter has not optimized the code (i.e. the user has not specified the -O optimization flag). The general format for the statement is:

```
assert TEST, DATA
```

which is essentially equivalent to:

```
if __debug__:
    if not TEST:
        raise AssertionError, DATA
```

Note the **__debug__** symbol is not enabled when the interpreter is optimizing the code.

BUILT-IN EXCEPTIONS

As we've already seen, Python comes with a number of base exceptions and exception classes. All of these can be used and trapped within your scripts to indicate or identify an error. If you are creating new exceptions (see p. 115) then you should consider using one of these exceptions as the base class. See Fig 6.1 for an example of the class structure for the exception system.

Exception

This is the root class used for all exceptions. Note that a string operation on the arguments returned from any exception should give a string representation of the error that occurred, irrespective of the number or type of arguments supplied. To obtain the individual arguments of any exception use the data format of the **except** statement passing a tuple of names into which the information should be placed:

```
try:
    pow(2,262)
except Exception,(args,):
    print args
```

Alternatively, if you fail to supply an explicit tuple of tuple, as in:

```
except Exception,args:
    print args
```

Then **args** will now hold the tuple of values returned by the exception.

```
Exception
    StandardError
        ArithmeticError
                FloatingPointError
                OverflowError
                ZeroDivisionError
        AssertionError
        AttributeError
        EnvironmentError
                IOError
                OSError
                        WindowsError
        EOFError
        ImportError
        KeyboardInterrupt
        LookupError
                IndexError
                KeyError
        MemoryError
        NameError
                UnboundLocalError
        RuntimeError
                NotImplementedError
        SyntaxError
        SystemError
        SystemExit
        TypeError
        ValueError
                UnicodeError
```

FIG 6.1 The Exception class structure

StandardError

The base class used for all the built-in exceptions, which also inherits the facilities offered by the **Exception** root class.

ArithmeticError

For exceptions arising due to arithmetic errors you will get one of the specific arithmetic exceptions, one of **OverflowError**, **ZeroDivisionError**, or **FloatingPointError**. This is the base class used by all three exceptions to indicate a general arithmetical fault. Since it's the base class, you can use this exception to trap all three specific arithmetic errors.

AssertionError

The exception raised when an **assert** statement fails.

AttributeError

The exception raised when an attribute reference or assignment fails. Note that if the type does not support attributes then a **TypeError** will be raised.

EnvironmentError

The class for errors that occur outside of Python's control, but that can be traced to the environment in which Python is operating. Used as the base class for **IOError** and **OSError** exceptions.

The standard arguments returned by the exception will be a two- or three-element tuple. In the two-element format the first element is the error number (**errno**) as returned by the operating system and the second element is the associated error string. In the three-element version, the third element will be the filename used when the exception was raised.

For example:

```
try:
    open('nosuchfile')
except EnvironmentError,(errno,string):
    print "Whoops!: %s (%d)" % (string, errno)
```

EOFError

The exception raised when the end-of-file (EOF) condition is detected by the built-in data handling functions. Note that this will only be raised if the EOF is raised without any data being read from the source. Also note that the built-in **read** and **readline** methods return an empty string on EOF.

FloatingPointError

Raised when a floating point operation fails – but only available if the interpreter has been compiled with floating point signal handling enabled. If not compiled with this option an **ArithmeticError** exception is raised instead.

ImportError

The exception raised when an **import** statement fails to find the specified module, or when **from** fails to find the specific symbol in the module. See the section on *Modules* in Chapter 7, (p. 118) for more information on import methods and semantics.

IndexError

The exception raised when you try to access a sequence element out of the range of the sequence's size. Note that a non-sequenced object will return **TypeError** if you try to access an element via the normal subscript notation.

IOError

The exception raised when an I/O operation fails, such as trying to open a non-existent file or writing to a device with no free space. The information supplied by the exception is the same as that given by any exception based on the **EnvironmentError** class.

KeyError

The exception raised when the dictionary or other mapping key requested does not exist within the mapping object.

KeyboardInterrupt

Raised when the interrupt key combination (Control-C or Command-. on the Mac) is pressed. The exception is raised even when the built-in **input** or **raw_input** functions have been called.

LookupError

The base exception class for the built-in **IndexError** and **KeyError** exceptions used to indicate an error when accessing information from a sequence (string, list, tuple) or mapping (dictionary).

MemoryError

The exception raised when the interpreter runs out of memory whilst executing a specific statement, but one that the interpreter still thinks it can recover from the situation if some objects are deleted to free up memory. It may not always be possible to recover from the situation, but by raising an exception a traceback for the program will be triggered. The data passed by the exception will describe what kind of internal operation triggered the exception.

NameError

The exception raised when the object specified cannot be found within either the local or global scope. The data passed by the exception will indicate the name that failed.

NotImplementedError

The exception raised when an abstract user-defined error requires methods that can't be found. Derived from the **RuntimeError** exception.

OSError

The exception raised when an operating system error occurs – usually through the **OS** module interface. Derived from the **EnvironmentError** exception.

OverflowError

The exception raised when an arithmetical operation exceeds the limits of the Python interpreter. Note that when doing long integer math the interpreter will raise a **MemoryError** rather than an **OverflowError**.

RuntimeError

The exception raised when there has been a runtime error that cannot be represented by one of the other exception types. This is included for compatibility only, since most errors now have their own exception class. The data passed by the exception will be a string indicating the error that occurred.

SyntaxError

The exception raised when a syntax error occurs, either within the original script, during an **import** or **exec** statement or within the built-in **eval** function.

The information returned by the exception will be a simple string of the error message. If you are accessing the exception object directly then the object will include the attributes **filename**, **lineno**, the **offset** within the line and the actual **text** of the line.

For a more detailed analysis, the data passed by the exception can be accessed as a tuple of the form (message, (filename, lineno, offset, text)). For example, the code

```
try:
    eval("print :")
except SyntaxError,(message,(filename,lineno,
offset,text)):
    print "Error in line %d, from file %s: \n" %
            (lineno, filename),\text,"\n",\
            ' ' * offset+"^", message
```

will generate the following output when executed:

```
Error in line 1, from file None:
print :
    ^ invalid syntax
```

SystemError

The exception raised when a system error occurs. This applies to internal Python errors that can be safely trapped and could potentially be recovered from. The data passed by the exception will be a string representing the error that went wrong.

Note that you should send **SystemError** exception information to the Python maintainers (see Appendix B) as it indicates a possible error with the interpreter.

SystemExit

The exception raised when the **sys.exit()** function is called. Normally the Python interpreter exits without any error or traceback being printed.

TypeError

Raised when a built-in operation or function is applied to an object of inappropriate type. The returned value is a string giving details about the type mismatch.

UnboundLocalError

The exception raised when a reference is made to a local variable (within the scope of a function or method) but no value has been bound to that variable.

UnicodeError

The exception raised when a Unicode-related encoding or decoding error occurs.

ValueError

The exception raised when a built-in operation or function receives an argument that has the right type but an inappropriate value, and the situation is not described by a more precise exception such as **IndexError**.

WindowsError

The exception raised when a Windows-specific error occurs. Also raised when the error number returned does not match a valid **errno** value. The actual values returned are populated using the **GetLastError** and **FormatMessage** Windows API calls.

ZeroDivisionError

The exception raised when the second argument of a division or modulo operation is zero. The returned value is a string indicating the type of the operands and the operation.

CREATING NEW EXCEPTION CLASSES

You can create your own exception classes simply by creating a new class which should be set to inherit from one of the existing exception classes. Alternatively, for backwards compatibility, you can also create a string-based exception, for example:

```
CustomError = 'Error'

raise CustomError
```

Note that exceptions match against values, thus raising a string exception, but checking against the object will still work:

```
CustomError = 'Error'

def test():
    raise 'Error'

try:
    test()
except CustomError:
    print "Error!"
```

However, it's bad practice to rely on this, so you should instead **raise** one of the predefined error strings.

If you want to create class-based exceptions create a new class, including any initialization information. You can then raise the exception, with any additional information, for parsing by an exception handler. The additional data collected by an **except** statement is extracted from the **args** attribute of an exception object. For example:

```
class MyNameException(Exception):
    def __init__(self, name, msg):
        self.args = (name, msg)
```

```
try:
    raise MyNameException('Marvin', 'Not my real name')
except MyNameException,(name, msg):
    print 'Sorry, but',name,'is',msg
```

As a rule, Python does not enforce the creation of new exception classes that are derived from existing classes. At least for the moment. Since any sub-class of the **Exception** hierarchy will automatically be trapped by an unspecified **except** clause, it's a good idea to inherit from the **Exception** classes.

RAISING AN EXCEPTION

You can manually raise an exception by using the **raise** statement. This accepts at least one argument, the name of the exception you want to use, with any additional arguments acting as additional data to the exception. For example:

```
raise TypeError, 'The type is not supported here'
```

This is syntactically equivalent to calling **die()** in Perl within an **eval** statement.

7

MODULES, CLASSES, AND OBJECT ORIENTATION

The last part of the core migration from Perl to Python is to understand how to import modules that we need to use and how to re-use and distribute your own code and libraries. Also related to this stage is the creation of classes, generally placed into modules in their own right, and how this relates to the Python object orientation system that pervades all parts of the language.

Both Perl and Python allow you to easily reuse your existing code base in new applications through the use of modules – Python is somewhat easier to use in this respect than Perl. The basic mechanics of putting your favorite routines into a module and loading that module on demand remain the same however.

In this chapter we're going to look at creating modules and creating new classes from which we can create new objects or, as Python calls them, class instances.

MODULES

Modules in Python work in a slightly different way to Perl. We still import the modules, but modules can be imported in different ways, and once imported accessing the information within them is also different. However, if you've followed the notes so far on using Python objects and methods you'll begin to see a familiar pattern.

Namespaces

Python uses a very simple system for controlling the namespaces for importing modules. Python uses these namespaces in the same way as

Perl uses packages (through the **package** statement). In Perl the package name for the main script is **main** and in Python **__main__**. The big difference between Perl and Python is how the namespaces affect how functions and objects in external modules are accessed.

In Perl, package namespaces are used as a way of indicating new modules (and classes), but through the **Exporter** module selected functions and variables are exported into the namespace of the caller. For example, in the module **Foo** exists a function **bar()** that is exported, to call the function you would simply refer to it by name:

```
use Foo;
bar();
```

In Python, the namespace, which is actually governed by the name of the module, is an integral part of the name we use within our script – i.e., we explicitly call the **bar()** function within the **Foo** module:

```
import Foo
Foo.bar()
```

This is in fact identical to the system we use when using the class/object system now employed by most Perl modules. Python uses the period to separate the individual elements (namespace/module/entity), for example **os.environ**, whilst Perl uses the double colon :: for separating individual components, for example **IPC::Open2**.

Note that with Python you cannot create multiple namespaces within a single file, there is no equivalent to the Perl **package** statement.

Importing a module

Using a module in Perl requires the **use** statement – the mnemonic there is that you want to 'use' the functions and variables (and by derivation classes) defined in the module. In Python we *import* the module into a script – the mnemonic here is that we are importing information about how to use the functions, objects and classes within the module, rather than importing the different entities into the script itself. The reason for this is related to the methods for importing modules, and what happens when you use the **import** statement.

Importing an entire module

The equivalent of the Perl **use** statement is the simple form of the Python **import** statement. For example, to import an entire module into a Perl script we would use:

```
use Net::FTP;
```

Within Python the same functionality is offered by the standard **ftplib** module, so this becomes:

```
import ftplib
```

The **import** statement in Python does three things:

1 Creates a new namespace to hold all the objects defined within the given module.

2 Executes the code in the module within the confines of the given namespace.

3 Creates a name within the caller that refers to the modules namespace.

In this case, a new namespace **ftplib** was created, the **ftplib.py** file within the Python library directory was found and executed within the **ftplib** namespace, and then an object called **ftplib** was created within the name-space of the current module – in this case our main script. See *Module loading/compilation* on p. 122 for information on how modules are searched for under Python.

The major differences between the two methods are:

▶ In Perl, the basic **use** statement only imports those entities that have been explicitly exported (through a mention in **@EXPORT** within the called module). In Python all entities are imported since there is no way to explicitly select objects to export.

▶ In Perl the **use** statement imports the functions and variables from a module into the current namespace; accessing function **foo()** from module **Bar** just means calling **foo()**. In Python, the basic **import** statement has it's own namespace into which the objects are made available; accessing function **foo()** from module **Bar** requires us to call **Bar.foo()**.

Another difference is that with Perl we can only import one module per **use** statement. For example, it's impossible within Perl to do:

```
use Getopt, Net::FTP;
```

In Python however we can place as many modules as we like into the **import** statement:

```
import os, sys, getopt, ftplib
```

Each is interpreted as an individual so the above is equal to:

```
import os
import sys
import getopt
import ftplib
```

Importing a module under an alias

An extension of the basic **import** method made available in Python 2.0 is the ability to import a module within a namespace different to the default namespace selected by the module's apparent name. For example, we can import the **ftplib** module as simple **ftp** using:

```
import ftplib as ftp
```

Now all calls to the **ftplib** module must be identified within the **ftp** namespace.

Using aliases can be a great way of testing a new version of a module without upsetting the original. For example, imagine you've got two modules, **mylib**, the stable version and, **newmylib**, the development version, you could change references in your test scripts to:

```
import newmylib as mylib
```

No changes would need to be made to the rest of the script for it to work – providing your new module doesn't break any of the API.

Importing specific module entities

In Perl, functions and variables that have been placed into the @EXPORT and @EXPORT_OK variables within the host package can be selectively imported into the namespace of the caller. For example we can explicitly request only to import the functions **foo** and **bar** from the module **Foobar** using:

```
use Foobar qw/foo bar/;
```

Under Python we can perform the same operation – the exact equivalent of the line above in Python is:

```
from Foobar import foo, bar
```

Note, however, that the above line imports the **foo** and **bar** objects into the current namespace – i.e., the following script is now valid:

```
from Foobar import foo, bar
foo()
bar()
```

The **from** version causes Python to import the specified objects into the namespace of the caller, which makes it operate in the same way as *all* Perl **use** statements. To import everything from the module into the current namespace, use *****:

```
from Foobar import *
```

Reloading a module

It's possible to reload a module that has already been loaded using the **reload**() built-in function. This re-evaluates and imports the module again, causing any changes to the module's code to be reflected within the caller, but it doesn't change the methods or operation of any existing objects that existed at the point of reload. There are some other traps too, check the **reload** function in Chapter 8, for more information.

Module loading/compilation

When we load a module in Perl what we are actually importing is the source code, the raw script that makes up the module. This in turn may load hooks for loading other raw script dynamically or the necessary hooks to load a dynamically-loadable module containing external C or C++ source code. Because Perl imports the raw script each time, it also has to compile the same module code each time the script is executed.

On a fairly simple script that is infrequently run this does not become a problem, but when working with scripts that are regularly executed, such as within a web application, the time taken to compile the module each time is prohibitive. There are solutions to this problem that rely on recording the compiled bytecode of the script, and simply executing this compiled version each time the script is required as used by **PerlEx** and **mod_apache**, but these solve the problem on a script by script basis, they do not solve the problem of working with many different modules and scripts, or the problem of running scripts outside of a webserver.

Python actually tries to load Python-compatible C/C++ extensions directly – during the import process it also compiles any module into bytecode so that next time you load the module you only need to load the pre-compiled bytecode for the module, not the source code. This results in fast execution times for all scripts.

What Python actually searches for is files within the Python library search path (see *Changing search directories*, on p. 127) for, in this order (assuming a module called **foo**):

1   A directory defining a package called **foo**.

2   A compiled extension or library named **foo.so**, **foomodule.so**, **foomodule.sl**, **foomodule.slb**, or **foomodule.dll**.

3   A file called **foo.pyo** (assuming the -**O** option has been used).

4   A file called **foo.pyc** (the precompiled bytecode version of **foo.py**).

5   A file called **foo.py**.

6   A built-in module called **foo**.

When Python finds the file **foo.pyc** (or **foo.pyo**) the timestamp is checked against **foo.py**, if **foo.py** is newer then the file is compiled and the compiled bytecode for the module is written into **foo.pyc** or **foo.pyo** if optimization has been enabled. Python always attempts to load a precompiled bytecode for modules loaded through **import**. Modules executed as a script are not precompiled and stored in any way.

If the -**O** command line option is in effect then Python loads an optimized form of the precompiled bytecode, as stored in **.pyo** files. These are identical in content to the **.pyc** file except the line numbers, assertions and other debugging information that could be used to trace the execution of the module.

If, after trying to load all these different components one still cannot be found, then the **ImportError** exception is raised.

Creating a new module

When writing an application in Perl creating a true module, that is one that can be imported using **use** and that defines and exports the functions and variables wanted, requires us to modify the header of a given file, change its file extension (and possibly its name), and place it into a location suitable for loading.

The process is somewhat easier in Python.

Modules in Perl

As a test case, imagine we have the script below, here written in Perl, that defines a single function **add()**. The entire script is in a file called **mymath.pl**:

```
sub add
{
    return $_[0]+$_[1];
}

print add(1,1);
```

To put the function **add** into its own module (let's call it **MyMath**), there are two possible solutions. The first solution creates a module that requires us to reference the module and entities within explicitly. To do this we need to place the function definition into a file called **MyMath.pm**. In addition we need to add a package definition and a trailing "true" value:

```
package MyMath;

sub add
{
    return $_[0]+$_[1];
}

1;
```

Now we can modify the original script to read:

```
use MyMath;
print MyMath::add(1,1);
```

The second solution will allow us to import functions and other entities into the namespace of the current script. For this to work we have to create the **MyMath.pm** file as before and then add some additional preamble to create the **import()** function that will be used by the **use** statement:

```
package MyMath;

require Exporter;
@ISA = qw/Exporter/;
@EXPORT = qw/add/;

sub add
{
    return $_[0]+$_[1];
}

1;
```

Now we can modify our original script to read:

```
use MyMath;
print add(1,1);
```

Modules in Python

Creating a new module in Python is as easy as writing the original script. In fact, we don't have to do anything. Given a script which performs the same task as the above, called **mymath.py**:

```
def add(a,b):
    return a+b
```

We can immediately access **add()** function simply by putting:

```
import mymath
print mymath.add(2,2)
```

in another script. The **import** statement automatically looks for the file **mymath.py**, and then creates a new namespace and imports the **add()** function into that namespace.

Furthermore, we can also explicitly import **add()** into the current namespace using:

```
from mymath import add
```

It really is that simple – here's a list of what we *don't* need to do to create a Python module compared to the steps required for a Perl module:

▶ We don't need to define the package and/or module name.

▶ We don't need to use **Exporter** (or any other module) to export objects to the caller.

▶ We don't need to populate the **@EXPORT** or other variables.

▶ We don't need to have a "true" value at the end of the module to indicate success.

Because of this flexibility all of the code and functions that you write and create in Python are available to all the other scripts and modules that you create without any form of modification.

Python module tricks

Python has a few more tricks up its sleeve when it comes to importing modules within a script. Some of these are in direct conflict with Perl, while others mimic or augment some of the ability we are already familiar with.

Import works anywhere

In Perl, the **use** statement is evaluated during the initial pass through the source script. This is partly to handle dependencies – Perl bails out of compilation if it can't find a module you've requested – but it also needs to import the text from the module it finds so that it can be compiled with the rest of the code. This is also in part why we need the **package** statement – it tells the Perl interpreter where the different packages that make up a script (including any loaded modules) start and, by implication, end. This leads to some problems – for example, we can't use the normal methods for importing a module depending on a variable, the following code just loads both modules:

```
if ($module = 'first')
{
    use First;
}
else
{
    use Second;
}
```

We can achieve the result we want by placing the **use** statements in a call to **eval()** or we could use **require**.

In Python the **import** statement is only executed at the point it is seen, which means that it will work within an **if** or other control statement:

```
if (module == 'os'):
    import os
else:
    import sys
```

This is actually used by modules like **os** which load a platform-specific module such as **posix** or **mac** depending on the host on which the Python interpreter is running.

It's also perfectly legal to load modules only when a function is actually called, i.e.:

```
def sendmymail():
    import smtplib
```

For all this flexibility, however, we cannot import a module using a variable or string without using the **exec** statement. Thus the typical Perl fragment:

```
$module = 'DBI';
eval("use $module");
```

can be re-written in Python as:

```
module = 'os'
exec 'import '+module
```

The **exec** statement is similar to the Perl **eval**(), executing a string as if it were a Python script or expression.

Changing search directories

Perl uses it's own internal table, stored in **@INC** to list the directories that are searched when you try to load a module. You can change the contents of this variable by using the **lib** pragma, for example:

```
use lib "./lib/perl";
```

What the **lib** pragma actually does is use a **BEGIN** block to modify the contents of **@INC**.

Python stores the list of directories that are searched when importing a module in the **sys.path** list as part of the **sys** module. Because Python only loads modules when it executes **import** statements, rather than as soon as the statements are seen (as in Perl), we can modify the **sys.path** list using the normal methods before we call **import**. For example, to add **./lib/perl** to the search list:

```
import sys
sys.path.append('./lib/python')
```

Now all future **import** statements will not only search the standard libraries, but also the directory we've just added.

To completely emulate the functionality of Perl's **lib** pragma you must use the **insert()** method to add the directory to the start, rather than the end of the list:

```
sys.path.insert(0,'./lib/python')
```

Trapping import *statements*

Because Python uses exceptions, and because an **ImportError** exception is raised if a module fails to load correctly we can trap the error safely within the script. For example:

```
try:
    import mymodule
except ImportError:
    print "Woah! We seem to be missing a module we
    require here"
    import sys
    sys.exit()
```

This is a cleaner way then using an **eval()** call in Perl to test for the existence of a particular module.

Identifying a module or script

Each module defines a variable, **__name__**, that contains the name of the module. You can use this as a way to determine within which module a particular piece of code is executing. However, it also becomes a handy way of determining whether a given module is running as a script, or whether it has been imported. Modules running as scripts set **__name__** to **__main__**, and we can test for this:

```
if __name__ == '__main__':
    # Work as a script
else:
    # Work as a module
```

Although this shouldn't be used to affect the functions or classes defined within the module, it can and often is used as a handy testing mechanism for a module. When you run the module as a script it tests itself, but when imported as a module it just defines the functions. This saves us from having a separate test script and also aids Python's code re-use because each module can be used as both script and library addition.

Checking any of the standard modules that come with Python you'll probably find such a block. For example, running the **smtplib** module as a script allows you to send an e-mail message:

```
$ python smtplib.py
From: mc@mcslp.com
To: mc@mcwords.com
Enter message, end with ^D:
Hello Doppleganger!
Message length is 20
send: 'ehlo twinsol\015\012'
reply: '250-twinsol.mchome.com Hello localhost
[127.0.0.1], pleased to meet you\015\012'
reply: '250-ENHANCEDSTATUSCODES\015\012'
reply: '250-EXPN\015\012'
...
```

I've trimmed the output for clarity, but you can see the effect. Importing **smtplib** as a module has no effect – the test code is only executed when the module is executed as a script.

Packages

Packages in Python allow a group of modules to be grouped under a common package name. This is analogous to the Perl system of nesting modules whereby the statement:

```
use Net::FTP;
```

actually causes Perl to look for the module **FTP** within the directory **Net**. By default, within Python, nesting modules in this manner does not work – importing the module **parent.child** does not look for the module **child** within a directory called **parent**.

The solution to this problem is to make use of the Python package system. A package is defined by creating a directory with the same name as the package and then creating the file **__init__.py** within that directory. The file contains the necessary instructions to the Python interpreter to allow the importing of modules, and module groups, within the package. For example, the directory structure below shows the layout of a project called MediaWeb which, as a network management tool, has been placed in a **Net** directory:

```
Net/
    __init__.py
    MediaWeb/
        __init__.py
        Weather.py
        Weblog.py
        Systemlog.py
```

Now, from within Python, we can import modules from this structure in a number of ways:

```
import Net.MediaWeb.Weather
```

would import the submodule **Weather** from the **Net/MediaWeb** directory – as with other **import** statements we would have to refer to functions in this module explicitly, i.e. **Net.MediaWeb.Weather.report()**.

```
from Net.MediaWeb import Weather
```

would import the same module, **Weather**, but without the package prefix, allowing us to use **Weather.report()**.

```
from Net.MediaWeb.Weather import report
```

imports **report** into the local namespace, enabling us to call it using **report()**.

In each case, the code in **__init__.py** is executed in order to perform any package specific initialization. All the **__init__.py** files are processed as they are seen within the import process, for example, importing **Net.MediaWeb.Weather** would execute **Net/__init__.py** and **Net/MediaWeb/__init__.py**.

The contents of **__init__.py** are entirely up to you – they may be empty, in which case nothing happens except to import the module you've selected. But they *must* exist for the directory nesting to work as you would expect it to within Perl.

On the other hand, you may want to enforce certain options. For example, the statement:

```
import Net.MediaWeb
```

does not automatically force Python to import the contents of the **Net/MediaWeb** directory and neither does the statement:

```
from Net.MediaWeb import *
```

In these instances you can do one of two things. In the first instance you may want to put the following into the **Net/MediaWeb/__init__.py** file:

```
# Net/MediaWeb/__init__.py
import Weather,Weblog
```

In the second instance, we can use the **__all__** attribute within the **__init__.py** file – this should be initialized with a list of modules that you want to import:

```
# Net/MediaWeb/__init__.py
__all__ = ['Weather', 'Weblog']
```

CLASSES

Perl provides a very simple method for creating classes and allowing you to create objects off of those classes. We can summarize Perl's approach to creating classes in three points:

▶ An object is simply a reference.

▶ A class is simply a package.

▶ A method is simply a subroutine.

For example, to create a new class and the constructor method required to create a new object, in this case an object for tracking banking accounts, is as simple as:

```
package Account;
sub new
{
    my ($package, $name, $balance) = @_;
    my $self = {'Name' => $name,
                'Balance' => $balance};
```

```
    bless $self, $package;
    return $self;
}

sub deposit
{
    my ($self, $value) = @_;
    $self->{'Balance'} += $value;
}

sub withdraw
{
    my ($self, $value) = @_;
    $self->{'Balance'} -= $value;
}
```

In this case we've created a hash-based object to contain our object data. The **new()** function is the constructor which will be used to create a new object, for example:

```
$bank = new Account('HSBC', 2000);
```

The functions defined within the scope of the package, i.e. **deposit()** and **withdraw()**, become methods to an instance of the class. We can make a deposit by calling **deposit()**:

```
$bank->deposit(1000);
```

To access the accounts balance:

```
print "You have ", $bank->{'Balance'},"\n";
```

Creating a class

Everything in Python is an object of some kind and when you create a new class you also create a built-in dictionary object (actually stored in the internal __dict__ attribute) which is used to hold the attributes for the object. Python does not support packages, instead we explicitly define that we are starting a new class. However, functions do form the basis of the methods we define within a particular class.

Creating a new class in Python requires the **class** statement which works like any other block definition in Python, everything contained within the **class** block becomes a part of the class you are defining. For example, we can rewrite the above Perl example in Python as:

```
class Account:
    def __init__(self, name, balance):
        self.name = name
        self.balance = balance
    def deposit(self, value):
        self.balance += value
    def withdraw(self, value):
        self.balance -= value
```

The __init__() function within a class is the constructor, the equivalent of the default new() function we typically define in a Perl class. Unlike the Perl constructor, the Python __init__() function is required in order to create a new instance of a given class. The other functions, deposit() and withdraw() are the other methods to the class.

We can create a new instance of the Account variable in Python using:

```
bank = Account('HSBC', 2000)
```

To deposit money in the account:

```
bank.deposit(1000)
```

Finally, to get the account's balance:

```
print "You have",bank.balance
```

All of the above are direct equivalents to the Perl examples we gave above.

Note as well, that creating a new class within Python is not reliant on us first defining a new package – although it is safe to think of the Python class statement as an equivalent of the Perl package statement when working with classes. Similarly, it's not a requirement that the module you import must match the name of the class it defines – there's no reason why a module called mymodule cannot contain the definition for the class MyFruit for example.

Additional class methods

The only method required by all classes is __init__() which creates a new instance of an object. All other methods, even those that relate to the internal operation of the object, are optional. However, the first argument that all methods within a class should accept is the object itself, typically called self – this follows the same basic format as Perl.

As well as __**init**__() there are a number of other "standard" methods which will be used internally by the Python interpreter if they are defined within a class.

Using __del__()

All class instances have a reference count for the number of times they have been referenced – i.e., each name that refers to it, each time the object is included as part of a list, tuple or dictionary, and so on. When the reference count reaches zero the instance is destroyed, freeing up the memory used to hold the object data. Python actually tries to call the __**del**__() method to perform the operation in the same way that Perl uses the special **DESTROY** method. Most basic objects, such as the example we've created here, don't require the method. If it's not defined then Python still deletes the object.

Be aware that the __**del**__() method cannot be relied on in situations where destroying the object requires the closing of files, network connections or releasing other system resources. In these situations you will need to explicitly define a **close**(), **disconnect**() or other method and then document it's use.

Operator overloading

All user-defined objects can be made to work with all of Python's built-in operators by adding implementations of the special methods which Python actually calls when an operator is used on any object, even the built-in types. For example, the __**add**__() method defines what happens when two objects of the same type are added together using the + operator. For example, we could merge two of the bank accounts we defined in the **Account** class using:

```
def __add__(self, other):
    return Account(self.name + ' and ' + other.name,
                   self.balance + other.balance)
```

In this case we return the balance of the two accounts, as in this example:

```
bank = Account('HSBC', 2000)
creditcard = Account('MBNA', -1000)
assets = bank + creditcard
```

Now **assets** contains a new object whose **name** attribute is "HSBC and MBNA" and **balance** is 1000.

Similar special function names exist for the other operators, including __repr__(), which is used when the **repr**() function is called and __coerce__() for when the **coerce**() function is called. Check the Python documentation for a full list of the operators supported.

Class inheritance

Inheritance in Perl is handled through the **@ISA** array – module names appearing in the array are taken as classes from which we can inherit additional methods. With Python the process is more explicit – you list the classes from which you want to inherit at the time you define the class. For example if you want the class **Citrus** to inherit from the class **Fruit**:

```
class Citrus(Fruit):
...
```

The actual list of classes to inherit values from can be as long you like so that:

```
package Recipe;
@ISA = qw/Fruit Vegetable Meat DryGoods/;
```

is equivalent to the Python:

```
class Recipe(Fruit, Vegetable, Meta, DryGoods):
```

>> SECTION 3
APPLYING PYTHON

8

BUILT-IN FUNCTIONS

Although Python does not rely on built-in functions to provide additional feature and functions such as network access or file control it does rely on built-in functions for providing and supplying the core functionality of the language. For example, there are built-in functions for converting strings to numbers and for manipulating tuples and lists.

In this chapter we'll look at these base functions and how they relate to Perl equivalent functions, where relevant. Appendix B contains a complete list of Perl functions and their Python equivalents.

PERL TO PYTHON TRAPS

There are quite a few traps for the unwary when migrating from Perl to Python in terms of the built-in function set. Primarily these relate to the way in which Python is object-oriented and therefore has class methods for certain operations that are covered by a Perl internal function – **keys**() and **each**(), for example. These traps apply as much to the built-in function set as to the methods on the base object types and other classes.

Other traps to look out for in all functions and methods, including the built-in ones dealt with in this chapter, are:

▶ Python has no "scratchpad" variable (**$_** in Perl) – if a function is expecting an argument and you don't supply one the interpreter will raise an exception.

▶ Python functions return values – if you ignore the return values then they are lost. Unlike Perl, Python built-in functions do not place the results of their operation into another variable (**$_** or **@_**) if no return value is supplied.

▶ Python does not distinguish between the core numeric, scalar, or list contexts. In Python there is no way to determine from within a function what the caller expects in return. Functions do not therefore return different values according to how they are called.

▶ Python doesn't assume anything – in Perl certain functions assume that you mean a particular operation based on the format in which you write them.

▶ Python functions (but *not* methods) do not edit variables in place. The Perl **chomp**() for example changes, in place, the contents of the variable you supply to it. Python can only do this as a method on an object.

Note that the information contained within this chapter was based on the documentation available for Python 2.0. Up-to-date lists of functions and Perl/Python equivalents can be found on the MCwords website. See the foreword for more information.

__import__ (name [, globals [, locals [, fromlist]]])
Perl equivalent: the Exporter *module*

The **__import__**() function is invoked automatically by the **import** statement. For example, the statement:

```
import module
```

results in the following call to **__import__**():

```
__import__('object',globals(),locals(),[])
```

Whilst the call

```
from module import class
```

would result in:

```
__import('object',globals(),locals(),['class'])
```

The **__import__**() function mainly exists so that you can optionally replace it with your own import function. See the **ihooks** and **rexec** modules for more examples.

Notes for Perl programmers

The __import__() function is very similar to the exporting function of the **Exporter** module. As with **Exporter** it's very unlikely that you will need to install your own version of this function. See Chapter 7 for more information on modules and how names are exported and imported to and from the caller.

abs(x)
Perl equivalent: abs(x)

Returns the absolute value of a number (plain or long integer or floating point number). If you supply a complex number then only the magnitude is returned.

For example:

```
>>> print abs(-2.4)
2.4
>>> print abs(4+2j)
4.472135955
```

apply(function, args [, keywords])
Perl equivalent: none

Applies the arguments **args** to **function**, which must be a function, method or other callable object. The **args** must be supplied as a sequence, lists are converted to tuples before being applied. The **function** is called using **args** as individual arguments, for example:

```
apply(add,(1,3,4))
```

is equivalent to:

```
add(1,3,4)
```

You need to use the **apply** function in situations where you are building up a list of arguments in a list or tuple and want to supply the list as individual arguments. This is especially useful in situations where you want to supply a varying list of arguments to a function.

The optional **keywords** argument should be a dictionary whose keys are strings, these will be used as keyword arguments to be supplied to the end of the argument list.

Notes for Perl programmers

The **apply()** function gets round the absence in Python of a way of dynamically calling a method or function. It also solves problems where you need to supply a list of arguments to a function that you are building dynamically. In Perl, arguments are progressively taken off an argument stack (@_), whereas Python uses fixed argument names. The **apply()** is frequently used where we need to supply a variable list of arguments to the function that we've probably built up in an array or tuple.

You can also use it to call a function or method based on a string by using the return value from a call to **eval()**. The **eval()** function returns a valid Python expression, which can include a valid method or code object. For example, here's a function called **run()** which runs the method **cmd** on the **imapcon** object, which is actually an instance of the **imaplib** class for communicating with IMAP servers:

```
def run(cmd, args):
    typ, dat = apply(eval('imapcon.%s' % cmd), args)
    return dat
```

The **imaplib** module provides methods for all of the standard IMAP commands. So, to obtain the number of messages you send the **select** function, which means calling the **select()** method on an **imaplib** instance. By using the function above we can execute the **select()** method using:

```
run('select',())
```

This in effect calls:

```
imapcon.select()
```

We can get the contents of a specific message using:

```
data = run('fetch', (message,'(FLAGS
RFC822.HEADER)'))[0]
```

In Perl, we'd do the same thing by using a symbolic reference, or by using the symbol table to determine the code reference we need to use. For example, a typical trick is to dynamically call a function based on a string supplied by the user, often within a web application:

```
my $func = sprintf("%s_%s",$action,$subaction);
*code = \&{$func};
&code($user,$group,$session);
```

buffer(object [, offset [, size]])
Perl equivalent: none

Creates a new buffer on the **object** providing it supports the buffer call interface (such objects include strings, arrays, and buffers). The new buffer references the **object** using a slice starting from offset and extending to the end of the **object** or to the length **size**. If no arguments are given then the buffer covers the entire sequence.

Buffer objects are used to create a more friendly interface to certain object types. For example, the string object type is made available through a buffer object which allows you to access the information within the string on a byte by byte basis.

Notes for Perl programmers

The **buffer()** is similar in principle to the **tie** system for tying complex data structures to a simplified structure. However, whereas the **tie** system is flexible enough to provide you with different methods for accessing scalar, array or hash data sources, the **buffer()** function is only suitable for sequence objects.

callable(object)
Perl equivalent: UNIVERSAL::can(METHOD) *or* exists() *when supplied a function reference*

Returns true if **object** is callable, false if not. Callable objects include functions, methods and code objects, and also classes (which return a new instance when called) and class instances which have the **call** method defined.

Notes for Perl programmers

The **callable()** function is slightly different to the closest suggestion given above. The **callable()** function only returns true if the method is defined within the given instance or class, it doesn't return a reference to the method itself. Also, **callable()** is designed to test any object or class that could be callable. This makes it appear to be as flexible as both UNIVERSAL::can() and **defined()**, when in truth all Python entities are objects or classes.

chr(i)

Perl equivalent: chr()

Returns a single character string matching the ASCII code **i**. For example:

```
>>> print chr(72)+chr(101)+chr(108)+chr(108)+chr(111)
Hello
```

The **chr()** function is the opposite of **ord()** which converts characters back to ASCII integer codes. The argument should be in the range 0 to 255, a **ValueError** exception will be raised if the argument is outside that limit.

cmp(x, y)

Perl equivalent: The <=> and cmp *operators*

Compares the two objects **x** and **y** and returns an integer according to the outcome. The return value is negative if **x** < **y**, zero if **x** == **y** and positive if **x** > **y**. Note that this specifically compares the values rather than any reference relationship, such that:

```
>>> a = 99
>>> b = int('99')
>>> cmp(a,b)
0
```

Notes for Perl programmers

The **cmp()** function in Python is similar to the **cmp** operator in Perl, in that it compares the values of the objects you supply as arguments, but unlike Perl's **cmp** it works on all objects. You should be using **cmp()** within a **sort()** method to guarantee the correct sorting order.

coerce(x, y)

Perl equivalent: none

Return a tuple consisting of the two numeric arguments converted to a common type, using the same rules as used by arithmetic operations. For example:

```
>>> a = 1
>>> b = 1.2
>>> coerce(a,b)
(1.0, 1.2)
>>> a = 1+2j
```

```
>>> b = 4.3e10
>>> coerce(a,b)
((1+2j), (43000000000+0j))
```

Notes for Perl programmers

Perl automatically translates between strings, integers and floating point numbers during any numerical expression. Although Python does not perform the automatic conversion of strings to numerical values (see the **float()** and **int()** functions later in this chapter), numbers are converted between integer, floating point, and complex types. The **coerce()** function exists to avoid constructs like:

```
$fpvalue = $intvalue/1.0;
```

compile(string, filename, kind)
Perl equivalent: anonymous subroutine

Compile **string** into a code object, which can later be executed by the **exec** statement to evaluate using **eval()**. The **filename** should be the name of the file from which the code was read, or a suitable identifier if generated internally. The kind argument specifies what **kind** of code is contained in **string**. See Table 8.1 for more information of the possible values.

TABLE 8.1 The kinds of code compiled by **compile()**

Kind value	Code compiled
exec	Sequence of statements
eval	Single expression
single	Single interactive statement

For example:

```
>>> a = compile('print "Hello World"','<string>','single')
>>> exec(a)
Hello World
>>> eval(a)
Hello World
```

Notes for Perl programmers

This is similar, but not identical to the process for creating anonymous functions within Perl, which internally create CV (Code Value) objects. However, **compile()** more closely matches the result of a parsed but unexecuted Perl **eval()** function call. Instead of returning a value, **compile()** returns the pre-compiled code ready to be executed.

complex(real [, imag])
Perl equivalent: none

Returns a complex number with the real component **real** and the imaginary component **imag**, if supplied.

delattr(object, name)
Perl equivalent: the delete() *function on hash/array based objects*

Deletes the attribute **name** from the object **object**, providing the object allows you to. Identical to the statement:

```
del object.name
```

However, it allows you to define **object** and **name** pragmatically, rather than explicitly in the code.

dir([object])
Perl equivalent: none

When supplied without an argument lists the names within the current local symbol table. For example:

```
>>> import smtplib, sys, os
>>> dir()
['__builtins__', '__doc__', '__name__', 'os', 'smtplib',
'sys']
```

When supplied with an argument, returns a list of attributes for that object. This can be useful for determining the objects and methods defined within a module:

```
>>> import sys
>>> dir(sys)
['__doc__', '__name__', '__stderr__', '__stdin__',
'__stdout__',
```

```
'argv', 'builtin_module_names', 'byteorder',
'copyright',
'exc_info', 'exc_type', 'exec_prefix', 'executable',
'exit',
'getdefaultencoding', 'getrecursionlimit',
'getrefcount',
'hexversion', 'maxint', 'modules', 'path', 'platform',
'prefix',
'ps1', 'ps2', 'setcheckinterval', 'setprofile',
'setrecursionlimit', 'settrace', 'stderr', 'stdin',
'stdout',
'version', 'version_info']
```

The information is built up from the __dict__, __methods__, and __members__ attributes of the given object and may not be complete – for example, methods and attributes inherited from other classes will not normally be included.

Notes for Perl programmers

Although there is no direct equivalent, the **dir()** function provides similar information to using **keys()** on a hash-based object, i.e.:

```
@attributes = keys %{$objref};
```

although it doesn't list any methods, or using **keys()** on a package's symbol table:

```
@entities = keys %main::;
```

divmod(a, b)
Perl equivalent: none

Returns a tuple containing the quotient and remainder of **a** divided by **b**. For example:

```
>>> divmod(7,4)
(1, 3)
```

For integers the value returned is the same as **a / b** and **a % b**. If the values supplied are floating point numbers the result is (q, a % b), where q is usually **math.floor(a / b)** but may be 1 less than that. In any case q * b + a % b is very close to a, if a % b is non-zero it has the same sign as b, and 0 <= abs(a % b) < abs(b).

eval(expression [, globals [, locals]])
Perl equivalent: eval()

Evaluates the string **expression**, parsing and evaluating it as a standard Python expression. When called without any additional arguments the expression has access to the same global and local objects in which it is called. Alternatively, you can supply the global and local symbol tables as dictionaries (see the **globals**() and **locals**() functions elsewhere in this chapter).

The return value is the value of the evaluated expression. For example:

```
>>> a = 99
>>> eval('divmod(a,7)')
(14,1)
```

Any syntax errors are raised as exceptions.

You can also use **eval**() to execute code objects, such as those created by the **compile**() function, but only when the code object has been compiled using the "eval" mode.

To execute arbitrary Python code incorporating statements as well as expressions, use the **exec** statement or use **execfile**() to dynamically execute a file.

Notes for Perl programmers

Although **eval**() appears to be identical to the Perl **eval**() function there are some differences:

1   Python's **eval**() function is designed to evaluate an expression and return a value.

2   Python's **eval**() can return an object, including a function or normal object type, rather than just a value or reference.

3   Python's **eval**() is not designed to execute an arbitrary piece of any Python code (although it will) but just a simple expression, use the **exec** statement instead.

execfile(file [, globals [, locals]])
Perl equivalent: do, *or* require, *or* eval()

Identical to the **exec** statement, except that it executes statements from a file instead from a string. The **globals** and **locals** arguments should be dictionaries containing the symbol tables that will be available to the file during execution. If **locals**, is omitted then all references use the **globals** namespace. If both are omitted, then the file has access to the current symbol tables as at the time of execution.

Notes for Perl programmers

The **execfile()** function most closely matches Perl's **eval()** function in that it will execute a file of code as if the code was executed within the realms of the current interpreter instance, with access to the same functions and variables. However, if you supply your own **globals** or **locals** dictionaries then it can function as an alternative to Perl's **Safe** module for executing code within a fixed environment.

filter(function, list)

Perl equivalent: grep() *or* map()

Filters the items in **list** according to whether **function** returns true, returning the new list. For example:

```
a = [1,2,3,4,5,6,7,8,9]
b = filter(lambda x: x > 6, a)
print b
```

If **function** is **None**, then the identity function is used and all the elements in **list** which are false are removed instead.

Notes for Perl programmers

The **filter()** function is a general purpose equivalent of the Perl **grep()** function. If you are looking for an alternative to Perl's **grep()** function consider using the example below:

```
def grep(pattern,list):
    import re
    retlist = []
    regex = re.compile(pattern)
    for element in list:
        if (regex.search(element)):
            retlist.append(element)
    return retlist
```

float(x)
Perl equivalent: none

Converts **x**, which can be a string or number, to a floating point number.

getattr(object, name [, default])
Perl equivalent: none

Returns the value of the attribute **name** of the object **object**. Syntactically the statement

```
getattr(x,'myvalue')
```

is identical to

```
x.myvalue
```

If **name** does not exist then the function returns **default** if supplied, or raises **AttributeError** otherwise.

Notes for Perl programmers

Because Perl's object system is based on the core scalar, array, and hash data types we can access an objects attribute pragmatically simply by supplying the variable name when accessing the array or hash element, for example:

```
$attribute = $object[$var];
$attribute = $object{$var};
```

However, we can't do this in Python – you must use **getattr**(). The above lines are equivalent to:

```
attribute = getattr(object, var)
```

globals()
Perl equivalent: none

Returns a dictionary representing the current global symbol table. This is always the dictionary of the current module – if called within a function or method then it returns the symbol table for the module where the function or method is defined, not the function from where it is called.

Notes for Perl programmers

The **globals()** function is normally used in conjunction with the **exec** statement and the **eval()** and **execfile()** functions, among others. The closest equivalent in Perl is to access the symbol tables directly:

```
@globals = keys %main::;
```

hasattr(object, name)

Perl equivalent: **exists()** *or* **defined()** *to determine data, or* UNIVER-SAL::can(METHOD) *to check for a particular method*

Returns true if the **object** has an attribute matching the string **name**. Returns zero otherwise.

Notes for Perl programmers

This is the Python equivalent of the Perl **exists()** method, but it also follows the inheritance tree, functionality only available in Perl through the universal **can()** method.

hash(object)

Perl equivalent: none

Returns the integer hash value for an object. The hash value is the same for any two objects that compare equally. Not applicable to mutable objects.

hex(x)

Perl equivalent: **printf("%x",$scalar)**

Converts an integer number to a hexadecimal string that is a valid Python expression.

Notes for Perl programmers

This is the *opposite* of the Perl **hex()** function which converts a hexadecimal or octal string to it's integer equivalent. The Python **hex()** function is equivalent to:

```
printf("%x",$value);
```

id(object)
Perl equivalent: none

Returns an integer (or long integer) – the identity – which is guaranteed to be unique and constant during the lifetime of the object.

input([prompt])
Perl equivalent: read() *or* sysread()

Equivalent to **eval(raw_input(prompt))**. See **raw_input()** in this chapter for more information.

Notes for Perl programmers

This is the equivalent of the **Term::Readline::readline**() function/method.

int(x [, radix])
Perl equivalent: int(), hex(), oct()

Converts the number or string **x** to a plain integer. The **radix** argument if supplied is used as the base to use for the conversion and should be an integer in the range 2 to 36.

intern(string)
Perl equivalent: none

Adds **string** to the table of "interned" strings, returning the interned version. Interned strings are available through a pointer, rather than raw string, allowing lookups of dictionary keys to be made using pointer rather than string comparisons. This provides a small performance gain over the normal string comparison methods.

Names used within the Python namespace tables and the dictionaries used to hold module, class or instance attributes are normally interned to aid the speed of execution of the script.

Interned strings are not garbage collected, so be aware that using interned strings on large dictionary key sets will increase the memory requirement significantly, even after the dictionary keys have gone out of scope.

isinstance(object, class)

Perl equivalent: UNIVERSAL::isa()

Returns true if **object** is an instance of **class**. Determination will follow the normal inheritance rules and subclasses. You can also use the function to identify if **object** is of a particular type by using the type class definitions in the **types** module. If **class** is not a class or type object then a **TypeError** exception is raised.

issubclass(class1, class2)

Perl equivalent: UNIVERSAL::isa()

Return true if **class1** is a subclass of **class2**. A class is always considered as a subclass of itself. A **TypeError** exception is raised if either argument is not a class object.

len(s)

Perl equivalent: **length()**, scalar @array, scalar keys %hash

Returns the length of a sequence (string, tuple, or list) or dictionary object.

Notes for Perl programmers

The Python **len()** function works for all sequence-based objects, so we can rewrite the following Perl code:

```
$length = length($string);
$length = scalar @array;
```

in Python as:

```
length = len(string)
length = len(array)
```

list(sequence)

Perl equivalent: The qw// *or* () *operators, or* split('',$string)

Returns a list whose items and order are the same as those in **sequence**. For example:

```
>>> list('abc')
['a', 'b', 'c']
>>> list([1,2,3])
[1, 2, 3]
```

Notes for Perl programmers

Because Python strings are sequences of individual characters, Python can convert a single sequence of characters into a list (or tuple) of individual characters.

locals()
Perl equivalent: none

Returns a dictionary representing the current local symbol table.

long(x)
Perl equivalent: int()

Converts a string or number to a long integer. Conversion of a floating point number follows the same rules as **int()**.

map(function, list, ...)
Perl equivalent: map()

Applies **function** to each item of **list** and returns the new list. For example:

```
>>> a = [1,2,3,4]
>>> map(lambda x: pow(x,2), a)
[1,4,9,16]
```

If additional lists are supplied then they are supplied to **function** in parallel. Lists are padded with **None** until all lists are of the same length.

If **function** is **None** then the identity function is assumed, causing **map()** to return **list** with all false arguments removed. If the **function** is **None** and multiple list arguments are supplied then a list of tuples of each argument of the list is returned, for example:

```
>>> map(None, [1,2,3,4], [4,5,6,7])
[(1, 4), (2, 5), (3, 6), (4, 7)]
```

The result is identical to that produced by the **zip()** function.

Notes for Perl programmers

The operation of the Python **map()** is identical to the Perl **map()** except for the treatment of multiple lists. In Perl, the following statement would apply **function** to each item in the remaining arguments to the function, just as if the arguments had been concatenated into a new list:

```
@chars = map(chr,(@list, $scalar, @array));
```

Trying the same in Python would result in **chr()** being passed as three arguments instead of one. Instead, concatenate the strings:

```
chars = map(lambda x: chr(x), list+scalar+array)
```

Also be aware that unless the function is predefined, you will have to use **lambda** to create an anonymous function. This is because Python doesn't have an equivalent to the **$_** 'scratchpad' variable.

max(s [, args...])
Perl equivalent: none

When supplied with a single argument, returns the maximum value in the sequence **s**. When supplied a list of arguments, returns the largest argument from those supplied. See **min()** for more details.

min(s [, args...])
Perl equivalent: none

When supplied with a single argument, returns the minimum value in the sequence **s**. When supplied a list of arguments, returns the smallest value from all the arguments. Note that sequences in a multi-argument call are not traversed – each argument is compared as a whole, such that:

```
min([1,2,3],[4,5,6])
```

returns:

```
[1, 2, 3]
```

And not the often expected 1.

oct(x)
Perl equivalent: **printf("%o",$scalar)**

Converts an integer number to an octal string. The result is a valid Python expression. For example:

```
>>> oct(2001)
'03721'
```

Note that the returned value is always unsigned, such that **oct(-1)** will yield "037777777777" on a 32 bit machine.

Note for Perl programmers

This is not the same as the Perl **oct()** function – this returns an octal number, it does not convert an octal string back to an integer.

open(filename [, mode [, bufsize]])

Perl equivalent: open() *or* sysopen()

Opens the file identified by **filename**, using the **mode** mode and buffering type **bufsize**. Returns a file object (see Chapters 3 and 6 for more information).

The **mode** is the same as that used by the system **fopen()** function – see Table 8.2 for a list of valid modes. If **mode** is omitted then it defaults to **r**.

TABLE 8.2 File modes for the **open()** function

Mode	Meaning
r	Reading
w	Writing
a	Appending (file position automatically seeks to the end during the open)
r+	Open for updating (reading and writing)
w+	Truncates (empties) the file and then opens it for reading and writing
a+	Opens the file for reading and writing, automatically changes current file position to the end of the file
b	When appended to any option opens the file in binary rather than text mode (Windows, DOS and some other OS unaffected)

The optional **bufsize** argument determines the size of the buffer to use while reading from the file. The different values supported are listed in Table 8.3. If omitted, the system default is used.

For example, to open a file for reading in binary mode using a 256 character buffer:

```
myfile = open('myfile.txt','rb', 256);
```

TABLE 8.3 Buffer sizes supported by the **open()** function

Bufsize value	Description
0	Disable buffering
1	Line buffered
>1	Use a buffer that is approximately **bufsize** characters in length
<0	Use the system default (line buffered for **tty** devices and fully buffered for any other file)

Notes for Perl programmers

See Table 8.4 for the Python equivalents of the Perl file opening formats.

TABLE 8.4 Python and Perl file opening formats

Perl format	Python mode
"" or "<file"	r
">file"	w
">>file"	a
"+<file"	r+
"+>file"	w+
"+>>file"	a+

The "b" option when opening a file is the equivalent of using **binmode**:

```
open(DATA, $file);
binmode DATA
```

The buffer option is far more extensive than Perl's. The Perl fragment:

```
open(DATA, 'myfile.txt');
autoflush DATA 1;
```

is equivalent to:

```
myfile=open('myfile.txt','r',0);
```

ord(c)
Perl equivalent: ord()

Returns the ASCII or Unicode numeric code of the string of one character c. This is the inverse of **chr()** and **unichr()**.

pow(x, y [, z])
Perl equivalent: x**y

Returns the value of **x** raised to the power of **y**. If **z** is supplied then calculate **x** raised to the power **y** modulo **z**, calculated more efficiently than using:

```
pow(x,y) % z
```

The supplied arguments should be numeric types, and the types supplied determine the return type. If the calculated value cannot be represented by the supplied argument types then an exception is raised. For example, the following will fail:

```
pow(2,-1)
```

But:

```
pow(2.0,-1)
```

is valid.

Note for Perl programmers

To protect yourself from accidentally supplying the wrong number type to **pow()**, you might want to consider using the **float()** function:

```
pow(float(mynumber),-1)
```

range([start,] stop [, step])
Perl equivalent: none

Returns a list of numbers starting from **start** and ending before **stop** using **step** as the interval. All numbers should be supplied and are returned as plain integers. If **step** is omitted then the step value defaults to one. If **start** is omitted then the sequence starts at zero. Note that the two arguments form of the call assumes that **start** and **stop** are supplied – if you want to specify a **step** you must supply all three arguments.

For positive values of **step**:

```
>>> range(10)
[0, 1, 2, 3, 4, 5, 6, 7, 8, 9]
>>> range(5,10)
[5, 6, 7, 8, 9]
>>> range(5,25,5)
[5, 10, 15, 20]
```

Note that the final number is **stop–step**, the range goes up to, but not including, the **stop** value.

If you supply a negative value to **step** then the range counts down, rather than up, and **stop** must be lower than **start** otherwise the returned list will be empty. For example:

```
>>> range(10,0,-1)
[10, 9, 8, 7, 6, 5, 4, 3, 2, 1]
>>> range (25,0,-5)
[25, 20, 15, 10, 5]
>>> range(0,10,-1)
[]
```

Notes for Perl programmers

The Python **range()** function gets round the limitation of the Perl .. range operator allowing you to create your own range with a suitable step in both ascending and descending order. Be aware however that the Python **range()** and **xrange()** functions return a list up to but *not* including the final value, unlike the Perl range operator.

raw_input([prompt])

Perl equivalent: **read()** *or* **sysread()** *on* **STDIN** *or* **Term::Readline::readline()**

Accepts raw input from **sys.stdin**, returning a string. Input is terminated by a newline, and this is stripped before the string is returned to the caller. If **prompt** is supplied, then it is output to **sys.stdout** without a trailing newline and used as the prompt for input. For example:

```
>>> name = raw_input('Name? ')
Name? Martin
```

If the **readline** module has been loaded then features such as line editing and history are supported during input.

Note for Perl programmers

Note that Python automatically strips the newline or carriage return character for you, you do not need to manually remove the line termination.

reduce(function, sequence [, initializer])

Perl equivalent: none

Applies the **function** (supporting two arguments) cumulatively to each element of **sequence**, reducing the entire statement to a single value. For example, to emulate the ! (factorial) mathematical operator:

```
reduce(lambda x,y: x*y, [1,2,3,4,5])
```

the effect is to perform the calculation:

```
((((1*2)*3)*4)*5)
```

which equals 120.

If **initializer** is supplied then it's used as the first element in the sequence:

```
>>> reduce(lambda x,y: x*y, [1,2,3,4,5],10)
1200
```

reload(module)

Perl equivalent: no direct equivalent, but you can use eval()

Reloads an already imported module. The reload includes the normal parsing and initializing processes employed when the module was imported originally. This allows you to reload a Python module without needing to exit the interpreter.

There are a number of caveats for using **reload**():

▶ If the module is syntactically correct, but fails during initialization, then the import process does not bind its name correctly in the symbol table. You will need to use **import** to load the module before it can be reloaded.

▶ The reloaded module does not delete entries in the symbol table for the old version of the module first. For identically named objects and functions this is not a problem, but if you rename an entity its value will remain in the symbol table after a reload.

▶ Reloading of extension modules (which rely on built-in or dynamically loaded libraries for support) is supported, but is probably pointless and may actually fail.

▶ If a module imports objects from another module using the **from...import...** form then **reload** does not redefine the objects imported. You can get round this by using the **import...** form.

▶ Reloading modules that provide classes will not affect any existing instances of that class – the existing instances will continue to use the old method definitions. Only new instances of the class will use the new forms. This also holds true for derived classes.

repr(object)
Perl equivalent: **Data::Dumper**

Returns a string representation of **object**. This is identical to using back-quotes on an object or attribute. The string returned would yield an object with the same value as that when passed to **eval()**.

Notes for Perl programmers

Both the `` operator and the **repr()** function generate a printable form of any object and also simultaneously create a textual representation that can be evaluated. This can be useful in situations such as configuration files where you want to output a textual version of a particular object or variable that can be re-evaluated.

round(x[, n])
Perl equivalent: **sprintf()**

Returns the floating point value **x** rounded to **n** digits after the decimal point. Rounds to nearest whole number if **n** is not specified. For example:

```
>>> round(0.4)
0.0
>>> round(0.5)
1.0
>>> round(-0.5)
-1.0
>>> round(3.14159264,2)
3.14
>>> round(1985,-2)
2000.0
```

As you can see, a negative number rounds to that many places before the decimal point. Also note that rounding is handled strictly on the point described by **n**, that is:

```
>>> round(1945,-1)
1950.0
>>> round(1945,-2)
1900.0
```

In the second example the "4" in 1945 is rounded to the next nearest, resulting in 1900, rather than rounding the "5" to make 1950 and then rounding 1950 up to 2000.

setattr(object, name, value)
Perl equivalent: none

Sets the attribute **name** of **object** to **value**. The opposite of the **getattr()** function which merely gets the information. The statement:

```
setattr(myobj, 'myattr', 'new value')
```

is equivalent to:

```
myobj.myattr = 'new value'
```

but can be used in situations where the attribute is known pragmatically by name, rather than explicitly as an attribute.

Note for Perl programmers

The **setattr()** function gets round the limitation of soft references and hash- or array-based objects used in Perl. In Perl you would be able to use:

```
$object{'myattr'} = $value;
```

Python does not support soft or symbolic references, the statement:

```
object.'myattr' = value
```

is invalid.

slice([start,] stop [, step])
Perl equivalent: none

Returns a slice object representing the set of indices specified by **range(start, stop, step)**. If one argument is supplied then it's used as **stop**, two arguments imply **start** and **stop**. The default value for any unsupplied argument is **None**. Slice objects have three attributes (**start, stop, step**) which merely return the corresponding argument supplied to the **slice()** function during the object's creation.

str(object)

Perl equivalent: none, although Data::Dumper *will show information for some objects*

Returns a string representation of **object**. This is similar to the **repr()** function except that the return value is designed to be a printable string, rather than a string that is compatible with the **eval** function.

tuple(sequence)

Perl equivalent: none

Returns a tuple whose items are the same and in the same order as the items in **sequence**. Examples:

```
>>> tuple('abc')
('a', 'b', 'c')
>>> tuple([1,2,3])
(1, 2, 3)
```

type(object)

Perl equivalent: the **ref()** *funcition returns the base object type or its class*

Returns the type of **object**. The return value is a type object, as described by the **types** module. For example:

```
>>> import types
>>> if type(string) == types.StringType:
    print "This is a string"
```

Notes for Perl programmers

The return value from **type** can be printed, for example:

```
>>> a = 1
>>> print type(a)
<type 'int'>
```

in the same way as the output from the Perl **ref**() function. However, it's more practical to compare the value to one of those in the **types** module if you are looking for a specific type. The full list of types supported by the **types** module is listed below:

BufferType	BuiltinFunctionType	BuiltinMethodType
ClassType	CodeType	ComplexType
DictType	DictionaryType	EllipsisType
FileType	FloatType	FrameType
FunctionType	InstanceType	IntType
LambdaType	ListType	LongType
MethodType	ModuleType	NoneType
SliceType	StringType	TracebackType
TupleType	TypeType	UnboundMethodType
UnicodeType	XRangeType	

unichr(i)

Perl equivalent: the Perl chr() *function natively decodes Unicode characters*

Returns a Unicode string of one character whose code is the integer **i** – this is the Unicode equivalent of the **chr**() function described earlier in this chapter. Note that to convert a Unicode character back into its integer form you use **ord**(), there is no **uniord**() function. A **ValueError** exception is raised if the integer supplied is outside the range 0. to 65535.

Notes for Perl programmers

Note that you must use the **unichr**() function if want to encode a Unicode character, the Python **chr**() function does not understand Unicode characters. However, the Python **ord**() function does decode them.

unicode(string [, encoding [, errors]])

Perl equivalent: none, Perl automatically decodes Unicode strings natively

Decodes the Unicode **string** using the codec **encoding**. The default behavior (when encoding is not supplied) is to decode UTF-8 in strict mode, errors raising **ValueError**. See the **codecs** module for a list of suitable codecs.

vars([object])
Perl equivalent: similar to accessing the symbol table directly using %main::

Returns a dictionary corresponding to the current local symbol table. When supplied with a module, class, or class instance, returns a dictionary corresponding to that object's symbol table. Does not modify the returned dictionary as the effects are undefined.

xrange([start,] stop [, step])
Perl equivalent: none

Works in the same way as the **range()** function, except that it returns an **xrange** object. An **xrange** object is an opaque object type which returns the same information as the list requested, without having to store each individual element in the list. This is particularly useful in situations where you are creating very large lists, the memory saved by using **xrange()** over **range()** can be considerable.

Notes for Perl programmers

The **xrange()** function gets around the similar problem in Perl of creating very large lists which are used for iteration in a loop. For example, in Perl it's a bad idea to do:

```
foreach $count (1..100000)
```

Instead we'd do:

```
for($count = 1;$count<=100000;$count++)
```

In Python the temptation is to use:

```
foreach count in range(1,100000):
```

However, it's more efficient to use:

```
foreach count in xrange(1,100000):
```

zip(seq1, ...)
Perl equivalent: none

Takes a series of sequences and returns them as a list of tuples, where each tuple contains the *n*th element of each of the supplied sequences. For example:

```
>>> a = [1,2,3,4]
>>> b = [5,6,7,8]
>>> zip(a,b)
[(1, 5), (2, 6), (3, 7), (4, 8)]
```

9

INTERFACING WITH THE OPERATING SYSTEM

There are two main aspects to talking with the operating system from within any language. The first is the basic interface between Python and the host – the environment and other system-specific information about the machine on which the Python interpreter is executing. The second aspect is the operating system itself and how to get information about and to/from the operating system.

In this chapter we're going to be taking a look at the Python equivalents of many of the system and operating system specific elements of Perl and the Python modules that support these operations.

COMMUNICATING WITH THE SYSTEM

The Python **sys** module provides us with the interface for determining information about the machine and environment in which Python is currently executing. Some of these elements are handled in Perl using built-in variables, others by built-in functions. We'll have a look at all of the compatibility information, and how to make the transition from using one system to another, as well as some of the Python specific elements.

Getting command-line arguments

Within Perl any arguments supplied to the script on the command line are supplied in the standard **@ARGV** variable. For example, we can accept a list of files to process using:

```
foreach my $file (@ARGV)
{
    print "Processing $file\n";
...
}
```

Under Python you must import the **argv** array from the **sys** module:

```
import sys
for argument in argv:
    print "Processing",argument
```

Note that **sys.argv** starts at zero, just like the C equivalent. However, unlike Perl, which stores the first *argument* to the script at index zero, Python stores the name of the script at index zero. Therefore **$ARG[0]** in Perl is equivalent to **sys.argv[1]** in Python. To determine the script name in Python use **sys.argv[0]** which is equivalent to the Perl **$0** or **$PRO-GRAM_NAME** variables.

Parsing command-line arguments

If you want to process arguments, as you would with the **GetOpt::Standard** or **GetOpt::Long** modules under Perl, use the **getopt** function within the getopt module. The format of the function is:

```
getopt(args, options [, long_options])
```

where **args** is the list of arguments you want to parse and **options** is a string containing the single letter arguments you want to interpret. If you append a colon to a letter within the **options** string then the argument will accept an additional argument as data to the argument. If supplied, the **long_options** should be a list of strings defining the words, rather than single letters, which should be identified and parsed. Note that in the arguments list word-based arguments must be prefixed with a double, rather than a single hyphen. The = suffix to an argument in **long_options** causes **getopt** to interpret the following argument as additional data.

The **getopt** function returns two objects. The first is a list of tuples containing the parsed argument and its value (if it has one), the second object is a list of the remaining, unparsed arguments.

For example:

```
>>> import getopt
>>> args = ['-a','-x','.bak',
'--debuglevel','99','file1','file2']
```

```
>>> opts, remargs = getopt.getopt(args,'ax:',
['debuglevel='])
>>> opts
[('-a', ''), ('-x', '.bak'), ('--debuglevel', '99')]
>>> remargs
['file1', 'file2']
```

Once you've extracted the information in this way you need to match up the arguments you were expecting with any information supplied. Typically this is done in two stages, the first stage converts our list of tuples into a dictionary, the second then decides what to do with the information. For example:

```
for o, a in opts:
    realopts[o] = a

if realopts.has_key('-a'):
    display_everything = 1
if realopts.has_key('-x'):
    file_extension = realopts['-x']
if realopts.has_key('--debuglevel'):
    debug_level = realopts['--debuglevel']
else:
    debug_level = 0
```

The **getopt** function raises an exception if an unrecognized option is seen in the argument list, or if the argument is expecting additional data but doesn't receive it.

Standard filehandles

Perl supports three main filehandles, **STDIN**, **STDOUT**, and **STDERR**. These are accessible through Python as **sys.stdin**, **sys.stdout** and **sys.stderr**. These are file objects, so you must use the file methods defined in Table 11.1 on p. 215. For example, to write an error to the Perl **STDERR** you would use:

```
print STDERR "Opening the log file for this session\n";
```

Under Python we can rewrite this as:

```
sys.stderr.write('Opening the log file for this
session\n')
```

Original filehandles

If you reassign any of the standard filehandles within Python the original objects as they were at the start of the scripts execution are available using the **sys.__stdin__**, **sys.__stdout__**, and **sys.__stderr__** objects.

Redirecting output

To redirect the output of **STDOUT** under Perl you can use the **select** function in its filehandle form:

```
select(MYSTDOUT);
```

or you can re-open **STDOUT** to point to a different file:

```
open(STDOUT,">mystdout.log")
    or die "Can't open output file: $!";
```

Now calls to **print()** which don't specify an alternative filehandle will send their output to a different location. For the **STDERR** and **STDIN** filehandles we can only use the latter **open()** method to redirect the output or input when information is sent to or received from those filehandles.

Within Python we can redirect any of the standard filehandles by using a similar **open()** trick, but with the added benefit that we can also restore the original destination:

```
import sys
sys.stderr = open('error.log','w')
sys.stderr.write('Error log!\n')
sys.stderr.close()
sys.stderr = sys.__stderr__
```

Terminating execution

The Perl built-in **exit()** function is identical to the Python **sys.exit()** function. Both accept a single argument which is the return value returned to the calling process. Python's implementation is slightly different in that to honor the request, Python actually raises a **SystemExit** exception – this forces any **finally** clauses of **try** statements to be honored, and it is possible to trap the exception and perform cleanup actions before final exit by using the normal **try** method. This is analogous to using the **END** blocks within a Perl script.

The optional argument to the function can either be an integer or an object. If it's an integer then by convention zero indicates successful execution whilst any non-zero value indicates an error.

If you supply an object then the object is printed to **sys.stderr** and a return value of 1 is returned to the caller. If the object is **None** then a zero is returned instead.

As an alternative to relying on trapping an exception you can use the **exitfunc** attribute to the **sys** module which allows you to define a function to be used as a cleanup function. For example:

```
import sys

def cleanup():
    print "Had enough, deciding to leave\n"

sys.exitfunc = cleanup
```

For a more extensive system use the **atexit** module.

Determining the interpreter version

The Perl variable **$^V** holds a v-string literal for the current version of the Perl interpreter. Under Python, you can get the same information using **sys.version**:

```
'2.0 (#71, Oct 22 2000, 22:09:24) [CW PPC w/GUSI2
w/THREADS]'
```

Note that the value is a Python string, rather than an array.

Determining the interpreter location

The Perl **$^X** variable contains the location of the Perl interpreter currently executing the script or program you are running. The **sys.executable** variable holds the same information under Python – for example with Python under Solaris:

```
>>> sys.executable
'/usr/local/bin/python2.0'
```

Or on the Mac:

```
>>> sys.executable
'Development:Applications:Python 2.0:PythonInterpreter'
```

Discovering the currently loaded modules

Perl populates the **%INC** hash each time you import a module using **do**, **use**, or **require**. The hash contains the key, which is the full name of the module with the corresponding value referring to the location of the module file that was loaded.

For example:

```
use Net::FTP;
use Getopt::Long;
use Net::Ping;

foreach my $key (keys %INC)
{
    print "$key => $INC{$key}\n";
}
```

would typically generate the following output:

```
Exporter.pm => /usr/local/lib/perl5/5.6.0/Exporter.pm
Carp.pm => /usr/local/lib/perl5/5.6.0/Carp.pm
XSLoader.pm => /usr/local/lib/perl5/5.6.0/i86pc-solaris-
thread/XSLoader.pm
...
Net/Ping.pm => /usr/local/lib/perl5/5.6.0/Net/Ping.pm
IO/File.pm => /usr/local/lib/perl5/5.6.0/i86pc-solaris-
thread/IO/File.pm
Fcntl.pm => /usr/local/lib/perl5/5.6.0/i86pc-solaris-
thread/Fcntl.pm
Cwd.pm => /usr/local/lib/perl5/5.6.0/Cwd.pm
AutoLoader.pm =>
/usr/local/lib/perl5/5.6.0/AutoLoader.pm
IO/Seekable.pm => /usr/local/lib/perl5/5.6.0/i86pc-
solaris-thread/IO/Seekable.pm
```

The Python **sys.modules** dictionary contains a similar mapping:

```
{'os.path': <module 'macpath' from 'development:
applications:python 2.0:lib:macpath.pyc'>,
 'os': <module 'os' from 'development:applications:python
 2.0:lib:os.pyc'>,
 'exceptions': <module 'exceptions' (built-in)>,
 '__main__': <module '__main__' (built-in)>,
 'Nav': <module 'Nav' (built-in)>,
```

```
 'mac': <module 'mac' (built-in)>,
 'Res': <module 'Res' (built-in)>,
 'sys': <module 'sys' (built-in)>,
 '__builtin__': <module '__builtin__' (built-in)>,
 'site': <module 'site' from 'development:applications: python
 2.0:lib:site.pyc'>,
 'macfsn': <module 'macfsn' from
'development:applications:python 2.0:mac:lib:macfsn.pyc'>,
 'macpath': <module 'macpath' from
'development:applications:python 2.0:lib:macpath.pyc'>,
 'macfs': <module 'macfs' (built-in)>,
 'struct': <module 'struct' (built-in)>,
 'stat': <module 'stat' from
'development:applications:python 2.0:lib:stat.pyc'>}
```

Note that format of each dictionary pair is specific – the key contains the name of the module and the corresponding value contains information about the module's real name and whether it is a built-in module or was loaded from an external file.

Modifying the library search path

Python modules are looked for within the standard system path. This is configured, as with Perl, during installation. For example, the following list comes from a Python 2.0 installation under Solaris 8:

```
['', '/usr/local/lib/python2.0',
'/usr/local/lib/python2.0/plat-sunos5',
'/usr/local/lib/python2.0/lib-tk',
'/usr/local/lib/python2.0/lib-dynload',
'/usr/local/lib/python2.0/site-packages']
```

This is the direct equivalent of the built-in **@INC**. We can modify the value of this list directly. Because **import** statements in Python are executed when they are seen, rather than at compile time, we can make modifications to the list at any time. In Perl, modifications to **@INC** must be made by the **lib** pragma or through the use of a **BEGIN** block to ensure that the modifications made occur before the compiler tries to execute a **use** statement. For example:

```
import sys
sys.path.append('/home/mc/lib')
import smtplib
```

Or to add paths you want placed earlier in the search sequence use the **insert()** method:

```
import sys
sys.path.insert(0,'/home/mc/lib')
import mymodule
```

Other variables in the *sys* module

There are some other variables defined within the **sys** module which can provide useful information about the Python environment available to us. These are listed here in Table 9.1 along with their Perl equivalents.

TABLE 9.1 Other variables supported by the **sys** module

Python **sys** variable	Perl equivalent	Description
builtin_module_names	None	A tuple containing the names of all the modules built into the Python executable
copyright	None	The copyright message from the current Python interpreter
exec_prefix	$Config{'archlib'}	Directory where the platform-dependent Python library files are kept
maxint	None, although it can be calculated	The largest integer supported by the **integer** object type
platform	$^O	The platform identifier string determined during installation/configuration. For example "sunos5" or "mac"
prefix	$Config{'privlib'}	Directory where platform-independent Python library files are kept
ps1, ps2	None	The strings containing the primary and secondary prompts used when using the interpreter interactively.By default these are set to ">>> " and "... " respectively

WORKING WITH THE OPERATING SYSTEM

Interacting with the operating system includes everything from determining the environment in which the interpreter and your script are running, the user and process environment and also controlling and communicating with external aspects such as files and filesystems.

In Perl many of these facilities are handled either through a built-in variable, for example %ENV or $>, or using one of the built-in functions such as **chdir()**. The rest of this functionality is augmented through certain external modules. For example the **Cwd** modules supply the interface to the **getcwd()** system call.

In Python most of this functionality is handled by the **os** module although some other modules provide generic interfaces to other systems. The **os** module is not itself the provider of functionality – instead it creates the necessary links between the **os** namespace and the built-in modules such as **posix** (for Unix/Windows NT and 2000) or **mac** which provide the real functionality on a system dependent basis. This allows the **os** module to act as a cross-platform module which provides all of the core APIs for communicating with the host system.

You can determine which of the various OS-dependent modules has been loaded by examining the **os.name** variable. For example:

```
Python 2.0 (#71, Oct 22 2000, 22:09:24) [CW PPC w/GUSI2
w/THREADS] on mac
Type "copyright", "credits" or "license" for more
information.
>>> import os
>>> os.name
'mac'
```

The **os.path** variable holds the name of the module that should be used for handling platform independent pathname operations. You can import the module required directly using:

```
import os.path
```

See Chapter 10 for information on how to manipulate path names as the equivalent of the Perl **File::Spec** module.

Manipulating environment variables

Perl provides a two-way interface between the system environment variables (those variables available and exported from the enclosing shell). The **%ENV** hash acts as a mapping between the real environment information for the Perl process and the internal hash information provided by the interpreter.

Initially the contents of **%ENV** match the contents of the environment in which the interpreter (and your script) were executed. From then on changes to **%ENV** affect the environment of the current process (and its children).

Under Python the **os.environ** dictionary works in the same way. The **os.environ** variable is actually a mapping object. During startup the contents of **os.environ** are populated with the current environment. You can access the information just as you would a standard dictionary:

```
print os.environ['PATH']
```

You can also assign a value to specific keys within **os.environ** to create and/or set the value of an environment variable in the same way as you would with Perl's **%ENV** hash. For example, the Perl fragment:

```
$ENV{'PATH} =
'/bin:/sbin:/usr/sbin:/usr/bin:/usr/local/bin';
```

is identical to the following fragment in Python:

```
os.environ['PATH'] =
'/bin:/sbin:/usr/sbin:/usr/bin:/usr/local/bin'
```

Alternatively, you can set the value of an environment variable using the **os.putenv()** function:

```
os.putenv('PATH',
'/bin:/sbin:/usr/sbin:/usr/bin:/usr/local/bin')
```

Note that although assigning a value to the mapping object provided by **os.environ** automatically calls **os.putenv()**, the **os.putenv()** function does not automatically update **os.environ**. This may mean that changes made to the environment using **os.putenv()** are not reflected in **os.environ** even though the real environment has actually been modified.

Line termination

Because the **os** module is loaded on a system dependent basis it also provides a handy way for setting and providing information that is system dependent. Most of this functionality is handled through the different functions and other system dependent modules loaded by **os**.

Line termination is a perennial problem with any cross-platform compatible language. Python solves this by automatically setting the value of the **os.linesep** variable to the correct line termination used by the current platform. The actual value is a string, either the single character newline ("\n") or carriage return ("\r") for POSIX or Mac OS machines, or the carriage-return/newline sequence ("\r\n") used by Windows.

Process environment

Most of the process environment, current user ID, process ID, and group ID, is handled by the various built-in variables in Perl. Python supports the same information through a series of functions in the os module. A list of the Python functions and their Perl equivalent expression or function is shown in Table 9.2.

TABLE 9.2 Process information functions in the **os** module

Python function	Perl equivalent	Description
chdir(path)	chdir(path)	Changes the current working directory to **path**
getcwd()	Cwd::getcwd()	Returns the path of the current working directory
getegid()	$)	Returns the effective group ID
geteuid()	$>	Returns the effective user ID
getgid()	$(	Returns the real group ID
getpgrp()	getpgrp()	Returns the ID of the current process group
getpid()	$$	Returns the process ID of the current process
getppid()	getppid()	Returns the ID of the parent process
getuid()	$<	Returns the real user ID
putenv(var,	%ENV = <VALUE>	Sets the value of the variable name **var** to value) **value**. See *Manipulating Environment Variables* on p. 175 for more information
setgid(gid)	$(= gid	Sets the group ID to **gid**

TABLE 9.2 *cont.*

Python function	Perl equivalent	Description
setpgrp()	setpgrp(0,0)	Creates a new process group for the current process. Returns the ID of the new process group
setpgid(pid, pgrp)	setpgrp(pid, pgrp)	Assigns the process ID **pid** to be a member of the group **pgrp**
setsid()	POSIX::setsid()	Creates a new session and returns the newly created session ID. Sessions are used with terminals and the shells that support them to allow multiple applications to be executed without the use of a windowing system
setuid(uid)	$< = uid	Sets the user ID of the current process
strerror(errno) the	$!	Returns the error message associated with error number in **code**
umask(mask)	umask(mask)	Sets the umask of the current process to **mask**
uname()	POSIX::uname()	Returns a tuple of strings containing the system name, nodename, release, version and machine for the current system

Process execution and management

You can execute and manage processes within Python. Execution involves either replacing the Python interpreter, starting a new process or communicating with a process either to read or write to the process or both. We can also install signal handlers to control how our process reacts when it is sent a signal. Most of this functionality is handled in Python by the **os** module.

Running external commands

Although we can do most things within Perl and Python using some form of module or extension there are times when we need to communicate with the outside world by running some external command.

The os.exec*() functions

The basic Python function for execution of an external command is **execv**, there are also variations on the same function that allow you to supply a dictionary of environment variables (**execve()**, **execvpe()**) or to search the environment path in **os.environ['PATH']** (**execvp()**, **execvpe()**). The format for each function is shown below:

```
os.execv(path, args)
os.execve(path, args, env)
os.execvp(path, args)
os.execvpe(path, args, env)
```

The **path** should be the full path to the file that you want to execute. When using **os.execvp()** or **os.execvpe()** the environment path directories are searched. Alternatively you can set a different path using the **os.defpath** variable. The **args** argument should be a list (or tuple) of arguments supplied to the program being called. The **env** argument should be a dictionary of environment variables – these will be used in place of the environment being used by the Python interpreter.

Here are some examples of running all of the above:

```
os.execv('/bin/ls', ('-la'))
os.execve('/usr/local/bin/cvs', ('commit'),
{'CVSROOT':'/export/cvs'})
os.execvp('ls',('-la'))
os.execvpe('cvs', ('commit'), {'CVSROOT':'/export/cvs'})
```

Note that in *all* cases the **exec*()** series of commands entirely replace the Python interpreter and therefore the current script in the same way as the Perl **exec()** function. In fact the Perl statement:

```
exec '/bin/ls', '-la';
```

is identical to the Python:

```
os.execv('/bin/ls', ('-la'))
```

If you want to start an additional process you will either need to use **os.fork()** to start a new child process, or use the **os.system()** command.

In addition to the base versions there are also multiple argument versions which can be used with a variable number of arguments rather than using a tuple or list argument.

The statement:

```
os.execl(path, arg0, arg1, ...)
```

is equivalent to **os.execv(path, (arg0, arg1, ...);**

```
os.execle(path, arg0, arg1, ..., env)
```

is equivalent to **os.execve(path, (arg0, arg1, ...), env)**; and

```
os.execlp(path, arg0, arg1, ...)
```

is equivalent to **os.execvp(path, (arg0, arg1, ...))**.

In all cases an **OSError** exception is raised if the program in **path** cannot be found, with additional arguments containing the precise error, for example:

```
>>> import os
>>> os.execv('nothing',('',))
Traceback (most recent call last):
  File "<stdin>", line 1, in ?
OSError: [Errno 2] No such file or directory
```

Starting a new process

The **os.system()** function starts a new process and command in the same way as the Perl built-in **system()** function such that:

```
system('emacs');
```

in Perl is equivalent to:

```
import os
os.system('emacs')
```

in Python. The return value from **os.system()** is the exit status of the called program. Under Windows, however, the value returned is always zero.

There is no equivalent to the Perl **qx{}** or backtick operator which starts a new program and executes it whilst also returning the output from the command. Use the Python **os.popen()** function instead (see the next section).

Communicating with an external process

Perl uses the **open** command as one of the primary methods for communicating to or from an external application. For example, we can read a directory listing using:

```
open(DIR,"ls -al|");
while(<DIR>)
{
```

```
    print $_;
}
```

The Python **open** function does not support the same ability. Instead, you need to use the **os.popen()** function:

```
import os
dir = os.popen('ls -al','r')
while(1):
    line = dir.readline()
    if line:
        print line,
    else:
    break
```

The **os.popen()** function works exactly the same as the built-in **open** function, returning a file object that we can read from in bytes or lines, as we have here. The actual format for the **os.popen()** function is:

```
os.popen(command [, mode [, bufsize]])
```

The **command** should be the string to be executed by the shell which is started when the function is called. The **mode** should be "r" for reading or "w" for writing, it defaults to "r" if no **mode** is supplied. The **bufsize** is the buffer size to be used when reading from the command, just like the **bufsize** argument to Python's **open()** function.

Note that just like the Perl **open()** function you cannot both read and write from a command when using the **os.popen()** function. Instead you need to use the **popen2** module, the Python equivalent of the **IPC::Open2** and **IPC::Open3** modules. The **popen2** module provides three functions, **popen2()**, **popen3()** and **Popen3()**.

The **popen2()** function spawns a new process and returns the child standard output and input filehandles:

```
(child_stdout, child_stdin) = popen2(cmd [, bufsize])
```

This is equivalent to the Perl statement:

```
open2(\*RDRFH, \*WTRFH, cmd);
```

popen3() returns the standard output, input and error filehandles:

```
(child_stdout, child_stdin, child_stderr) = popen3(cmd
[, bufsize])
```

which is equivalent to the Perl statement:

```
open3(\*WTRFH, \*RDRFH, \*ERRFH, cmd);
```

Once opened we can read and write to/from **child_stdout**, **child_stdin**, or **child_stderr** using the same methods as for a normal file.

The **Popen3()** function returns an instance of the **Popen3** class:

```
child = Popen3(cmd [, capturestderr [, bufsize]])
```

The **capturestderr** argument if true forces the instance to capture standard error as well as input and output. The default is not to capture standard error. The new instance has the following methods and attributes:

```
child.poll()
```

returns the exit code of the child or -1 if the child is still running;

```
child.wait()
```

waits for the child process to terminate, returning the exit code;

```
child.fromchild
```

the file object that captures the child's standard output;

```
child.tochild
```

the file object that sends input to the child's standard input;

```
child.childerr
```

the file object that captures the child's standard error.

Creating a new child process

Forking off a new process under Perl is a common method used to provide multi-channel access for both file and network based services. Perl provides support for the operating system **fork()** function through a built-in function of the same name. We can therefore spawn a new child process using:

```
unless ($pid = fork())
{
    # Start of the child process
}
# End of child
```

```
#Continuation of parent
```

The **os.fork()** function within Python works in the same way, the above script can be rewritten in Python as:

```
pid = os.fork()
if not pid:
    # Start of child process

else:
    # Continuation of parent process
```

When waiting for a child process to terminate you can use either the **os.wait()** or **os.waitpid()** functions which work in the same fashion as the Perl equivalents:

```
(pid, exitcode) = wait([pid])
(pid, exitcode) = waitpid(pid, options)
```

The **pid** should be the process ID of the process that you want to wait for. The **options** should be 0 for the normal operation (wait until the process terminates) or **os.WNOHANG** if you want the call to immediately return. This is equivalent to calling the Perl **waitpid()** with the **WNOHANG** flag in effect.

However, unlike the Perl versions, the Python versions return a tuple consisting of the pid and the exit status. The exit status is available within Perl through the **$?** Variable. The exit status is a 16-bit number, the low byte of this is the signal number that killed the process and the high byte is the exit status.

Therefore we can rewrite the Perl fragment:

```
$newpid = waitpid($pid, 0)
print "Process $newpid terminated with $?\n"
```

within Python as:

```
(newpid, exitcode) = os.waitpid(pid, 0)
print "Process",newpid,"terminated with",exitcode
```

Python also supports the same facilities for checking the exit code of a child according to a series of predefined values. In Perl these are macros defined in the **POSIX** module:

```
use POSIX qw/:sys_wait_h/;

while(1)
{
```

```
    $exitcode = waitpid($pid, WNOHANG);
    last if (WIFSIGNALED($exitcode));
}
```

In Python we would write:

```
import os

while(1):
    (newpid, exitcode) = os.waitpid(pid, os.WNOHANG)
    if (WIFSIGNALED(exitcode)): break
```

Python provides error checking functions called **WIFSTOPPED()**, **WIFSIGNALED()**, **WIFEXITED()**, **WEXITSTATUS()**, **WSTOPSIG()**, and **WTERMSIG()**. All accept an exit status as their only argument, and return true only if the exit status matches the given flag. These equate to the flags supported by most Unix implementations within Perl.

Signals

The Python **os.kill()** function works in the same way as the Perl **kill()** function – the arguments to the two functions are identical although the order is reversed:

```
kill(signal, pid); # Perl's version
kill(pid, signal)  # Python's version
```

The **signal** module contains the symbolic constants for the different signals with each constant in the form **SIG***. For example the alarm signal can be sent to the current process using:

```
kill(os.getpid(), signal.SIGALRM)
```

Other signals such as quit (**SIGQUIT**) and termination (**SIGTERM**) along with all the other signals supported under a typical POSIX/Unix system are also supported.

Signal handlers

Perl's flexible signal handler system is controlled through the **%SIG** hash – you assign signal handlers, and assigning the undefined value disables the handler. Under Python you must use the **signal.signal()** function to install a handler for a given signal. For example, the code below installs a signal handler for the alarm signal, sets the alarm timer (using **signal.alarm()** and then sleeps for a period beyond the alarm time:

```python
import signal,time,sys

def alarm_handler(signum, frame):
    print "Wake Up!"
    sys.exit()
signal.signal(signal.SIGALRM, alarm_handler)

signal.alarm(5)
time.sleep(10)
```

Note that Python signal handlers must accept two arguments – any failure to handle these will cause a **TypeError** exception to be raised. The two arguments are **signum**, the signal raised when the handler was called, and **frame**, which is a frame object describing the Python execution stack at the point the signal was raised.

The above Python script is identical to the Perl script:

```perl
sub alarm_handler
{
    print "Wake Up!\n";
    exit();
}

$SIG{ALRM} = \&alarm_handler;

alarm(5);
sleep(10);
```

As you can see, the Python **signal.alarm()** function is identical to the Perl **alarm()** function.

Getting the current signal handler

To obtain the handler for a given signal you must use the **signal.getsignal()** function of the Perl fragment:

```perl
$handler = $SIG{ALRM};
```

is identical to:

```python
handler = signal.getsignal(SIGALRM);
```

Note that in Python's case the returned object is callable so we could immediately invoke the handler using:

```python
handler()
```

Disabling a signal handler

The **signal** module defines two standard handlers which can be used to modify the behavior of the signal handling process. The **signal.SIG_IGN** handler forces Python to ignore the specified signal, whilst the **signal.SIG_DFL** handler causes Python to invoke the default signal handler.

Thus the Perl statement:

```
$SIG{ALRM} = 'IGNORE';
```

equates to:

```
signal.signal(SIGALRM, signal.SIG_IGN)
```

in Python, and:

```
$SIG{QUIT} = 'DEFAULT';
```

is equal to the Python statement:

```
signal.signal(SIGQUIT, signal.SIG_DFL)
```

Signal differences

There are some significant signal differences between Python and Perl:

▶ Python automatically installs signal handlers for the SIGPIPE, SIGINT and SIGTERM signals. SIGPIPE signals are ignored, SIGINT signals raise a **KeyboardInterrupt** exception and SIGTERM attempts to cleanup the interpreter before calling the callable object assigned to **sys.exitfunc**.

▶ There is no way to trap an exception using a signal handler in the same way as you would trap calls to **warn()** or **die()** using the $SIG{__WARN__} and **$SIG{__DIE__}** handlers. You should instead use the normal exception trapping system.

User/group information

The user and group information stored in the Unix **/etc/passwd** and **/etc/group{s}** files is available through the grp and pwd modules. These duplicate the built-in functions offered by Perl. In each case the functions raise a **KeyError** if the group does not exist. See Table 9.3 for a list of the supported functions and their Perl equivalents.

TABLE 9.3 Getting user and group entries with Python

Python	Perl	Description
grp.getgrgid(gid)	getgrgid(gid)	Returns a tuple containing the information for the group matching **gid**. The tuple consists of the group name, group password, group ID, and a list of the members of the group. For example **grp.getgrgid(0)** returns: (**'root', '', 0, ['root']**)
grp.getgrnam (name)	getgrnam(name)	Identical to **getgrgid()** but looks for a group matching **name**
grp.getgrall()	getgrent() and aloop	Returns a list of tuples, where each tuple contains the information returned by **getgrgid()**
pwd.getpwuid(uid)	getpwuid(uid)	Returns the user information for the user ID **uid**. Information is returned as a tuple containing username, password, user ID, group ID, gecos (full name and/or contact detail), home directory and shell. For example **pwd.getpwuid(0)** returns (**'root', 'x', 0, 1, 'Super-User', '/', '/usr/bin/bash'**). Note that list returned by **pwd.getpwuid()** is shorter than that returned by Perl
pwd.getpwnam	getpwnam (name)	Identical to **getpwuid()** but looks for (name) a user matching **name**
pwd.getpwall()	getpwent() and a loop	Returns a list of tuples, where each tuple contains the information returned by **getpwuid()**

For example, to get the home directory and shell for the current user under Perl you would probably use:

```
($name, $gecos, $homedir, $shell) = (getpwuid($<))[0,6..8];

print <<EOF;
You are $name ($gecos)
Home Directory is $homedir
Shell is $shell
EOF
```

We can rewrite that in Python as:

```
import pwd,os

pwinfo = pwd.getpwuid(os.getuid())
name = pwinfo[0]
fullname, homedir, shell = pwinfo[4:]
print "You are %s (%s)\nHome Directory is %s\nShell is %s" \
        % (name, fullname, homedir, shell)
```

You might also want to investigate the **getpass** and **crypt** modules which provide a safe way of getting a password from a terminal and for changing a text password into its encrypted equivalent respectively. For example, the script below prompts and then checks the current user's password:

```
import getpass,pwd,crypt

password = getpass.getpass()
realpw = pwd.getpwnam(getpass.getuser())[1]
if realpw == crypt.crypt(password,password[:2]):
    print "Password validated"
else:
    print "Password invalid"
```

File management

Although the **os** modules provides most of the basic file manipulation functionality, we'll cover the different methods for file management in the next chapter.

10

DATA MANIPULATION

Manipulating information of any form – especially text – is something that Perl is very well known for. Perl was originally a text processing language and over the years the expansion of the Internet and the increase in text-based information has kept Perl in the forefront of people's minds.

Python doesn't have quite the same heritage, partly because many people migrating from Perl to Python can't see how a language without the =~ and built-in regular expression system can possibly be used for processing text. Python is also better known for its mathematical abilities over its text- and data-processing abilities, largely because of its built-in support for large integers and complex numbers.

We'll look at the specifics later, but to dispel a few myths about Python's text processing abilities:

▶ Strings can be extracted and manipulated directly in Python because they operate as just another sequence. The reason Python doesn't have a **substr**() function is because it doesn't really need one.

▶ For more complex string processing use the **string** module – this supports all of the familiar **split**(), **join**(), transliteration and case conversion operations provided by Perl in addition to some new ones.

▶ Formatting strings in Python can be handled using the % operator rather than **sprintf**() or **printf**().

▶ Python *does* support regular expressions through an external module called **re**. The module actually supports Perl regular expression semantics so you won't need to make any changes to the regular expressions, just the way you execute and operate on them.

▶ DBM databases are handled in Python like other features through an external module. We also have the ability to open any supported DBM file format using the **anydbm** module.

▶ Python doesn't have a database independent interface such as DBI, but what it does have is an army of developers providing solutions for connecting to mySQL, PostGreSQL, and many other database systems.

BASIC STRING HANDLING

Python supports the basic text extraction from strings supported by the Perl **substr()** function using slices on a string, since strings are just another type of sequence. For the other functions traditionally supported through internal functions such as **split()** and **chomp()** we need to use the string module. We'll look in detail at the specifics later, but a quick list of the compatible functions are shown in Table 10.1.

TABLE 10.1 Perl and Python functions for handling strings

Perl function	Python equivalent
substr(text, offset)	text[offset:len]
index(text, substr, start)	string.index(text, substr, start)
rindex(text, substr, start)	string.index(text, substr, start)
split(expr, text, max)	string.split(text, expr, max)
join(expr, args...)	string.join(list, expr)
lc(text)	string.lower(text)
lcfirst(text)	None
uc(text)	string.upper(text)
ucfirst(text)	string.capitalize(text)
chop(text), chomp(text)	string.lstrip(text), string.rstrip(text), string.strip(text)
tr/from/to/	string.translate(text, maketrans(from, to))

In addition to the functions that we'll look at shortly, the **string** module also defines some constant string sequences which can be used in most of the functions in Table 10.2.

TABLE 10.2 String sequences

Perl expression	Python equivalent
[0–9]	digits
[0–9A–F]	hexdigits
[a–zA–Z]	letters
[a–z]	lowercase
[A–Z]	uppercase
[0–7]	octdigits
\s	whitespace

With all functions, especially when working on strings, you must remember to capture the return value from any operation as Python does not modify variables or objects in place, it only returns copies of the objects with the modifications.

Finding string segments

The Perl and Python **index()** and **rindex()** functions work identically, even down to the argument order and operational arguments that they accept. We can therefore make direct comparisons between the Perl and Python functions – the Perl fragment

```
$loc = index('The cat sat on the mat', 'cat');
$lastat = index('The cat sat on the mat', 'at', 8);
$rloc = rindex('The cat sat on the mat', 'on');
```

is directly equivalent to the following in Python:

```
loc = string.index('The cat sat on the mat', 'cat')
lastat = string.index('The cat sat on the mat', 'at', 8)
rloc = rindex('The cat sat on the mat', 'on')
```

Extracting string segments

For extracting components of a string in Perl we have to use the **substr()** function – in Python we can use slices on the string, since a string is just another type of sequence. In Perl, the format of the **substr()** function is:

```
substr(text, start [, length [, replacement]])
```

Ignoring the **replacement** argument for the moment, we can translate the function call to using slices. For example the Python statement:

```
text[start:]
```

is equivalent to the two argument version of **substr()** and

```
text[start:(start+length)]
```

for the three argument version. Note the calculation required here, the **substr()** function accepts the starting offset and the length, whereas using a slice requires the start and end locations.

For example, the Perl fragment:

```
$text = 'The cat sat on the mat';
print substr($text,4),"\n";
print substr($text,4,3),"\n";
print substr($text,-3),"\n";
```

and the Python fragment

```
text = 'the cat sat on the mat'
print text[4:]
print text[4:7]
print text[-3:]
```

both yield:

```
the cat sat on the mat
cat
mat
```

Replacing string segments

Ignoring the use of regular expressions for the process, replacing strings in Perl is easy, you either use the four argument version of **substr()** or you assign a value to the **substr()** expression. For example the Perl statement:

```
substr($text,4,3) = 'tyrannosaurus rex';
```

changes our original string into "the tyrannosaurus rex sat on the mat."

In Python, the string object does not support assignment, so the following still will *not* work:

```
text[4:7] = 'tyrannosaurus rex'
```

A **TypeError** exception will be raised if you try this. Instead, the most straightforward solution is to use slices to extract the text before and after the portion that you want to replace and then use concatenation to reassemble the string, i.e.:

```
text = text[:4] + 'tyrannosaurus rex' + text[7:]
```

For a more generic version, the statements:

```
substr(text, start, length) = replacement
substr(text, start, length, replacement)
```

are equal to:

```
text = text[:start] + replacement +
text[(start+length):]
```

Alternatively, if you can be sure that the string you are searching can be found without skipping over elements then you can use the **string** module's **replace()** function:

```
replace(text, old, new [, max])
```

This replaces **old** with **new** in the string **text** either as many times as seen, or **max** times if the argument is supplied. We can therefore rewrite our example above as:

```
text = string.replace(text, 'cat', 'tyrannosaurus rex')
```

We can also use the **replace()** method directly on the string:

```
text.replace('cat', 'tyrannosaurus rex')
```

Note however that searches *always* start from the beginning of the string. Replacing "at" once will change "cat," we can't start the search from the start. If you want to replace a word that appears at the end of a string, either use a regular expression, or use slices to make the change only in the component of the original string that you want to modify. For example:

```
text = text[:-3] + string.replace(text[-3:], 'at',
'oon')
```

will change the **text** variable to read "the cat sat on the moon."

Splitting

The Python **split()** function that comes as part of the **string** module is not quite as flexible as its Perl equivalent as it only allows you to split by a single or multicharacter sequence, not a regular expression. In all other respects though it's identical. It splits a string into component parts returning a list. The general format of the Python function is:

```
split(text, [, expr [, max]])
```

The **text** argument is the string that you want to split and **expr** is the separator. If you do not supply **expr** then Python assumes you want to split by white space – this is the same as using the Perl **split()** function without arguments on **$_** or with /**\s+**/ as the split expression – i.e.:

```
@words = split /\s+/, $text;
```

in Perl is equivalent to:

```
words = string.split(text)
```

If the **max** argument is supplied then it operates in the same way as the Perl version, limiting the number of times that the split operation occurs.

If you want to perform a regular expression based split then use the **split()** function that comes with the **re** module:

```
fields = re.split(r'[\s,:;]+', text)
```

The above statement splits the characters in **text** whenever it sees one or more whitespace, comma, colon, or semicolon. The Perl equivalent is:

```
@fields = split /[\s,:;]+/, $text;
```

See the section *Regular expressions* on p. 196.

Joining

You can join a sequence of words together in Python using the **join()** function in the **string** module, but care needs to be taken since the Python versions accept arguments in the opposite order. For example, the Perl statement:

```
$string = join(', ', 'martin', 'sharon',
               'wendy', 'rikke');
```

is equivalent to the Python:

```
string = string.join(['martin', 'sharon',
                      'wendy', 'rikke'], ', ')
```

Note the first argument is a sequence, either list or tuple, rather than a series of arguments to the function directly. Obviously this also works directly with list objects, such that:

```
$string = join(', ', @list);
```

is identical to:

```
string = join(list, ', ')
```

Trimming

You can trim the leading and/or trailing whitespace from a string in Python using the **lstrip()**, **rstrip()**, and **strip()** functions. The mnemonic here is that **lstrip()** strips the left and **rstrip()** strips the right:

```
string = '    leading space trailing '
lstrip(string) # returns 'leading space trailing '
rstrip(string) # returns '    leading space trailing'
strip(string)  # returns 'leading space trailing'
```

The closest equivalent to **chomp()** is therefore **rstrip()**, but note that the Python **rstrip()** and **lstrip()** functions remove all whitespace (tabs, spaces, linefeed/carriage returns), including repetitions, not just linefeed/carriage return characters. Also be aware that **rstrip()/lstrip()** do not take any notice of what platform you are on – they always strip linefeed and carriage return characters, regardless of the line termination sequence used by the current platform.

The closest equivalent to **chop()** is probably to take the last character directly off the string:

```
string = 'hello world\n'
string[:-1]
```

Remember however that you must capture the output from the functions, as Python does not change the variables in place. This means that the Perl statement:

```
$_ = "string\n";
chomp;
```

is equivalent to the Python:

```
text = "string\n"
text = string.rstrip(text)
```

Changing case

Most of the basic case translation operations are supported by a series of functions in Python's **string** module, as detailed here in Table 10.3.

TABLE 10.3 Case translation functions in Perl and Python

Description	Perl	Python equivalent
Change to lower case	lc(text)	string.lower(text)
Change first to lower case	lcfirst(text)	None
Change to upper case	uc(text)	string.upper(text)
Change first to upper case	ucfirst(text)	string.capitalize(text)
Change first of each word to upper case	None	string.capwords(text)
Swap case (lower to upper/upper to lower)	None	string.swapcase(text)

In addition to the equivalents of the Perl functions, Python also supports two additional functions, **capwords()** and **swapcase()**. These simplify the statements:

```
$string = join(' ', map { ucfirst($_) } split /\s+/,
$string);
```

and

```
$string = join('', map { /[a-z]/ ? uc($_) : lc($_) }
split //,$string);
```

or

```
$string =~ tr/a-zA-Z/A-Za-z/;
```

respectively.

Translating characters

There is no built-in equivalent to the **tr//** translation/transliteration operator. Instead, you need to use the **string.translate()** function. The function takes two arguments, the text to be translated, and string mapping characters that you want to exchange. You cannot make up the string yourself you need to use the **string.maketrans()** function. This makes the following statement in Perl:

```
$text =~ tr/a-z/A-Z/;
```

equivalent to the following in Python:

```
string.translate(text,
maketrans('abcdefghijklmnopqrstuvwxyz',
          'ABCDEFGHIJKLMNOPQRSTUVWXYZ'))
```

If you simply want to translate lowercase to uppercase characters then use one of the case specific functions.

REGULAR EXPRESSIONS

Regular expressions are a large part of the Perl language and they are used just about everywhere. In addition to the =~ and !~ operators, regular expressions are also supported by **split()**, **grep()**, and other functions, and they become a standard part of just about every text processing script you write. The regular expression system in Perl is one of the contributing factors to why Perl is so popular when it comes to processing information.

Python's regular expression system is not so much of an integral part of the language. There is no built-in regular expression parser, instead we have to use an external module to provide the facilities. Although we have access to the same basic methods of matching and replacing regular expression information they need to be accessed through a series of functions or classes rather than operators.

The Python **re** module replaces the older (and now obsolete) **regex** module as the regular expression engine. The main benefit of the **re** module, aside from some improvements in both speed and memory footprint, is that the **re** module works exactly like the regular expression parser in Perl, supporting the same semantics and regular expression language, but without the operator interface to the regular expression engine.

For cross reference, the list of supported character sequences, expressions and other characters supported by the **re** module in Python are shown in Table 10.4. We'll look at specific solutions for working with regular expressions in Python shortly.

TABLE 10.4 Character sequences recognized by the **re** module in Python

Character sequence	Description
text	Matches the string **text**
.	Matches any character except newline (unless the **s** flag is in use)
^	Matches the start of a string
$	Matches the end of a string
*	Matches zero or more repeats of the preceding expression, matching as many repetitions as possible
*?	Matches zero or more repeats of the preceding expression, matching as few repetitions as possible
+	Matches one or more repeats of the preceding expression, matching as many repetitions as possible
+?	Matches one or more repeats of the preceding expression, matching as few repetitions as possible
?	Matches zero or one repeats of the preceding expression, matching as many repetitions as possible
??	Matches zero or one repeats of the preceding expression, matching as few repetitions as possible
{m, n}	Matches from **m** to **n** repetitions of the preceding expression, matching as many repetitions as possible
{m, n}?	Matches from **m** to **n** repetitions of the preceding expression, matching as few repetitions as possible
[...]	Matches a set of characters; for example [a-zA-Z] or [,./;']
[^...]	Matches the characters not in the set
A|B	Matches either expression **A** or **B**
(...)	Expression group
\number	Matches the text in expression group **number**
\A	Matches only at the start of the string
\b	Matches a word boundary
\B	Matches not a word boundary
\d	Match any decimal digit – equivalent to **r'[0-9]'**
\D	Match any non-digit character – equivalent to **r'[^0-9]'**

TABLE 10.4 *cont.*

Character sequence	Description
\s	Match any whitespace (space, tab, newline, carriage-return, form feed, vertical tab)
\S	Match any non-whitespace character
\w	Match any alphanumeric character
\W	Match any non-alphanumeric character
\Z	Match only the end of the string
\\	Match backslash
(?iLmsux)	The group matches the empty string, with the **iLmsux** characters matching the corresponding regular expression options as defined in Table 10.5. Note that these affect the portion of the regular expression following, rather than the entire expression. They can also be used when you want the affects to be defined by the search expression, rather than the regular expression function
(?:...) not	Matches the expression defined between the parentheses, but does populate the grouping table
(?P<name>)	Matches the expression defined between the parentheses, but the matched expression is also available as a symbolic group identified by name. Note that the group still populates the normal group match variables. To refer to a group by name, supply it directly to the **match.end**() or **match.group**() methods, or use **\g<name>**
(?P=name)	Matches whatever text was matched by the earlier named group
(?#...)	Introduces a comment – the contents of the parentheses are ignored
(?=...)	Matches if the text supplied matches next, without consuming any text. This allows you to look ahead in an expression, without affecting the rest of the regular expression parsing. For example **Martin (?=Brown)** will only match "**Martin**" if it's immediately followed by "**Brown**"
(?!...)	Matches only if the specified expression doesn't match next (the opposite of **(?=...)**)
(?<=...)	Matches if the current position in the string is preceded by the supplied text, with the whole expression terminating at the current position. i.e. (?<=abc)def will match 'abcdef'. Matching is precise to the number of characters preceding such **abc** and **a|b** would match but **a*** would not
(?<!...)	Matches if the current position in the string is not preceded by the specified match (opposite of **(?<=...)**)

Some general notes that apply to all Python regular expressions:

▶ Regular expressions should be supplied as raw strings using the **r"** operator – this ensures that the string is interpreted as seen, rather than run through the normal parser for escaping character sequences as used on all other single, double and triple quoted blocks.

▶ Note that expression groups are available using the old style, and now deprecated in Perl, form of **number** as opposed to the newer Perl format of **$number**.

Most regular expressions also support a number of flags, just like the Perl expressions, as listed here in Table 10.5:

TABLE 10.5 Flags supported by regular expression processes

Flag	Description
I or IGNORECASE	Ignores the case of expression and match text
L or LOCALE	Use locale settings for determining the **b**, **B** and **w**, **W** sequences
M or MULTILINE	Makes ^ and **$** apply to the start and end of lines rather than strings in multiline strings
S or DOTALL	Forces **.** to match all characters, including newline
X or VERBOSE	Allows regular expressions to ignore unescaped whitespace and comments

You'll notice that there is no equivalent of the /**g** option which in Perl forces a matches to occur globally – this is because Python's **re** functions instead accept a fourth argument, **count**, which restricts the number of modifications to the given **count** value. See the *Substitution* section on p. 202 for examples.

Basic searches/matches

You can perform a basic search using the **re.search()** function:

```
search(pattern, string [, flags])
```

this is syntactically equivalent to the Perl:

```
$string =~ /pattern/flags;
```

For example, to determine whether the string 'cat' is in the string **$string** in Perl we'd use:

```
if ($string =~ /cat/) { ... }
```

In Python this translates to:

```
if re.search(r'cat', string): ...
```

The **search()** function actually returns a **MatchObject** if the search was successful, or **None** if it wasn't. See the *Using MatchObjects* section on p. 202 for more information.

The **match()** function is a more restrictive version of **search()**, only matching expressions at the beginning of the supplied string, rather than anywhere within the string. This can be used to enforce within a script for a match to start at the beginning of a string, irrespective of a user-supplied regular expression. In essence it provides no advantages over preceding the search expression with \A.

Extracting matched components

If you want to find and match specific expressions then the simplest method is to use the **findall()** function – this returns a list of the matches in a given expression, rather than a **MatchObject**. The function returns the matched text if no groups are used – if a group is used then it returns a list of all the matches, and if multiple groups are used then each item in the returned list is a tuple containing the text for each group, for example:

```
>>> import re
>>> string = 'the cat sat on the mat at ten'
>>> print re.findall(r'at',string)
['at', 'at', 'at']
>>> print re.findall(r'm.*?\b',string)
['mat']
>>> print re.findall(r'(at)',string)
['at', 'at', 'at']
>>> print re.findall(r'(cat)(.*?)(mat)',string)
[('cat', ' sat on the ', 'mat')]
```

This makes the **findall()** function the equivalent of the Perl statements:

```
@matches = ($string =~ s/at/);
```

or

```
($animal, $doing, $where) = ($string =~ m/(cat)(.*?)(mat)/);
```

Using MatchObjects

The **search()** and **match()** functions return **MatchObjects** which contain information both about the contents of the matched groups as well as the locations within the original strings at which the matches occurred. It's probably easiest to think of a **MatchObject** as a super variable containing the information that Perl populates through the **$number**, **@+** and **@LAST_MATCH_START** built-in variables. I've listed the methods available to the **MatchObject** indicated by **m** in Table 10.6.

TABLE 10.6 Methods for a given MatchObject

MatchObject method	Description
m.group([group, ...])	Returns the matched text for the supplied **group** or groups as defined by their index number, returning a tuple. If no group name is given then all of the matches are returned
m.groups([default])	Returns a tuple containing the text matched by all the groups in the pattern. If supplied then **default** is the value returned for those groups that did not match the supplied expression. The default value for **default** is **None**
m.groupdict([default])	Returns a dictionary containing all the name subgroups of the match. If supplied **default** is the value returned for those matches that didn't match the default is **None**
m.start([group])	Returns the start location of the specified **group**, or the start location of the entire match
m.end([group])	Returns the end location of the specified **group**, or the end location of the entire match
m.span([group])	Returns a two element tuple equivalent to (**m.start(group)**, **m.end(group)**) for a given group or the entire matched expression
m.pos	The value of **pos** as passed to the **match()** or **search()** function
m.endpos	The value of endpos as passed to the **match()** or **search()** function
m.re	The regular expression object that created this **MatchObject**
m.string	The string supplied to the **match()** or **search()** function

For example the Perl fragment:

```
$datetime = 'The date and time is 11/2/01 16:12:01 from
MET';
$datetime =~ m'((\d+)/(\d+)/(\d+)) ((\d+):(\d+):(\d+))';
$date = $1;
$time = $5;
($day, $month, $year) = ($2, $3, $4);
```

can be re-written in Python as:

```
datetime = 'The date and time is 11/2/01 16:12:01 from
MET';
dtmatch = re.match(
r'((\d+)/(\d+)/(\d+)) ((\d+):(\d+):(\d+))', datetime)
date = dtmatch.group(1)
time = dtmatch.group(5)
(day, month, year) = dtmatch.group(2,3,4)
```

Substitution

The **sub()** function performs the same operation as the **s///** substitution operator in Perl. The basic format for the command is:

```
sub(pattern, replace, string [, count])
```

We can therefore rewrite the Perl fragment:

```
$text = 'the cat sat on the mat';
$text =~ s/cat/slug/;
```

with:

```
text = 'the cat sat on the mat'
text = re.sub(r'cat', 'slug', text)
```

Note once again that the text or variable that you perform the substitution on is not modified in place, we must re-assign the result of the function to the original variable to make the change.

The replacement can also contain group references in the form **\n** where **n** is the group number. The Perl fragment below converts an international date (yyyymmdd) into a British date:

```
$date = '20010416';
$date =~ s/(\d{4})(\d{2})(\d{2})/$3.$2.$1/;
```

Which we can rewrite in Python as:

```
date = '20010416';
date = re.sub(r'(\d{4})(\d{2})(\d{2})', '\3.\2.\1', date)
```

The **replace** argument will also accept a function which will be supplied a single **MatchObject** argument. For example the Perl statement below is used to replace sequences of the form **%xx** as used in URLs with their single character equivalent:

```
$value =~ s/%([a-fA-F0-9][a-fA-F0-9])/pack("C",
hex($1))/eg;
```

We can rewrite this in Python as:

```
value = re.sub(r'%([a-fA-F0-9][a-fA-F0-9])',
               lambda x: chr(eval('0x'+x.group(1))), value)
```

To get the number of substitutions that took place use the **subn()** function which returns a tuple containing the substituted text and the number of substations, i.e.:

```
text = 'the cat sat on the mat'
(text, subs) = re.subn(r'at', 'ow', text)
```

sets **subs** to three.

As previously mentioned there is no **/g** flag to force substitutions to take place globally within a given string. In fact, by default all of Python's substitution functions replace all occurrences. To limit the number of modifications made, use the optional fourth argument **count**. For example, to change only the first occurrence of "at" to "oelacanth:"

```
text = 'the cat sat on the mat'
text = re.sub(r'at', 'oelacanth', text, 1)
```

which produces "the coelacanth sat on the mat."

Using compiled regular expressions

The **compile()** functions compiles a regular expression into a regular expression object in much the same way as the **qr{}** operator in Perl. To compile a new regular expression object use the **compile()** function:

```
compile(str [, flags])
```

Where **str** is the regular expression you want to use and **flags** as listed in Table 10.5 that you want to use on the new object. The new object has methods with the same name and purpose as the main functions in the **re** module.

For example we can rewrite the Python fragment:

```
text = 'the cat sat on the mat'
text = re.sub(r'at', 'oelacanth', text, 1)
```

as:

```
text = 'the cat sat on the mat'
cvanimal = compile(r'at')
text = cvanimal.sub('oelacanth', text)
```

The benefit of the compiled regular expression object is that we can use it many times on different strings without implying the additional compilation overhead on the regular expression itself. This is particularly useful when processing log or other text files.

The other methods supported by a regular expression object are listed in Table 10.7.

TABLE 10.7 Methods/attributes for a regular expression object

Regular expression method	Description
r.search(string [, pos [, endpos]])	Identical to the **search()** function, but allows you to specify the start and end points for the search
r.match(string [, pos [, endpos]])	Identical to the **match()** function, but allows you to specify the start and end points for the search
r.split(string [, max])	Identical to the **split()** function
r.findall(string)	Identical to the **findall()** function
r.sub(replace, string [, count])	Identical to the **sub()** function
r.subn(replace, string [, count])	Identical to the **subn()** function
r.flags	The flags supplied when the object was created
r.groupindex	A dictionary mapping the symbolic group names defined by r'(?Pid)' to group numbers
r.pattern	The pattern used when the object was created

Escaping strings

The **quotemeta()** function in Perl translates all the characters in a string that may be interpreted as regular expression character sequences, allowing you to use a string directly as pattern of a regular expression pattern or replacement. The Python **escape()** function in the **re** module performs a similar operation:

```
$string = quotemeta($expr)
```

is therefore equivalent to:

```
string = re.escape(expr)
```

SORTING SEQUENCES

In Perl we can place the sort function in front of any potential list to **sort** the results and if we want a sort ordered in the opposite direction then we can use the **reverse** function. All of the following are common occurrences:

```
sort @list;
sort keys %hash;
sort grep(/cat/,@names);
reverse sort getlistofcats();
```

We can of course also qualify the sort further by supplying a block or function to be used when comparing values, with **$a** and **$b** providing the two values that need to be compared:

```
sort { $a <=> $b } @list;
sort currency @money;
```

The only problem with the Perl solution is that we must make judgements at sort time about whether we are sorting numbers (in which case we use the <=> operator) or strings (when we use **cmp**).

With Python there is no separate sorting function; instead the list and string built-in object types support a **sort()** method which sorts the contents in place. There are therefore three things to be wary of when sorting Python lists:

▶ Calling **list.sort()** sorts the list permanently – unless you make a copy of the list there is no way to preserve the original order of the list.

▶ Dictionaries cannot be sorted without extracting their key or value lists and then sorting the list.

▶ Tuples cannot be sorted at all – if you've received a tuple as a return value from a function (and many do return tuples rather than lists) then you need to make a copy in a list. before sorting the values.

There are some advantages with Python – numeric and string based lists are automatically sorted numerically and alphabetically without requiring you to choose a special operator.

When sorting a list the Python statement:

```
list.sort()
```

will normally do what you expect with any given list.

Sorting tuples

Because a tuple is immutable we cannot sort it in place – the tuple built-in object doesn't even support a **sort()** method. The solution is to use the built-in **list()** function to create a copy of the tuple as a list, and then sort the list, i.e.:

```
tuplecopyaslist = list(mytuple)
tuplecopyaslist.sort()
for item in tuplecopyaslist:
    print item
```

Sorting dictionaries

We've already seen an example of this when looking at dictionaries in Chapter 4, but it's worth a quick recap. Essentially, we cannot get a sorted list of the keys from a dictionary that we can use directly from within another statement. For example, the following **for** statement just won't work:

```
for item in dict.keys().sort():
```

Instead, we need to get a list of keys into a new variable, before sorting that:

```
keylist = dict.keys()
keylist.sort()
for item in keylist:
    print '%s is %s' % (item, dict[item])
```

Sort functions

When sorting non-standard data, or when we want to normalize the data to be sorted without affecting the contents of the list itself, we need to use functions – either anonymous or named – to do the sort operating for us. For example, we can do a case independent sort in Perl using:

```
@sorted = sort { lc($a) cmp lc($b) } keys %hash;
```

With Python, we need to use either the **lambda** statement to create an anonymous function (which is in principle what the {} block in a **sort()** statement in Perl does) or create a separate function.

In either case, the function is supplied two arguments – the two elements that are being compared which are equivalent to the Perl **$a** and **$b** variables. For example we can recreate the above using **lambda** in Python like this:

```
list.sort(lambda x,y: return cmp(string.lower(x),
string.lower(y)))
```

Or using a separate function:

```
def noncasesort(x,y):
    return cmp(string.lower(x), string.lower(y))

list.sort(noncasesort)
```

Note that when calling the sorting function we supply the code object for the **noncasesort()** function rather than actually calling the function.

COPYING VARIABLES

One of the problems with Python using references to data all of the time is that it can play havoc with data structures which are using references, rather than copies of data from other variables. For example, the following fragment creates two variables, **alist** and **blist**:

```
>>> alist = [25,50,75,100]
>>> blist = alist
```

The **blist** variable is a reference to the same array object as **alist**, which means changing a value in the *variable* **alist** modifies the same list to which **blist** points, such that:

```
>>> alist[3] = 2000
>>> alist
```

```
[25, 50, 75, 2000]
>>> blist
[25, 50, 75, 2000]
>>>
```

We get the same value – both **alist** and **blist** point to the same array, so modifying values in one modifies the values we get back from the other.

To make a copy of a list or other sequence we can extract a full length slice – for example:

>>> blist = alist[:]

By assigning the values from a slice of the list we copy the individual objects from **alist** to **blist**, thus:

```
>>> alist[3] = 100
>>> blist
[25, 50, 75, 2000]
```

The above operation creates what is called a shallow copy and will not copy nested structures:

```
>>> alist = [1,2 [3,4]]
>>> blist = alist[:]
>>> alist.append(5)
>>> blist
[1, 2, [3, 4]]
>>> alist[2][1] = 5
>>> blist
[1, 2, [3, 5]]
```

To perform a deep copy, which copies all elements (including nested structures) to a completely new variable, you need to use the **deepcopy()** function in the **copy** module, for example:

```
>>> import copy
>>> alist = [1,2 [3,4]]
>>> blist = copy.deepcopy(alist)
>>> alist[2][1] = 5
>>> blist
[1, 2, [3, 4]]
```

EXTERNAL DATA SOURCES

Gathering information from external data sources, including files, databases, and even remote connections, is a common part of any program. Communicating with these external sources is not always straightforward. Working with simple text files is easy with any language, by accessing data stored in a binary format requires more work. With Perl we have a number of choices. Built-in we have the ability to open the popular Unix DBM files, or better still we can use one of the *DBM modules to **tie** a hash to a particular database. To communicate with any database system the obvious and time honored solution is the excellent DBI module written by Tim Bunce.

In Python we have access to most of the DBM formats using modules supplied in the standard Python library, but accessing a database system is more difficult. There is no standard interface, but there are lots of different modules available to talk in different ways to Oracle, mySQL, PostGreSQL, and other systems.

We'll be looking at how to work with simple files in Chapter 11. Below, we'll look at the methods available for working with DBM files and other database systems under Perl and Python.

DBM databases

Most DBM databases are Unix bound, and often used in places where quick access to fairly simple information is required. For example, DBM files are used by the alias system used by **sendmail** to map e-mail addresses to mailbox names.

Under Perl the best solution is to use one of the many different tied classes for working with the DBM/NDBM/GDBM and Berkeley database systems. For example, to open a GDBM database in this manner, we'd use:

```
use GDBM_File;
use Fcntl;

tie (%dbmhash, 'GDBM_File', 'mydbmdatabase',
     O_RDONLY, 0444)
    || die "$0: Error opening source $old: $!\n";
```

The resulting hash, in this case **%dbmhash**, then works like a normal hash – updating a value in the hash creates and/or updates the value in the corresponding DBM database and using **delete** to remove an entry from the hash removes the entry from the file.

Python supports similar functionality through a number of modules – dbm, gdbm and dumbdbm – which provides a DBM file-like ability without the use of an external C library. Python also supports the Berkeley DB system using the bsddb module. The only format that Python doesn't support natively is the special SDBM format, which is actually a Perl-only implementation of a DBM-style database. As an alternative, all versions of Python come with dumbdbm, an implementation of a DBM-style database written entirely in Python.

A full comparison list can be seen in Table 10.8.

TABLE 10.8 DBM file modules under Perl and Python

Perl Module	Python Module
ODBM_File	dbm
NDBM_File	ndbm
GDBM_File	gdbm
SDBM_File	None
DB_File	bsddb

For example, to open our GDBM database we write:

```
import gdbm

dict = gdbm.open('mydbmdatabase')
```

Like Perl, we end up with a dictionary which supports all of the normal functionality, including the **has_key()** and **keys()** methods.

The other modules work in the same way, providing the same **open()** function in each case, the general format of which is:

```
open(file [, flag [, mode]])
```

The optional **flag** allows you to specify which mode to open the database in – these follow the generic file opening modes used with the built-in **open()** function seen in Chapter 4 and Chapter 11. The default is read-only mode. The optional **mode** argument is the octal value used to create the database if it does not already exist; the default is 0666.

In a strict sense therefore the following is a closer equivalent of the Perl fragment above:

```
dict = gdbm.open('mydbmdatabase, 'r', 0666)
```

There is also an equivalent to the **Any_DBM** module in Perl through the **anydbm** Python module – unlike the Perl equivalent, the Python version attempts to identify and open an existing database even in read mode

Storing objects

As with the Perl versions, the Python DBM modules do not allow you to store nested data structures or objects within a DBM database – this is because the DBM format is designed to store textual rather than binary data. Under Perl we have access to the MLDBM module through CPAN which uses the **Data::Dumper** to convert the nested data structures into a serial data stream suitable for storing in a DBM database.

Python provides the **shelve** module which supports the same functionality as the MLDBM module. For serializing the information into a format for the DBM database the **shelve** module uses the **pickle** module.

Commercial databases

Although there are many alternative solutions, the primary method for communicating with a commercial database such as PostGreSQL or mySQL in Perl is to use Tim Bunce's **DBI** module in combination with one of the various **DBD** database drivers. Unfortunately there is no similar system in Python, instead we have the same situation with Python as we did with Perl in the early nineties where we have 40–50 different tools for accesses to a variety of database systems.

In essence most of these work in a similar way to the DBI system – we open a connection to the database, execute a statement, and then use a loop to extract the information from the query we supplied. In Perl, using the DBI module and mySQL for example, we can open a database connection and print out the results using something like this:

```
use DBI;
$dbh = DBI->connect('DBI:mysql:database=clients);

my $query = "select firstname, lastname from clients";
my $sth = $dbh->prepare($query);
```

```
$sth->execute();
while(my $row = $sth->fetchrow_hashref())
{
    print "$row->{firstname} $row->{lastname}\n";
}
$sth->finish();
$dbh->disconnect();
```

In Python, using the MySQL-Python module (available through the Vaults of Parnassus, **www.vex.net/parnassus/**) we can do the same:

```
import MySQLdb

dbh = MySQLdb.Connect(db='clients')
mycursor = mydb.cursor()

stmt = "select firstname, lastname from clients"
cursor.execute(stmt)
results = cursor.fetchall()

for firstname, lastname in results:
        print firstname, lastname

mydb.close()
```

Other modules are available for talking to other database systems. Check the Python site and the Vaults of Parnassus (see Appendix A for more information) where you can search the modules available.

There is work underway to produce a standard interface to database systems under Python. You can find out more information on the Python website – look under Sigs (Special Interest Groups), the db-sig is responsible for design and implementations. If you want to help out, there is a fairly well specified API (mirroring the functionality offered by DBI) already, all they need is developers to handle the programming.

11

FILE MANIPULATION

Processing information is one of Perl's major strengths – it's easy to read in, split, identify, and summarize information largely because Perl was designed entirely with this process in mind. Because we can use **split**(), **join**(), hashes, and regular expressions we have access to a powerful toolkit for interpreting just about any text file. For manipulating file systems – including permissions and ownership – Perl also has strong built-in facilities, although many of them are Unix-related.

Although Python does not have these abilities built-in, it does come with modules that provide you with basic string handling (**string**), regular expressions (**re**), and powerful facilities with basic string, list, and dictionary manipulation. Despite information to the contrary, Python is just as powerful as Perl when it comes to manipulating text files.

For manipulating file systems Python also comes with a series of modules for obtaining file lists, navigating through file systems, and determining file permission and ownership information.

In this chapter we'll look at all of the different solutions in Perl and Python for processing files and manipulating and navigating file systems.

FILE PROCESSING

The basic processes of opening a file have already been covered in Chapters 4 and 8. Once the file has been opened you end up with a file object which is then used to access the information from the file. The methods supported by a file object closely mimic the functions and operators we would normally use in Perl and other oddities, such as using line based input (as opposed to free-form or byte based input) are supported natively by the file object.

The basic Perl functions and equivalent Python file methods are listed in Table 11.1. We'll have a look at the specifics of reading, writing, and locating our position within a file in this section.

TABLE 11.1 Reading and writing files in Perl and Python

Perl operation	Python equivalent	Description
read() or sysread()	f.read([count])	Read **count** bytes
$line = <FILE>	f.readline()	Read a single line
@lines = <FILE>	f.readlines()	Read all the lines
print FILE $string	f.write(string)	Write **string**
print FILE @lines	f.writelines(list)	Write the lines in **list**
close(FILE)	f.close()	Close the file
tell(FILE)	f.tell()	Get the current file pointer
seek()	f.seek(offset [, where])	Seek to **offset** relative to **where**
POSIX::isatty()	f.isatty()	Returns 1 if file is an interactive terminal
IO::Handle->flush()	f.flush()	Flush the output buffers
truncate FILE, size	f.truncate([size])	Truncates file to **size**
fileno(FILE)	f.fileno()	Return the integer file descriptor

Reading

Perl supports two methods of reading information from a file, either on a line basis using the **<FILE>** construct or using the **read()**, **sysread()**, and other functions to read information from a file. As you can see from Table 11.1 most of the basic Perl file handling operations are supported by similar methods under Python.

Line by line

If you want to emulate the functionality of the Perl line input construct:

```
$line = <FILE>;
```

then you need to use the Python **readline()** method to an opened filehandle:

```
line = file.readline()
```

The method reads a single line from the file, and is platform-aware so that the same operation should work fine for reading standard text files on any platform. Also note that like **<FILE>** the **readline()** method also returns the line terminate sequence – use **string.strip()** or **string.rstrip()** to remove this (see Chapter 10 for more information).

Getting all the lines

You can get all of the lines from a file using the **readlines()** method on an active file object. This works in the same way as the **<FILE>** construct when used in list context. For example, we can import an entire file into an array in Perl using:

```
open(FILE, "myfile.txt");
@lines = <FILE>;
```

In Python we can rewrite this as:

```
myfile = open('myfile.txt')
lines = myfile.lines()
```

To read the entire contents of a file into a string object use the **read()** method without any arguments. For example:

```
myfiledata = myfile.read()
```

This is equivalent to using **<FILE>** in scalar context in Perl when the **$/** has been set to **undef**. A common trick for this in Perl is to create a new block and localize **$/**:

```
{
    local $/;
    $myfiledata = <FILE>;
}
```

Byte by byte

We can also use the **read()** method to get a specific number of bytes from a file. For example, to read a 512 byte record from a file we'd use a statement like this:

```
record = file.read(512)
```

Which is identical to the **read**() function in Perl – we can perform the same operation as the Python fragment above in Perl using:

```
read FILE, $record, 512;
```

End of file

Python does not support the notion of an "end of file" status for an open file object. Although an **EOFError** exception does exist, it is actually used by the **input**() and **raw_input**() built-in functions to identify when an end of file character has been found when reading input from the keyboard.

Instead, the **read**() and **readline**() methods return an empty string when they see the end of the file. This means that Python naturally supports the special behavior provided by Perl when using the **while(<FILE>)** construct.

For example, in Perl to read and print all of the lines from a file we'd probably use:

```
open(FILE, 'myfile.txt');
while(<FILE>)
{
    print;
}
close(FILE);
```

which we can rewrite in Python as:

```
myfile = open('myfile.txt')
while 1:
    line = myfile.readline()
    if !line: break
    print line,
myfile.close()
```

The **if** test breaks us out of the loop when we see an empty line. The other alternative is to use a **for** loop and the **readlines**() method to step through each individual line:

```
myfile = open('myfile.txt')
for line in myfile.readlines():
    print line,
myfile.close()
```

Processing example

Processing a file in Python requires more than just the basic ability of reading lines or information. Because Python does not include the built-in ability to split or otherwise manipulate strings with more than sequence syntax we need to import a few modules to perform the operations we'd do natively in Perl. In all other respects, the basics of the processing system remain the same – we read in a line, extract the components we want and work on them before moving to the next line.

As an example, here's a very simple script in Perl which uses **split()** to compile a count of the hosts and URL access from a standard web log:

```perl
my (%hostaccess, %urlaccess) = ((),());

if (@ARGV < 1)
{
    print "Usage: $0 logfile\n";
    exit(1);
}

open(FILE, $ARGV[0]) or die "Woah! Couldn't open
$ARGV[0]: $!\n";

while(<FILE>)
{
    @splitline = split;
    if (@splitline < 10)
    {
        print;
        next;
    }
    ($host,$ident,$user,$time,$offset,$req,
     $loc,$httpver,$success,$bytes) = @splitline;

    $hostaccess{$host}++;
    $urlaccess{$loc}++;
}

foreach my $host (sort keys %hostaccess)
{
    print "$host: $hostaccess{$host}\n";
}

foreach my $loc (sort keys %urlaccess)
```

```
{
    print "$loc: $urlaccess{$loc}\n";
}
```

For comparison, here's the same script in Python:

```python
import string
import sys

def cmpval(tuple1, tuple2):
    return cmp(tuple2[1],tuple1[1])

hostaccess = {}
urlaccess = {}

if len(sys.argv) < 2:
    print "Usage:",sys.argv[0],"logfile"
    sys.exit(1)

try:
    file = open(sys.argv[1])
except:
    print "Whoa!","Couldn't open the file",sys.argv[1]
    sys.exit(1)

while 1:
    line = file.readline()
    if line:
        splitline = string.split(line)
        if len(splitline) < 10:
            print splitline
            continue
        (host,ident,user,time,offset,req,
         loc,httpver,success,bytes) = splitline
        try:
            hostaccess[host] = hostaccess[host] + 1
        except:
            hostaccess[host] = 1
        try:
            urlaccess[loc] = urlaccess[loc] + 1
        except:
            urlaccess[loc] = 1
    else:
        break
```

```
hosts = hostaccess.items()
hosts.sort(lambda f, s: cmp(s[1], f[1]))

for host, count in hosts:
    print host, ": ", count

urls = urlaccess.items()
urls.sort(cmpval)

for url, count in urls:
    print url, ": ", count
```

There are a few major differences between the two scripts, most of which we've already covered elsewhere, but to recap:

▶ Python requires that we import the **sys** module – required for accessing the command line arguments and **exit()** function.

▶ We import the **string** module to gain access to the **split()** function so that we can extract the input.

▶ The **try** statement is used in place of **die** and **or** to determine whether we can open the file correctly.

▶ The **hostaccess** and **urlaccess** dictionaries need to be sorted first by extracting a list of key/value pairs and second by using a separate function (I've used both a **lambda** define function and a separate **cmpval** function) to sort the list according to the value in each tuple.

Writing

Writing back to a file in Perl is easy, in nearly all cases we can use **print()** to send the output to a specific filehandle. In Python the **print** function has not always worked this way, although since version 2.0 the facility has been added.

Using **write()** or **writelines()**

The **write()** and **writelines()** methods are the most obvious way of writing information back to a file in Python. Both can be used to write binary data and unlike **print** they do not automatically add a newline to each string written to the file. The **write()** method writes a single string and despite the name the **writelines()** method actually only writes a list of strings to the file. This means that the Perl statement:

```
print FILE 'Some text';
```

is directly equivalent to:

```
file.write('Some text')
```

and

```
print FILE @lines;
```

is directly equivalent to:

```
file.writelines(lines)
```

Using print

New in Python 2.0 is the ability to write direct to an open file without using the **write()** or **writelines()** methods. You can use this method as a direct replacement for the **print FILEHANDLE** construct in Perl. For example, we can rewrite the Perl fragment:

```
open(FILE, '>file.out');
print FILE "Some kind of error probably occurred\n"
```

in Python and this becomes:

```
file = open('file.out','w')
print >>file 'Some kind of error occurred'
```

Because we're using **print** the newline character is automatically appended, so be careful when using **print** in Python – appending a comma will stop Python from appending the line termination sequence.

Changing position

The **seek()** and **tell()** functions in Perl move to and return the current position within a given file and the Python **tell()** and **seek()** methods work in exactly the same way. Even the **where** argument, which determines from which point (start of file, current position, end of file) is the same. However, you have to use the numeric values (0, 1, and 2 respectively) as there are no handy definitions for these values.

FILE MANAGEMENT

Getting file lists

Perl provides two basic methods for getting file lists – you can use the special <spec> construct – for example <*.c> – or the preferred option now which is to use the **glob()** function to get a list. In either case the result is the same: a list of file names according to the file specification that you supply.

For example, to get a list of all the HTML files in a given directory:

```
@files = glob('*.html');
```

In Python, the **glob()** function in the **glob** module provides the same functionality:

```
import glob
files = glob.glob('*.html')
```

The **glob** module supports file expansion based on the Unix shell semantics which is the same as that supported by Perl in most circumstances. However, be aware that it's not identical to the extensions supported by Perl under Windows.

The various directory handle functions (**opendir()**, **readdir()** etc.) are not supported under Python – you'll need to translate these into a **glob()** statement or if you are using regular expressions to pick out filenames in Perl, then use **glob()** in combination with a loop and the **re** module to extract the items.

For example, the Perl fragment:

```
opendir(DIR,'.');
while(my $file = readdir(DIR))
{
    push @filelist, $file if ($file =~ /[A-Z]*?[0-9].
    [a-z]*/);
}
```

can be translated into Python as:

```
import glob, re
for file in glob.glob('./*'):
    if (re.search(r'[A-Z]*?[0-9].[a-z]*', file)):
        filelist.append(file)
```

Moving, renaming, and deleting files/directories

Most of the functions for moving, renaming, and otherwise manipulating directories can be found in the **os** module. All of these work in the same way as the Perl equivalents – see Table 11.2 for a comparative list between the Perl and Python functions.

TABLE 11.2 Moving, renaming, and deleting files in Perl and Python

Perl	Python	Description
link(source, dest)	link(source, dest)	Creates a hard link between **source** and **dest**
mkdir(path, mode)	mkdir(path [, mode])	Make the directory **path**, using the mode **mode**. Under Python **mode** defaults to 0777 if not supplied
File::Path::mkpath (path, debug, mode)	makedirs(path [, mode])	Identical to **mkdir()** except that the function will make all of the directories defined in the path, such that **makedirs('/a/b/c')** would create **'/a'**, **'/a/b'**, and **'/a/b/c'** if they didn't already exist
unlink(path)	remove(path) or unlink(path)	Removes a given file
File::Path::rmtree (path, debug, ownonly)	removedirs(path)	Remove the directory specified in path, including any subdirectories or files (identical to **rm -r**). Raises an **OSError** exception if the directory could not be removed
rename(source, dest)	rename(source, dest)	Renames **source** to **dest**
None	renames(source, dest)	Identical to **rename()** except that any directories specified in **dest** which do not exist will be created in an identical fashion to that used by **makedirs()**
rmdir(path)	rmdir(path)	Remove the directory **path**
symlink(source, dest)	symlink(source, dest)	Create a symbolic link between **source** and **dest**

Access and ownership

Perl supports a very strong system for determining the ownership and accessibility of a given file or directory, mostly through the –**X** tests. For example, we can determine whether a file exists using the –**e** test:

```
print "It's there!\n" if (-r $file);
```

Python's system is less straightforward and it's common to have to use more than one module to get the information we want. The primary source for information about accessibility is the **os.access()** function, this accepts the path to the file that you want to test and a number of constants that check the read, write, execute, and existence status of the file. For example, we could rewrite the above state in Python as:

```
if (os.access(file, os.F_OK)):
    print "It's there!"
```

Other tests are not quite so clearly determined. For ownership and other information you'll need to compare information gleaned from **os.stat()** and other functions with known values – as an example, the -O test in Perl returns true if the file is owned by the real ID of the current user:

```
print "Mine!\n" if (-O $file);
```

To get the same information from Python we need to use:

```
if (os.stat(path)[4] == os.getuid()):
    print "Mine!"
```

The final trick is used when determining the type of file. For simple files the information can be extracted using the **os.path.is*()** functions – for example, the **os.path.isdir(path)** function returns true if the given **path** is a directory. For others you need to use the **stat** module in combination with the mod information returned by the **os.stat()** function. For simple file determinations such as block or character special files the **stat.S_IS*()** functions work by accepting element zero from **os.stat()**. For example, we can determine if a file is a socket (including network or Unix domain sockets) using:

```
if (stat.S_ISSOCK(os.stat(path)[0])):
    print "Socket!"
```

With other settings we need to do some octal logic math to get the results – we can determine whether the sticky bit has been set on a file using:

```
if (stat.S_IMODE(os.stat(path)[0]) & 01000):
    print "Sticky!"
```

I've listed the different solutions in Python compared to the Perl -X tests in Table 11.3.

TABLE 11.3 Perl and Python file tests

Perl test	Python equivalent	Result
-r	os.access(path, os.R_OK)	File is readable by effective uid/gid
-w	os.access(path, os.W_OK)	File is writable by effective uid/gid
-x	os.access(path, os.X_OK)	File is executable by effective uid/gid
-o	os.stat(path)[4] == os.geteuid()	File is owned by effective uid
-R	None	File is readable by real uid/gid
-W	None	File is writable by real uid/gid
-X	None	File is executable by real uid/gid
-O	os.stat(path)[4] == os.getuid()	File is owned by real uid
-e	os.access(path, os.F_OK)	File exists
-z	stat(path)[6] == 0	File has zero size
-s	stat(path)[6]	File has non-zero size (returns the file size in bytes)
-f	os.path.isfile(path)	File is a plain file
-d	os.path.isdir(path)	File is a directory
-l	os.path.islink(path)	File is a symbolic link
-p	stat.S_ISFIFO(os.stat(path)[0])	File is a named pipe (**FIFO**), or **FILEHANDLE** is a pipe
-S	stat.S_ISSOCK(os.stat(path)[0])	File is a socket
-b	stat.S_ISBLK(os.stat(path)[0])	File is a block special file
-c	stat.S_ISCHR(os.stat(path)[0])	File is a character special file
-t	None	File is opened to a tty (terminal)
-u	stat.S_IMODE(os.stat(path)[0])	File has setuid bit set & 04000
-g	stat.S_IMODE(os.stat(path)[0])	File has setgid bit set & 02000
-k	stat.S_IMODE(os.stat(path)[0])	File has sticky bit set & 01000
-T	None	File is a text file
-B	None	File is a binary file (opposite of **-T**)

TABLE 11.3 *cont.*

Perl test	Python equivalent	Result
-M	None	Age of file in days when script started
-A	None	Time of last access in days when script started
-C	None	Time of last inode change when script started

When setting the permissions and ownership under Python care has to be taken. Although Python provides both the **chmod()** and **chown()** functions, they accept only two arguments, rather than the settings and a list of files to change. For single files this doesn't make any difference, the Perl statement:

```
chmod(0666, 'file.txt');
```

and the Python:

```
os.chmod('file.txt', 0666)
```

are identical. But when working with multiple files the statement:

```
chmod(0666, 'file.txt', 'fileb.txt', 'filec.txt')
```

has to be translated to:

```
for file in ('file.txt', 'fileb.txt', 'filec.txt'):
    os.chmod(file, 0666)
```

For cross reference, Table 11.4 contains the format of the functions under Perl and Python.

Getting file information

The **stat()** and **lstat()** functions are supported by Python through the **os** module, but the information returned by these two functions is not in an identical order as that provided by Perl. See Table 11.5 for more information. Also note that Python only accepts a file path to get this information, you cannot use a file handle (object) as you do with Perl.

For example, to get the file size in Perl we can use:

```
$filesize = -s $file;
```

TABLE 11.4 Setting access modes under Perl and Python

Perl function	Python function	Description
chmod(mode, path [, ...])	os.chmod(path, mode)	Change the **mode** of **path**. Note that Python accepts only one path to **chmod()**, if you want to change multiple paths use a loop or multiple calls to **chmod()**
chown(uid, gid, path [, ...])	os.chown(path, uid, gid)	Change the user ID and group ID of **path**. Note that Python accepts only one path, if you want to change multiple paths use a loop or multiple calls to **chown()**

TABLE 11.5 Elements returned by **stat()** under both platforms

Perl element	Python element	Description
0	2	Device number of file system
1	1	Inode number
2	0	File mode (type and permissions)
3	3	Number of (hard) links to the file
4	4	Numeric user ID of file's owner
5	5	Numeric group ID of file's owner
6	Not Returned	The device identifier (special files only)
7	6	File size, in bytes
8	7	Last access time since the epoch
9	8	Last modify time since the epoch
10	9	Inode change time (*not* creation time!) since the epoch
11	Not Returned	Preferred block size for file system I/O
12	Not Returned	Actual number of blocks allocated

or

```
($filesize) = (stat($file))[7];
```

In Python we can get the same information using:

```
filesize = os.stat(file)[6]
```

Alternatively you can use the **os.path** module which provides a lot of this information through a series of separate functions, listed in Table 11.6.

TABLE 11.6 Alternative methods for getting file information in Python

Function	Description
getatime(path)	Returns the time of last access as the number of seconds since the epoch
getmtime(path) of	Returns the time of last modification as the number of seconds since the epoch
getsize(path)	Returns the size of the file in bytes

Note that Python does not support the _ filehandle for getting information from a file in multiple calls – if you want to get different pieces of information from the same file in Python you need to specify the file path each time.

Manipulating file paths

Although not a built-in feature, Perl provides a series of modules for manipulating file paths in a platform portable way through the **File::Spec** module. You can use this to build up path components which are valid on the current platform with respect to directory and/or file names. In addition, the **File::Basename** module allows you to extract the directory, filename and extension from a given path.

All of these different functions are provided in Python through the **os.path** module. The **os.path** module is automatically loaded according to the current platform and is therefore also platform independent.

The main functions and their equivalents are summarized in Table 11.7.

TABLE 11.7 Path manipulation functions in Perl and Python

Perl function	Python function	Description
File::Spec(patha [, pathb …])	os.path.join(patha [, pathb …])	Joins the components **patha**, **pathb** into a valid path using the correct path separators for the current platform
File::Spec::canonpath (path)	os.path.abspath(path)	Returns a cleaned up version of **path** removing references to current and parent directories
File::Basename:: basename(path)	os.path.basename(path)	Extract the base name (filename or final directory) for a given path
File::Basename:: dirname(path)	os.path.dirname(path)	Extract the directory name for a given path

12

COMMUNICATING OVER A NETWORK

Perl has always had strong networking communication support built in through **socket()**, **bind()**, and other functions. Since Perl 5 we've also been able to use the **IO::Socket** module for an easier way of creating a socket object which automatically connects to a remote machines or sets up a socket suitable for providing a service through which we can communicate with another machine. In all cases, what we end up with is a filehandle that we can read and write to using the usual **read()**, **sysread()** and **print()** functions.

For communicating with Internet services we can to use one of the various modules available on CPAN – Graham Barr's libnet module, for example, provides connectivity with FTP, SMTP, NNTP, and other network services, whilst Gisle Aas's LWP toolkit provides methods for downloading and parsing web pages through the HTTP protocol.

The Python distribution comes with the **socket** module which provides all of the same functions as provided internally by Perl. It also comes with modules for communicating with SMTP, FTP, NTTP, HTTP, and various other protocols. It even comes with two HTTP server classes for building your own HTTP servers within your Python scripts.

In this chapter we're going to have a look both at the basic socket-based functionality and at some of the protocol specific modules that we can use, both in Perl and Python.

BASIC SOCKET FUNCTIONS

Whether you are used to using the built-in Perl socket functions or the **IO::Socket** module, you shouldn't have any problems making the move to using Python's object based model. With Perl the first stage is to create a new generic socket using the **socket** function, we then use that as a base from which to bind to a service port in order to provide a network service, or to connect to a remote service. For example, the Perl fragment below creates a socket and then connects to a remote host:

```perl
use Socket;

sub open_tcp_socket
{
    my ($SOCKETHANDLE, $remotehost, $service_name) = @_;
    socket($SOCKETHANDLE,PF_INET,SOCK_STREAM,'tcp');
    my $port_num = (getservbyname($service_name,'tcp'))[2];
    my $remote_socket = sockaddr_in($port_num,
                                    scalar gethostbyname
                                    ($remotehost));
    connect($SOCKETHANDLE, $remote_socket);
}
```

We can open a connection and read some data using:

```perl
open_tcp_socket(*SOCKETHANDLE,'mail.mchome.com','smtp');
recv(SOCKETHANDLE, $message, 1024, 0);
print $message;
close(SOCKETHANDLE);
```

Python shortens some of these operations – for example we don't need to use the **sockaddr_in()** function to pack the port number and remote host address before calling **connect()** – the Python **connect()** accepts a tuple containing the port number and remote address and opens the connection. For example, we can rewrite the **open_tcp_socket()** function above in Python like this:

```python
def open_tcp_socket(remotehost,servicename):
    s = socket.socket(socket.AF_INET, socket.SOCK_STREAM)
    portnumber = socket.getservbyname(servicename,'tcp')
    s.connect((remotehost,portnumber))
    return s
```

The code for using the function is remarkably similar:

```python
mysock = open_tcp_socket('mail.mchome.com','smtp')
message = mysock.recv(1024)
print message
mysock.close()
```

As expected, the biggest difference is that Python creates a new **socket** object on which we use methods to **connect()**, **listen()**, and **accept()** connections, just as we use functions in Perl. The list of Perl functions, the arguments they accept and their Python equivalents are listed in Table 12.1.

TABLE 12.1 Perl and Python **socket** functions

Perl built-in function	Python **socket** method
socket(S,family,type)	S = socket(family, type)
accept(S)	S.accept()
bind(S,address)	S.bind(address)
close(S)	S.close()
connect(S, sockaddr_in(serviceport, scalar gethostbyname(address)))	S.connect((address,serviceport))
getpeername(S)	S.getpeername()
getsockname(S)	S.getsockname()
getsockopt(S, level, option)	S.getsockopt(level, option)
listen(S, waitqueue)	S.listen(waitqueue)
recv(S, message, buflen [, flags])	message = S.recv(buflen [, flags])
send(S, message [, flags])	S.send(message [, flags])
send(S, message, flags, address)	S.sendto(message [, flags], (address, port))
setsockopt(S, level, option, value)	S.setsockopt(level, option, value)
shutdown(S, how)	S.shutdown(how)

Note that the **connect()** method accepts a single argument, a tuple with two elements the IP address and the serviceport number that we would normally supply to the **sockaddr_in()** Perl function to create a packed address for the Perl **connect()** function.

The most important thing to remember when working with sockets under Python is that the socket is not a filehandle and so we can't use the **readline()** or other methods to read information from the socket. Instead, we need to use the **recv()** and **send()** methods to exchange data with a remote host. In most cases this shouldn't cause too many problems as most protocols work on a challenge/response system such as that used by SMTP or HTTP.

If you want to be able to read and write to a network socket then use the **fdopen()** function within the **os** module to create a new file object based on the file descriptor number. File descriptors are shared between files and sockets on most operating systems and you can obtain the file descriptor number of any file or socket object using the **fileno()** method. For example, we could rewrite the code we used earlier for reading from an SMTP server:

```
mysock = open_tcp_socket('mail.mchome.com','smtp')
message = mysock.recv(1024)
print message
mysock.close()
```

to:

```
mysock = open_tcp_socket('mail.mchome.com','smtp')
file = os.fdopen(mysock.fileno())
line = file.readline()
print line,
file.close()
mysock.close()
```

This opens the socket, creates a file object based on the sockets file number and then uses **readline()** to read the information. With the **socket** module we can do this automatically (without the need for **os**) using the **makefile()** method:

```
mysock = open_tcp_socket('mail.mchome.com','smtp')
file = mysock.makefile()
line = file.readline()
print line,
mysock.close()
file.close()
```

If you are communicating with one of the standard Internet services such as SMTP, HTTP or FTP then use one of the modules that comes with Python – we'll be looking at some alternatives later in this chapter.

RUNNING A SERVER

You can use the usual methods of calling **os.fork()** or the **select** module or even threads to support the multiple connections required by most network servers. If you are creating a network service however you might be better off using the **SocketServer** module which provides a number of different classes designed to handle network communication. The module provides eight different classes which provide all of the mechanisms required to support basic network services similar to HTTP, SMTP, and others. You can see a list of the classes supported in Table 12.2.

TABLE 12.2 Network servers supported by the **SocketServer** module

Class	Description
TCPServer(address, handler)	A basic TCP-based server. The **address** should be a tuple containing the host name and port number to set up the service – if **hostname** is set to an empty string then the server binds to the default address for the current host. The **handler** should be an instance of the **BaseRequestHandler** class – see the main text for information on how to create the handler required
UDPServer(address, handler)	A basic UDP-based server
UnixStreamServer(address, handler)	A server which uses the Unix domain sockets in stream mode for communication
UnixDatagramServer(address, handler)	A server which uses the Unix domain sockets in datagram mode for communication
ForkingUDPServer(address, handler)	Identical to **UDPServer** except that the server handles multiple requests by using **os.fork()**
ForkingTCPServer(address, handler)	Identical to **TCPServer** except that the server handles multiple requests by using **os.fork()**
ThreadingUDPServer(address, handler)	Identical to **UDPServer** except that the server handles multiple requests by using threads to set up multiple client handler threads
ThreadingTCPServer(address, handler)	Identical to **TCPServer** except that the server handles multiple requests by using threads to set up multiple client handler threads

In order to create a server using these base classes you need to create a new subclass of the **BaseRequestHandler** class provided by the module. The class needs to define at the bare minimum the **handle()** method which is called each time a connection from a client is obtained. The object instance (**self**) contains a number of different attributes including the **socket** object used to communicate with the server as **request** and the address of the client that made the connection as **client_address**.

Once the new subclass has been created all you need to do is create a new instance of the desired server class, passing the handler subclass you just created. Finally you need to call either the **handle_request()** method, which handles a single request, or the **serve_forever()** method which processes request until you terminate the server process.

For example, the script below creates a handler called **TimeHandler** which returns the date or time of the server, or its epoch value when requested from the client:

```
import SocketServer, socket, string, time

class TimeHandler(SocketServer.BaseRequestHandler):
    def handle(self):
        socketfile = self.request.makefile()
        self.request.send(
            'Hello %s, What do you want?\r\n' %
            (self.client_address,))
        while 1:
            line = socketfile.readline()
            print "Got %s\n" % (line,)
            line = string.strip(line)
            if not line:
                break
            if line == 'time':
                self.request.send("The time is: %s\r\n"
                        % (time.strftime('%H:%M:%S',
                            time.localtime(time.time
                            ()))),)
            if line == 'date':
                self.request.send("The time is: %s\r\n"
                        % (time.strftime('%d/%m/%Y',
                            time.localtime(time.time
                            ()))),)
            if line == 'datetime':
```

```
                self.request.send("The time is: %s\r\n"
                    % (time.strftime('%d/%m/%Y %H:%M:%S',
                            time.localtime(time.time()))),))
            if line == 'rawtime':
    self.request.send('%d\r\n' % (time.time(),))
    socketfile.close()

server = SocketServer.TCPServer(('', 8000), TimeHandler)
server.serve_forever()
```

Using this script we can easily get the time of the remote machine:

```
$ telnet twinsol 8000

Hello ('198.112.10.135', 43712), What do you want?
time
The time is: 15:09:39
date
The time is: 14/04/2001
datetime
The time is: 14/04/2001 15:09:43
rawtime
987257386
```

This is a basic example but you could extend the service to just about any network-based solution you needed. For further examples, see the **BaseHTTPServer**, **SimpleHTTPServer** and **CGIHTTPServer** modules all of which provide a classes for servicing HTTP requests.

OBTAINING NETWORKING INFORMATION

The **socket** module is also responsible for talking with the host operating system to determine information such as the protocol and service lists and for communicating with the host domain name resolver to resolve hostnames into their IP addresses.

The information returned by most of the Python equivalent matches the information returned by the Perl functions when called in scalar context. However, all IP addresses are returned in the form of a string on dotted-quads, rather than the packed format returned by Perl.

TABLE 12.3 Perl and Python network information functions

Perl function	Python equivalent
gethostbyname(hostname) (scalar context)	gethostbyname(hostname)
gethostbyname (hostname) (list context)	gethostbyname_ex(hostname)
gethostbyaddr(address) (scalar context)	None
gethostbyaddr(address) (list context)	gethostbyaddr(address)
getprotobyname(protocolname) (scalar context)	getprotobyname(protocolname)
getservbyname(name, protocol) (scalar context)	getservbyname(name, protocol)

We can therefore shorten the Perl fragment:

```
$address = join('.',
        unpack('C4',scalar gethostbyname
        ('www.python.org')));
```

or

```
$address = inet_aton('www.python.org');
```

to the following in Python:

```
address = gethostbyname('www.python.org')
```

Also note that Python functions also accept IP addresses as strings, rather than as 32-bit packed bytestring.

Also be aware that the **gethostbyname_ex()** function in Python does not return the address type or length. What it does return is the primary name for the given name, a list of aliases for the name, and a list of addresses for that name. For example:

```
>>> socket.gethostbyname_ex('www.python.org')
('parrot.python.org', ['www.python.org'],
['132.151.1.90'])
>>> socket.gethostbyname_ex('www.yahoo.com')
('www.yahoo.akadns.net', ['www.yahoo.com'],
['216.32.74.53', '216.32.74.52', '64.58.76.177',
'64.58.76.179', '216.32.74.50', '64.58.76.176',
'64.58.76.178', '216.32.74.51', '216.32.74.55'])
```

CLIENT MODULES

Python comes with a number of modules for communicating with network servers as a client. Most of these provide the same functionality as their Perl equivalents and because the Perl modules work on a class/object basis migrating from a Perl based client to a Python based client shouldn't be too difficult. For reference, I've listed the common Perl modules and their Python equivalent modules in Table 12.4.

TABLE 12.4 Perl network client modules and their Python equivalents

Perl module	Python equivalent
Net::SMTP	smtplib
Net::FTP	ftplib
Net::NNTP	nntplib
Net::POP3	poplib
Net::xMAP	imaplib
LWP::Simple	urllib
URI	urlparse
URI::Escape	urllib

We'll take a look at some of the more commonly used modules and some Perl and Python equivalent scripts to see how easy the migration can be.

Working With SMTP

The libnet bundles includes the **Net::SMTP** module which provides us with a simple method for talking direct to SMTP servers – you create a new **Net::SMTP** object and then use methods with the same name as the commands you would supply to the SMTP server. For example, ignoring errors, we could open a connection a send a message using:

```
use Net::SMTP;

$smtp = Net::SMTP->new('mail.mchome.com');
$smtp->mail('mc@mcwords.com');
$smtp->to('mc@mcwords.com');
$smtp->data();
$smtp->datasend("Subject: Reminder\n\nDon't Mail
```

```
Self\n");
$smtp->dataend();
$smtp->quit();
```

Python's **smtplib**, which comes as standard with the Python distribution, uses the same model – once we've created a new instance of the **smtplib** class we use methods with the same name as SMTP commands to setup and send the e-mail. In addition, Python also provides a **sendmail()** method which accepts three arguments, the sender, recipient, and e-mail message, which will do all the work for us.

We can therefore rewrite the above Perl script as:

```
import smtplib

server = smtplib.SMTP('localhost')
server.sendmail('mc@mcwords.com','mc@mcwords.com',
               "Subject: Reminder\n\nDon't Mail Self\n")
server.quit()
```

Here's a more extensive example that also gets input from the user – this fragment is taken from the bottom of the **smtplib** module:

```
import sys, rfc822
from smtplib import *

def prompt(prompt):
    sys.stdout.write(prompt + ": ")
    return string.strip(sys.stdin.readline())

fromaddr = prompt("From")
toaddrs = string.splitfields(prompt("To"), ',')
print "Enter message, end with ^D:"
msg = ''
while 1:
    line = sys.stdin.readline()
    if not line:
        break
    msg = msg + line
print "Message length is " + `len(msg)`

server = SMTP('localhost')
server.set_debuglevel(1)
server.sendmail(fromaddr, toaddrs, msg)
server.quit()
```

Working with HTTP

The most obvious use on the client end of the HTTP protocol is generally to download a remote page to disk. Within Perl this is generally handled through the LWP toolkit from Gisle Aas. The **LWP::Simple** module provides the **mirror()** function which downloads a URL putting the contents directly into a file – for example we can download the homepage of the Perl website to a file using:

```
use LWP::Simple;

$rc = mirror('http://www.perl.com',
            'perlhomepage.html');
```

The Python **urllib** provides the same functionality through the **urlretrieve()** function such that we can get the home page of the Python website using:

```
import urllib

urllib.urlretrieve('http://www.python.org',
                    'pythonhomepage.html')
```

We can also open a URL and access the input using the same methods as we would use on a typical file object by using **urlopen()**. For example, we could rewrite the above as:

```
import urllib

url = urllib.urlopen('http://www.python.org')
file = open('pythonhomepage.html','w')

while 1:
    line = url.readline()
    if len(line) == 0:
    break
    file.write(line)
```

If you actually want to parse the information in an HTML page that you download then you need to use the **httmllib** module.

Working with IMAP

IMAP (Internet Mail Access Protocol) is quickly replacing POP (Post Office Protocol) as the e-mail solution used, especially in large companies. The Perl **Net::xMAP** is somewhat temperamental and IMAP itself is not always the easiest protocol to work with. The Python **imaplib** module provides a class-based interface to an IMAP server – the script below downloads the e-mail from a single e-mail account, displaying the results as HTML. I use this script as a very quick way of checking my e-mail remotely without having to fire up a full e-mail client.

```
#!/usr/local/bin/python

import imaplib
import sys,os,re,string

# Set up a function that we can use to call the
# corresponding method on a given imap connection when
# supplied with the name of an IMAP command
def run(cmd, args):
    typ, dat = apply(eval('imapcon.%s' % cmd), args)
    return dat

# Get the mail, displaying the output as HTML

def getmail(title,login,password):
# Login to the remote server, supplying the login and
# password supplied to the function
    run('login',(login,password))

# Use the select method to obtain the number of
# messages in the users mail account. The information is
# returned as a string, so we need to convert it to an
# integer
    nomsgs = run('select',())[0]
    nomsgs = string.atoi(nomsgs)

# Output a header for this email account
    print "<p><font size=+2><b>"+title+"</b></font></p>"

# Providing we've got some messages, download each
# message and display the sender and subject
    if nomsgs:
# Output a suitable table header row
    print "<table border=0 cellpadding=0 cellspacing=0>"
    print
"<tr><td><b>Sender</b></td><td><b>Subject</b></td></tr>"
# Process each message
    for message in range(nomsgs,0,-1):
    subject,sender,status = '','','U'
```

```
# Send the fetch command to the server to obtain the
# email's flags (read, deleted, etc.) and header
# from the email
    data = run('fetch', (message,'(FLAGS
    RFC822.HEADER)'))[0]
    meta,header = data
# Determine the email's flags and ignore a message if
# it's marked as deleted
    if string.find(meta,'Seen') > 0:
        status = ''
    if string.find(meta,'Deleted') > 0:
        continue
# Separate the header, which appears as one large
# string, into individual lines and then extract
# the subject and sender fields
                for line in string.split(header,'\n'):
                    if not line:
                        sender = re.sub(r'\<.*\>','',
                                    re.sub
                                    (r'\"','',sender))
# If the message is unread, then mark the subject and
# sender in red
                        if (string.find(status,'U') == 0):
                            subject = '<font color=red>'
                                    + subject + '</font>'
                            sender = '<font color=red>'
                                    + sender + '</font>'
                    print "<tr><td>%s</td><td>%s</td></tr>"
                            % (sender,subject)
                    break
# Extract the sender/subject information by looking
# for the field prefix
                    if line[:8] == 'Subject:':
                        subject = line[9:-1]
                    if line[:5] == 'From:':
                        sender = line[6:-1]
        print "</table>"
    else:
        print "No messages"
# Logout from the server
    run('logout',())
```

```
# Set the server information
server='imap'
# Print out a suitable HTTP header and HTML page header
print "Content-type: text/html\n\n"
print """
<head>
<title>Mail</title>
</head>
<body bgcolor="#ffffff" fgcolor="#000000">
"""

# Connect to the server, and then call getmail to get
# the mail from the server
try:
    imapcon = imaplib.IMAP4(server)
except:
    print "Can't open connection to ",server
    sys.exit(1)
getmail('MC','mcmcslp','PASSWORD')
```

You can see the results of using the script in Fig 12.1.

FIG 12.1 Checking your e-mail using IMAP

13 WEB DEVELOPMENT

The Internet, and some form of HTML or web environment-based development, is hard to avoid these days.

Perl has for years supported web and HTML projects, largely because of its text processing abilities. Parsing the data supplied by a client through a web server is relatively easy in Perl using a combination of **split()** and a regular expression. Furthermore when outputting the information the ease with which we can output text, interpolate variable data and communicate and integrate with outside data sources makes Perl an obvious choice. In fact, I doubt Perl would be as popular a scripting language as it is today if it wasn't for its extensive use in web development.

To make the whole development process easier Perl includes the **CGI** module. The module provides the basic functions required to get form data into a suitable format internally within your CGI script. In addition, it provides a host of support functions that also allow you to setup and communicate back with the browser, accept multipart forms and through additional modules such as **CGI::Cookie** to support more advanced options.

An even bigger part of the **CGI** module is its structured support for outputting HTML to different standard levels. Using the **CGI** functions we can output genuine HTML 2.0, HTML 3.0, and HTML 4.0 code, as well as code supporting the HTML extensions in Internet Explorer and Netscape browsers.

Python has less of a web heritage, although there are stalwart users who make use of Python and, as we'll see later, some of the most advanced web tools available. Unfortunately, the CGI tools provided with Python are not nearly as extensive or advanced as those provided with Perl.

The core **cgi** module in Python provides very basic form parsing abilities, including the ability to parse multiple fields with the same name, multi-part forms and to accept files during an upload. Unfortunately this is the limit of its abilities. Cookies, HTTP header generation, and any form of HTML generation has to be handled manually.

That's not to say that Python is not good at web development. Python has Zope, one of the best known web development environments that runs entirely on a scripting language, which in this case, is Python. A large number of sites also use Mailman, a mailing list manager, also written entirely in Python. Mailman includes a web environment which allows both users and administrators to manage their mailing lists through a web browser.

Finally, one of the coolest Python development projects ever is Jython (formerly JPython). Jython is an implementation of Python written entirely in Java. It's possible, for example, to write a Python-based script which we supply over a network as part of a Java applet – we don't have to worry whether the client has Python, because we can supply it in the form of Jython. As if that wasn't enough, we can also use Java objects within Python and Python objects within Java.

In this chapter we're going to have a look at the basic mechanics of parsing an HTML form and setting up a Python-based CGI script. We'll also look at the **urllib** and **urlparse** modules which parse, extract, and translate information in URLs into a more usable form in the same way as Gisle Aas' URI modules. For information on downloading URLs or setting up HTTP or other network servers see Chapter 12. If you are working with XML and HTML you might also want to check out the **xmllib** and **htmllib** modules.

BASIC CGI PROGRAMMING

The basic process of setting up your Python based CGI application is to start by sending back the HTTP header. The Python **cgi** module does not provide any solutions for generating this information for you. This means that you will need to translate any **CGI** module instructions of the form:

```
use CGI;

my $query = new CGI;
print $query->header('text/html');
```

into a Python **print** statement:

```
print 'Content-type: text/html\r\n\r\n',
```

To get the information supplied to fields in a form, the easiest method is to use the **param()** function in the Perl **CGI** module:

```
use CGI;

my $name = param('name');
my @options = param('options');
```

In Python this translates to using the **getvalue()** function:

```
import cgi

name = cgi.getvalue('name')
options = cgi.getvalue('options')
```

The **getvalue()** function also accepts a second argument, which is the value returned if the form doesn't have a field matching the name you've requested, you can use this in the same way as you would use the || operator in Perl. For example:

```
$name = param('name') || 'nobody';
```

can be rewritten as:

```
name = cgi.getvalue('name', 'nobody')
```

That is, unfortunately, where it ends when it comes to migrating from Perl to Python. All of the other options supported by the **CGI** module are unsupported in Python, either in the **cgi** module or any others.

Generating HTML

For generating HTML the easiest way to do this in Python is to generate the HTML manually using **print** statements. Although not elegant, it's the easiest solution available if you don't want to use any additional third party modules. Alternative, you can get hold of the HtmlKit module extensions (**www.dekorte.com/Software/Python/HtmlKit/**) these provide some basic methods for most of the HTML kit, albeit with less of a focus than that provided by the Perl **CGI** module.

For example, in Perl we can generate a table using:

```
use CGI qw/:html3/;
print table(Tr([th(['Name','Title', 'Phone'])]),
            Tr([td(['Martin','MD','01234 567890'])])));
```

Using the **HtmlKit** module we could rewrite this as:

```
import HtmlKit

table = HtmlKit.Table()
row = table.newRow()
row.newColumn('Name')
row.newColumn('Title')
row.newColumn('Phone')
row = table.newRow()
row.newColumn('Martin')
row.newColumn('MD')
row.newColumn('01234 567890')
print str(table)
```

It's not quite as neat, but **HtmlKit** does provide an easier and more struct-ured way of defining some HTML elements, especially fonts and basic layout properties. Be warned that **HtmlKit** implies many different options in the HTML that is generated explicitly where **CGI** relies on implicit options. This is because the **CGI** module only outputs what you supplied to the various functions, as you can see here in the HTML generated by our earlier sample:

```
<table><tr><th>Name</th> <th>Title</th>
<th>Phone</th></tr> <tr><td>Martin</td> <td>MD</td>
<td>01234 567890</td></tr></table>
```

In comparison, the **HtmlKit** module adds options to the table, column, and cell definitions which you would otherwise have to explicitly disable:

```
<table border="0" cellpadding="3" cellspacing="1"
width="100%"><tr><td nowrap
bgcolor="#dddddd">Name</td><td nowrap bgcolor="#dddddd
">Title</td><td nowrap
bgcolor="#dddddd">Phone</td></tr><tr><td nowrap
bgcolor="#dddddd">Martin</td><td nowrap
bgcolor="#dddddd">MD<
/td><td nowrap bgcolor="#dddddd">01234
567890</td></tr></table>
```

HANDLING COOKIES

In Perl the **CGI::Cookie** module will create a cookie HTTP header for you by supplying the cookie data, domain, and expiry date to a new cookie object. For example

```perl
my $query = new CGI;
my $cookietext = $query->cookie(-name => 'sample',
                                -value => { login =>
                                               $login,
                                            other =>
                                            'Other'
                                -path => '/',
                                -domain =>
                                    'mcwords.mchome.com',
                                -expires => '+1y');
print "Set-Cookie: $cookietext\n";
```

In Python there is a third party module called **Cookie** which will build a new cookie for you. For example, we could rewrite the above using the **Cookie** module like this:

```python
import Cookie
cookie = Cookie.SmartCookie()
cookie['sample'] = 'login=%s; other=Other' % (login)
cookie['sample']['path'] = '/'
cookie['sample']['domain'] = 'mcwords.mchome.com'
cookie['sample']['expires'] = 365*24*3600
print cookie
```

Note that we have to actually calculate the future value ourselves (in seconds) rather than using relative strings.

To actually parse a cookie you need to use the **load()** method on a **SmartCookie** object to load the information supplied in the **HTTP_COOKIE** environment variable:

```python
import Cookie, os

cookie = Cookie.SmartCookie()
cookie.load(os.environ['HTTP_COOKIE'])
print cookie['sample']
```

URL PROCESSING

The **urllib** module actually provides methods for downloading files, as we've already seen in Chapter 12. It also contains a number of functions for processing/converting URLs into useful formats in the same way as the Perl **URI::Escape**. The functions in each are summarized in Table 13.1.

TABLE 13.1 Converting URL to/from escaped versions

Perl URI::Escape	Python urllib	Description
uri_escape(string)	urllib.quote (string)	Escapes characters in **string** with URL compatible formats. Note that the Python **quote()** does not convert spaces to **+** characters by default (**uri_escape()** does). Use the **quote_plus()** function instead
uri_unescape(string)	urllib.unquote (string)	Converts a string that has URL escape sequences embedded into it in a normal string. Note that the **unquote()** function does not convert + characters back to spaces, use **unquote plus()**

For example, in Perl we would convert the string "file=/path/to/an/odd file" using:

```
use URI::Escape;
print uri_escape(' file=/path/to/an/odd file');
```

and in Python:

```
import urllib
print urllib.quote_plus('file=/path/to/an/odd file')
```

If you want to change the list of characters that are escaped during this process both the Perl and Python functions accept an additional argument to set these values, but they work in opposite ways. In Perl, the second argument defines which characters are "unsafe" and therefore should be escaped. For example, to mark all characters to be escaped we'd use:

```
uri_escape($url,'\x00-\xff');
```

or to escape everything except alphanumeric characters:

```
uri_escape($url,'^a-zA-Z0-9');
```

In Python, the second arguments defines which characters are safe, and therefore do not need to be escaped:

```
urllib.quote(url,'a-zA-Z0-9')
```

For more complex translations you'll need to be more careful about which characters you do (or more importantly don't) include.

ZOPE

Zope is actually an acronym for Z-Objects Publishing Environment which should give you a clue as to its capabilities. Zope is a completely Python-based solution for publishing information on the web. Rather than just filling the gap of a traditional web server, Zope also supports online page editing, change tracking, and multi-user access so it's possible to have a team of people working on stories and pages without needing to teach them HTML.

Zope also works through a series of templates and other content, so you can provide personalized and custom content whilst still providing the same basic structure to your users. Even better is the ability change the layout and content dynamically based on the user's preferences, and because we're all inside Python we can make complex but still intelligent choices about what to display.

Furthermore, because Zope is served through Python we also have access to all of the abilities of Python to create, deliver, and interface to other data sources. For example, you could develop a complete project management system entirely in Zope which means that everything from the HTML used to display the information to the database itself is provided by the same tool.

If that isn't enough for you, you can also interface to most other SQL databases, including mySQL, PostgreSQL, Oracle, and many others. You can also interface to e-mail, Usenet and other services and if necessary write your own interfaces. Finally, Zope supports a huge range of standards including HTML, XML, WebDAV, CSS, DOM, XML-RPC, SQL, RSS, and LDAP.

All these different sources are still programmable and accessible through an online interface and most can be used by editors and writers without the need of a programmer or web developer to provide the interface and information.

Zope is already used by a large number of companies including Bell Atlantic Mobile, Red Hat, NASA, the US Navy, ishophere.com, i-Gift, IDG (Brazil), GE, Digital Garage, Verio, www.HireTechs.com, and Storm Linux.

Installing, using, and developing a Zope service is beyond the scope of this book, especially when there is no direct competition with a comparable Perl-based service. To find out more about Zope visit the website at www.zope.org.

GUI DEVELOPMENT WITH TK

Python has always been seen as a tool for rapid application development (RAD) and, whilst there is a huge push towards development of web based applications, there are still sites that require GUI-based applications to interface to internal databases and systems.

There are many different toolkits out there for GUI development, including those that build on the popular QT, KDE, and Gnome GUI systems which fit on top of the X Window System. Many of these tool-kits are supported under both Perl and Python but they are limited to being used on Unix-like operating systems as they all build on the core X Windows technology.

The only cross-platform solution available is Tk which was developed along with Tcl by John Ousterhout. Tcl and Tk are available free even though Scriptics also supports a number of commercial products and systems to help in the development.

Perl and Python both support Tk, but Python has a small advantage in that it supports Tk on Unix, Windows and MacOS – Perl is limited to only Unix and Windows. Beyond that, the only other advantage of using Python over Perl for Tk development is that the Tk environment relies heavily on an object-, class-, and method-based interface to the underlying widgets. The advantage of using Python/Tk over Tcl/Tk is that that Tcl was born and designed out of the need to produce a macro language for the Unix shell to make certain operations easier. Tcl is therefore relatively limited in its abilities. Although Perl supports an object based system it is less natural to use than Python's implementation.

With all this mind, migrating from a Perl based Tk application to a Python based application is relatively easy. Because Tk is an external toolkit we only need to learn the interface to it – both languages use the same widget names and basic methods for creating and manipulating those widgets into an interface. Your most difficult job will be converting the non-Tk elements.

In this chapter we'll have a look at some of the basics of creating and using Tk widgets within the two languages. You will need to know how to create Tk widgets in Perl – we won't be looking at the specifics of individual widgets and their properties or methods. For a more complete guide to the Tkinter interface check out the online documentation written by Fredrik Lundh which you can find in the documentation section of the main Python site.

BASIC OPERATIONS

The major difference between Perl- and Python-based Tk programming is how we interact with the widgets that we create. Both systems work by creating new widgets which return objects and it's through these objects that you set their properties and create additional widgets, containers, and other interface elements to build up the individual window.

We'll have a look at four different aspects of Tk programming in relation to Perl and Python. We'll start with the basics of creating widgets before moving on to look at how we set their properties and other values. Then we'll look at how to define widget callback before finally looking at the different widget geometry systems (Packer, Placer, and Grid).

Creating widgets

To actually load the Perl interface to Tk we use:

```
use Tk;
```

With Python the interface is called **Tkinter** – you can import this module by name as:

```
import Tkinter
```

It's actually more convenient to import the objects in the module into the current namespace, because there are so many object classes defined within the module that always using the explicit name gets tiresome. It's usually enough to use:

```
from Tkinter import *
```

Although we use objects in both cases, the interaction between the objects you create and Perl and Python differs slightly. In Perl, to create a window and then to create a button widget within it, we first create our window object and then call the **Button** method on the new window to create the button, i.e.:

```
$root = MainWindow->new();
$button = $root->Button();
```

With Python, we do refer to the window that we created, but don't use a method on the window object to create the button, i.e.:

```
root = Tk()
button = Button(root)
```

Note that we've also essentially set up the relationship in reverse. In Perl the root window (or other container widget) creates the objects it owns through a series of methods. Python uses classes to create new instances of widgets which in turn accept the object to which they belong as an argument. In short, a Perl/Tk widget creates widgets it owns, and a Python/Tk widget adopts a parent widget when created.

For cross reference, I've included a list of widgets that are supported by both Perl and Python in Table 14.1.

TABLE 14.1 Some of the widgets supported by Tk

Widget class	Description
BitmapImage	A subclass of the **Image** widget for displaying bitmap images
Button	A simple push-button widget with similar properties to the **Label** widget
Canvas	A drawing area into which you can place circles, lines, text, and other graphic artefacts
Checkbutton	A multiple-choice button widget, where each item within the selection can be selected individually
Entry	A single-line text entry box
Frame	A container for arranging other widgets
Image	A simple widget for displaying bitmaps, pixmaps (color bitmaps), and other graphic objects

TABLE 14.1 *cont.*

Widget class	Description
Label	A simple box into which you can place message text (noneditable)
Listbox	A multiline list of selection choices
Menu	A list of menu selections that can be made up of **Label**, **Message**, **Button**, and other widgets
Menubutton	A menu (within a single menu bar) that lists the selections specified in a **Menu** object
Message	A multiline **Label** object (noneditable)
OptionMenu	A special type of **Menu** widget that provides a pop-up list of items within a selection
PhotoImage	A subclass of the **Image** widget for displaying full-color images
Radiobutton	A multiple-choice button widget, where you can choose only one of a multiple of values
Scale	A slider that allows you to set a value according to a specific scale
Scrollbar	A slider for controlling the contents of another widget, such as **Text** or **Canvas**
Text	A multiline text widget that supports editable text that can be also be tagged for display in different fonts and colors
Toplevel	A window that will be managed and dressed by the parent window

For a simple example of this process in action, here's a Perl script to display a simple "Hello world" button which terminates the application when pressed:

```
use Tk;

$root = MainWindow->new();
$root->title("Hello world!");
$button = $root->Button(text => 'Hello world',
                        command => \&quit_callback);

$button->pack();
MainLoop();

sub quit_callback
{
    exit(0);
}
```

The same script in Python looks like this:

```
import sys
from Tkinter import *

def main():
    root = Tk()
    button = Button(root,
                    text = 'Hello world',
                    command = quit_callback)

    button.pack()
    root.mainloop()

def quit_callback():
    sys.exit(0)

main()
```

There is only one slight difference between the overall layout of these two scripts. In the Python version we create a **main** function which actually does all the work of setting up the environment. Using a separate function is not a requirement, just the normal mode of operation for most Python scripts.

The other major difference is how we create a container window for our widgets. In Perl we do this by calling the **new**() method on the **MainWindow** class:

```
$root = MainWindow->new();
```

In Python, we create a new instance of the **Tk** class:

```
root = Tk()
```

Finally, the two scripts differ in the way we call the main loop function which then services requests and handles the callbacks and events that make up the application. In Perl we call the **MainLoop**() function. In Python we need to call the **mainloop**() method for the main window.

Setting properties

Widget properties are set in Perl by supplying the property names and values as list, using hash notation, when the widget was created. For example, to set the text label and callout for a button we'd probably use something like this:

```
$button = $root->Button(text => 'Hello, world',
                        command => \&quit_callback);
```

In Python we can more or less do the same – we supply the properties as part of the call when creating a class instance for the widget you are creating. With Python though we use keyword arguments:

```
button = Button(root, text = 'Hello, world', command =
quit_callback)
```

For reference, a list of the generic properties supported by most widgets is shown in Table 14.2.

TABLE 14.2 Generic widget properties

Property	Description
font	The font name in X or Windows format
background, bg	The color of the background, specified either by a name or hexadecimal RGB value
foreground, fg	The color of the foreground, specified either by a name or hexadecimal RGB value
text	The string to be displayed within the widget, using the foreground and font values specified
image, bitmap	The image or bitmap file to be displayed within the widget
relief	The style of the widget's border, which should be one of raised, sunken, flat, ridge, or groove
borderwidth	The width of the relief border
height	The height of the widget, specified in the number of characters for labels, buttons, and text widgets, and in pixels for all other widgets
width	The width of the widget, specified in the number of characters for labels, buttons, and text widgets, and in pixels for all other widgets
textvariable	The name of a variable to be used and/or updated when the widget changes
anchor	Defines the location of the widget within the window, or the location of the text within the widget; valid values are **n**, **ne**, **e**, **se**, **s**, **sw**, **w**, **nw**, and center

Note that some properties in some widgets share the same name as a Python keyword. These will often generate errors if you try to use a keyword argument as a property name as Python will misinterpret the name as the keyword. Most notably the **from** property used in Scale and Scrollbar widgets is known to cause problems. In this instance an alias normally exists – for example **from** becomes **from_**.

Changing existing properties

To change the properties of a widget after it has been created we need to use the **configure** method in Perl, again supplying a hash as the arguments:

```
$button->configure(text => 'Not hello world');
```

With Python each widget object operates like a dictionary, so we can update values directly by setting the corresponding property:

```
button['text'] = 'Hello, world'
```

To set multiple properties use the **configure()** method as in Perl:

```
Button.configure(text = 'Hello, world',
                 command = quit_callback)
```

Obtaining existing properties

To get a property back under Perl you must use the **cget()** method:

```
$buttontext = $button->cget('text');
```

The same method works in Python:

```
buttontext = button.cget('text')
```

However, it's probably easier to get the dictionary element directly:

```
buttontext = button['text']
```

Widget variables

When working with widgets that use variables to store their information Python and Tkinter is much more strict about the type of variable that it will work with. In Perl for example when creating a Checkbutton that has an on or off value you simply assign a reference to the variable that will hold the Checkbutton's value:

```
Checkbutton(variable => \$cbvalue)
```

The same rule applies to other variables used in conjunction with other widgets – for example, the script below uses two Scale widgets to allow you to convert between measurements in metres and feet, with the variables holding this information being the scalars **$feetscale** and **$metrescale**:

```
use Tk;

my ($feetscale, $metrescale) = (0,0);

$main = MainWindow->new();

$feetframe = $main->Frame()->pack(side => 'left');

$feetframe->Scale(command     => \&update_feet,
                  variable    => \$feetscale,
                  width       => 20,
                  length      => 400,
                  orient      => 'vertical',
                  from        => 0,
                  to          => 328,
                  resolution  => 1,
                  tickinterval => 25,
                  label       => 'Feet'
                  )->pack(side => 'top');

$feetframe->Label(textvariable => \$feetscale)-
>pack(side => 'top',
    pady => 5);

$metreframe = $main->Frame()->pack(side => 'left');

$metreframe->Scale(command     => \&update_metre,
                   variable    => \$metrescale,
                   width       => 20,
                   length      => 400,
                   orient      => 'vertical',
                   from        => 0,
                   to          => 100,
                   resolution  => 1,
                   tickinterval => 10,
                   label       => 'Metres'
                   )->pack(side => 'top');
```

```
$metreframe->Label(textvariable => \$metrescale)-
>pack(side => 'top',
    pady => 5);

MainLoop();

sub update_feet
{
    $metrescale = $feetscale/3.280839895;
}

sub update_metre
{
    $feetscale = $metrescale*3.280839895;
}
```

In Python we need to create a suitable Tk variable to hold the Checkbutton's value – you cannot use standard Python variables:

```
cbvar = IntVar()
cb = Checkbutton(master, text="Expand", variable=cbvar)
```

Tkinter actually defines a number of different variable types which you can use, these include **IntVar()**, **FloatVar()**, **StringVar()**, and **BooleanVar()**.

You cannot set or get the values in these variables directly, instead, use the **set()** and **get()** methods. You can see this more clearly in the Python version of the metre/feet conversion application shown here:

```
from Tkinter import *

def main():
    main = Tk();

    global feetscale, metrescale
    feetscale = IntVar()
    metrescale = IntVar()
    feetframe = Frame(main)

    Scale(feetframe,
            command     = update_feet,
            variable    = feetscale,
            width       = 20,
            length      = 400,
```

```
            orient      = 'vertical',
            from_       = 0,
            to          = 328,
            resolution  = 1,
            tickinterval = 25,
            label       = 'Feet'
            ).pack(side  = 'top')

    Label(feetframe,
            textvariable = feetscale
            ).pack(side = 'top',
                    pady = 5)

    feetframe.pack(side = 'left')

    metreframe = Frame(main)

    Scale(metreframe,
            command     = update_metre,
            variable    = metrescale,
            width       = 20,
            length      = 400,
            orient      = 'vertical',
            from_       = 0,
            to          = 100,
            resolution  = 1,
            tickinterval = 10,
            label       = 'Metres'
            ).pack(side  = 'top');

    Label(metreframe,
            textvariable = metrescale
            ).pack(side = 'top',
                    pady = 5)

    metreframe.pack(side = 'left');

    main.mainloop()

def update_feet(self):
    global metrescale, feetscale
    metrescale.set(int(feetscale.get()/3.280839895))
```

```
def update_metre(self):
    global metrescale, feetscale
    feetscale.set(int(metrescale.get()*3.280839895))

main()
```

You can see here that the two callbacks which contain the calculations required to convert between the two measurements require the **get()** and **set()** methods.

Widget callbacks

Callbacks in both languages are just functions that you define which are called when a particular event occurs. With Perl the function is "dumb" and not provided with information when it is called, although you could conceivably discover this information through closures. This means that to modify the value of a widget you must use global variables to hold the widgets you expect to modify. It also means that we cannot change the properties within the widget that triggered the event. For example, to change our 'Hello world' example so that it changed the message text to 'Quit' and changed the callback method to the real **quit_callback()** function:

```
sub change_message
{
    $button->configure(text => 'Quit!',
                       command => \&quit_callback);
}
```

Under Python, all callback functions are called with a single argument – the widget which invoked it. Using this object we can modify the widget that invoked the callback directly:

```
def change_message(self)
{
    self.configure(text = 'Quit!',
                   command = quit_callback);
}
```

Also note that when assigning a callback to a property in Python we do not need to explicitly pass a reference to the callback function – Python automatically supplies a reference to the function.

Widget geometry

Both language's implementations of Tk support three different geometry systems for organizing widget layouts within windows or other container widgets. The three systems are Packer, Grid, and Placer. The basic operation for all three systems is identical – you call the corresponding method (**pack()**, **grid()**, or **place()**) supplying options. In Perl you do this through a hash and in Python through a series of keyword arguments.

For example, to pack a widget aligned to the top of a parent frame widget in Perl we'd probably use something like:

```
$button->pack(side => 'top');
```

Whilst in Python we'd use:

```
button.pack(side = 'top')
```

Also note that because of the way Tkinter works there are some small differences in the order in which you should pack your objects. In Perl it's popular to both create and pack the widget at the same time, i.e.:

```
$feetframe = $main->Frame()->pack(side => 'left');
```

We can then populate the frame with the other widgets without having to redefine the geometry options for the container widget.

In Python we can do the same direct operation:

```
feetframe = Frame(main).pack(side = 'left')
```

But we don't physically get the same results. What actually happens is that Packer tries to pack the widget into the frame *before* being aware of the other objects. In this example, taken from our earlier metre/feet conversion scale application, we end up with two scale widgets, one on top of the other, rather than next to each other, even though in all other respects the formatting and definition of the widgets and calls to Packer are the same.

DIALOG BOX SAMPLE

For one final example, here are two scripts which define functions for creating simple dialog boxes in Tk. The Perl version is shown below. The dialog box accepts a list of arguments which set the parent widget, dialog box title, lead-in text, bitmap, the default button selection (activated when you press

Return), and a list of further button options. The return value is the number of the button that was pressed, or zero if the default was selected.

```perl
#! /usr/local/bin/perl -w

use Tk;

sub dialog
{
    my ($master, $title, $text, $bitmap, $default,
    @butdefs) = @_;

    $w = MainWindow->new();
    $w->title($title);
    $w->iconname('Dialog');

    $top = $w->Frame(relief => 'raised', borderwidth => 1);
    $top->pack(side => 'top', fill => 'both');
    $bot = $w->Frame(relief => 'raised', borderwidth => 1);
    $bot->pack(side => 'bottom', fill => 'both');

    $msg = $top->Message(width => '3i',
                        text => $text,
                        font=>'-Adobe-Times-Medium-R-
                        Normal-*-180-*');

    $msg->pack(side    => 'right',
                expand => 1,
                fill    => 'both',
                padx    => '3m',
                pady    => '3m');

    if (defined($bitmap))
    {
    $bm = $top->Label(bitmap => $bitmap);
    $bm->pack(side => 'left',
            padx => '3m',
            pady => '3m');
    }
my $i = 0;
my $retval = 0;
my %buttons;
```

```perl
my %revbutton;
foreach $but (@butdefs)
{
    my $b = undef;
    if ($i == $default)
    {
        $bd = $bot->Frame(relief      => 'sunken',
                          borderwidth => 1);
        $bd->pack(side   => 'left',
                  expand => 1,
                  padx   => '3m',
                  pady   => '2m');

        $b = $bd->Button(text => $but);
        $b->configure(command => sub {$retval =
        $revbutton{$b} });

        $b->pack(in    => $bd,
                 side  => 'left',
                 padx  => '2m',
                 pady  => '2m',
                 ipadx => '2m',
                 ipady => '1m');
    }
    else
    {
        $b = $bot->Button(text => $but);
        $b->configure(command => sub { $retval =
        $revbutton{$b} });
        $b->pack(side   => 'left',
                 expand => 1,
                 padx   => '3m',
                 pady   => '3m',
                 ipadx  => '2m',
                 ipady  => '1m');
    }
    $buttons{$i} = $b;
    $revbutton{$b} = $but;
    $i++;
}
```

```
    if ($default >= 0)
    {
        $w->bind('<Return>',
                 sub { $buttons{$default}->flash(),
                       ($retval = $default) });
    }

    $w->waitVariable(\$retval);
    $w->destroy();
    return $retval;
}

$ret = dialog(undef,"Warning","Overwrite file?",
              'warning',1,"OK","Cancel");
print "Button $ret was pressed\n";

MainLoop();
```

For example, to create a dialog box that asks the user to confirm whether they want to delete a file you'd probably use:

```
$ret = dialog(undef,"Warning","Overwrite file?",
              'warning',1,"OK","Cancel");
```

The resulting window would look something like the window shown in Fig 14.1.

FIG 14.1 Dialog box from Perl

The Python version is shown below.

```python
#! /usr/bin/env python

from Tkinter import *
import sys

def dialog(master, title, text, bitmap, default, *args):
    w = Toplevel(master, class_='Dialog')
    w.title(title)
    w.iconname('Dialog')

    top = Frame(w, relief=RAISED, borderwidth=1)
    top.pack(side=TOP, fill=BOTH)
    bot = Frame(w, relief=RAISED, borderwidth=1)
    bot.pack(side=BOTTOM, fill=BOTH)

    msg = Message(top, width='3i', text=text,
                  font='-Adobe-Times-Medium-R-Normal-*-
                  180-*')
    msg.pack(side=RIGHT, expand=1, fill=BOTH,
             padx='3m', pady='3m')
    if bitmap:
        bm = Label(top, bitmap=bitmap)
        bm.pack(side=LEFT, padx='3m', pady='3m')

    var = IntVar()
    buttons = []
    i = 0
    for but in args:
        b = Button(bot, text=but, command=lambda
        v=var,i=i: t(i))
        buttons.append(b)
        if i == default:
            bd = Frame(bot, relief=SUNKEN, borderwidth=1)
            bd.pack(side=LEFT, expand=1,
                    padx='3m', pady='2m')
            b.lift()
            b.pack (in_=bd, side=LEFT,
                    padx='2m', pady='2m',
                    ipadx='2m', ipady='1m')
```

```
        else:
            b.pack (side=LEFT, expand=1,
                    padx='3m', pady='3m',
                    ipadx='2m', ipady='1m')
        i = i+1

        if default >= 0:
            w.bind('<Return>',
                    lambda e, b=buttons[default], v=var,
                    i=default:
                    (b.flash(),
                     v.set(i)))

        oldFocus = w.focus_get()
        w.grab_set()
        w.focus_set()

        w.waitvar(var)
        w.destroy()
        if oldFocus: oldFocus.focus_set()
        return var.get()
```

To call the function to provide the same dialog box as before we'd use:

```
i = dialog(None,'Warning','Overwrite file?',
            'warning',1,'OK','Cancel')
```

The resulting dialog box should be identical to the one in Fig 14.1.

>> APPENDICES

PYTHON RESOURCES

Like most modern scripting languages – and indeed any modern, open-source development project – Python is heavily supported in the programming community through the Internet. The main web site is www.python.org, which provides the most comprehensive guide to the Python language and its available resources, both on and off the web.

WEB RESOURCES

Much of Python's success comes from the users who provide feedback to the Python development team, suggest new features and changes to the language semantics, and help identify and fix bugs. This information ultimately reaches Guido van Rossum, the designer and developer of the Python language, although there are now many other people who aid the development of the language. Most of this information is exchanged on the Internet, either through e-mail, newsgroups, or the various Python websites. Of course, we can't describe everything available, due to the sheer fluidity of the Internet. But there are some choice areas of the main Python site, as well as other sites that deserve a special mention. The entries listed here should give you a good spread of the most useful resources.

www.python.org

The main focus point for everything to do with Python. This site is managed by volunteers from Python Software Activity. They include a number of Python fanatics, all dedicated to the long-term success of Python as a scripting language. The site also contains all the online documentation, which is available both for searching online and for downloading from the site. Included here are HTML, PostScript, and Acrobat PDF versions of the documentation for you to use at home.

python.sourceforge.net

PythonLabs, the development team responsible for Python development, moved to SourceForge, one of the many free software communities in October 2000. Although most of the development and news about Python continues on the main Python website, new versions and daily snapshots of the current development versions of Python and its documentation appear here on SourceForge.

www.python.org/psa

The site is the homepage of Python Software Activity. PSA raises funds, supports new development, hosts conferences, and operates the various Internet-based services that support Python development. PSA requests membership fees from people who wish to help in the further development of Python. At the time of writing, this membership cost $50 for an individual, or $500 for an organization.

www.python.org/sigs

A significant portion of the Python development and promotion comes from various special interest groups (SIGs). These have limited lives while different development projects are in progress. The list at the beginning of February 2001 looked like Table A.1, but use the URL above for a more up-to-date list. Note that the expiry dates were correct at the time of going to press, most of the discussion have become continuing works in progress.

Each list is supported via a mailing list. Anybody can join a SIG and get involved in the discussion and even in the development of a particular part of the Python development process.

www.python.org/cgi-bin/todo.py

This URL points to a Python CGI script that provides a list of all the currently requested and outstanding "To Do" items for Python development.

www.jython.org

The homepage of the Jython project, includes the downloadable components, documentation, samples, and pointers to further information on Jython and where it's used.

TABLE A.1 Python PSA special interest groups

Name	Description	Coordinator	Expires
catalog-sig	The Python software catalog, dealing with cataloging Python's modules, packages and other resources	Andrew Kuchling	June 2002
db-sig	Databases (currently working on creating a common tabular database API, amongst other things)	Andrew Kuchling	June 2002
distutils-sig	Distribution utilities	Greg Ward	June 2002
do-sig	Distributed Object Technologies	David Arnold	June 2002
doc-sig	Documentation (covering both tools and content)	Fred Drake	June 2002
edu-sig	Python in Education (spreading the word on Python, and getting Python promoted as programming for everybody)	Timothy Wilson	December 2002
i18n-sig	Internationalization and localization, including Unicode	Andy Robinson	June 2002
image-sig	Image Processing	Fredrik Lundh	June 2002
import-sig	Import architecture redesign	Gordon McMillan	June 2002
meta-sig	SIG about the SIGs	Guido van Rossum	Never
pythonmac-sig	On Apple Macintosh	Jack Jansen	Never
types-sig	Static typing design	Paul Prescod	June 2002
xml-sig	XML Processing	Andrew Kuchling	June 2002

www.mailman.org

The home of the Mailman mailing list software. Mailman is written entirely in Python and provides all of the normal features of a mailing list manager, from e-mail-based subscriptions, digests, and secure authentication of subscribers. In addition, it sports a web front end, both for subscribers to existing lists, and also for the managers of the lists themselves.

www.zope.org

Zope is a web publishing and content management system that allows multiple people to manage the content of a website. In addition to the basic content facilities, Zope also provides conduits (called factories) for importing information from external sources including the traditional database and less-conventional POP, IMAP, and NNTP sources.

starship.python.net

The Python Starship site was set up as an extension to the main www.python.org site to provide a medium for community cooperation on Python projects. Starship Python is supported by Digital Creations, the people behind the development of Zope, and also now the people supporting the developers of Perl itself.

www.pythonjournal.com

The Python Journal was an online magazine for Python programmers. The first issue was a huge success, and the second issue appeared in June 1999. However, no further issues have been forthcoming and more attention has been paid to some of the daily resources, such as the O'Reilly Python update and sites like LinuxProgramming.com.

python.ora.com

The home of the O'Reilly Python effort, including information on their books, and also regularly updated news and related articles on the Python development and programming.

www.pythonware.com

Python has spawned a number of commercial companies aiming to provide a more stable, and obviously attractive, Python solution. One of these companies is Secret Labs AB, and PythonWare is their website. They are currently developing a RAD (Rapid Application Development) environment called PythonWorks for Python based on the core Python language with some specific extensions developed in house for interfaces, graphics, and image processing.

www.activestate.com

ActiveState are perhaps better known for their work in producing the original Windows port of Perl. However, in recent years they have concentrated on extending their product range by not only supporting an extended Perl installation (with additional documentation and features) for Windows, but also a similar product for Linux and Solaris.

More recently still they have been licensed to release a similar product for Python. In addition to all of the core functionality offered by the ActivePython product, ActiveState are also working on a development environment and debuggers and other platform specific extensions for Python.

Most interestingly, ActiveState are working with Microsoft (who help fund them) to produce VisualPerl and VisualPython products. These will allow owners of the VisualStudio development environment to have access to the same integrated development environment, debugger, and other tools, available to existing C/C++/VisualBasic developers.

www.cdrom.com

Walnut Creek, who run www.cdrom.com, produce a number of free CDs, including the Python Tools CD. Python Tools includes both the Python language in all of its different platform versions, with all of the modules available and a huge amount of online documentation archived from the main Python Internet site. This CD is a must have if you don't want to download the information from the website manually.

E-MAIL, NEWSGROUP, AND MAILING LIST RESOURCES

Most of the general, day-to-day discussion and support for Python is handled by a variety of Usenet newsgroups and mailing lists. Beyond those listed below, you will find that specific topics are also discussed by the different Python SIGs; see the information on the websites above for more details.

comp.lang.python

This is the primary, high-volume, and open newsgroup for general discussion about Python. You can also pose questions here and have them answered by other readers. Obviously this newsgroup generates a lot of traffic, but the information content is quite high.

You can also subscribe to a mailing list of the messages posted to the newsgroup. You can use this if you don't have direct access to Usenet newsgroups, or if you'd just prefer to get information sent to you by e-mail.

The list itself is actually maintained by Mailman, a mailing list system endorsed by the FSF (Free Software Foundation) and written entirely in Python. You can join either by visiting www.python.org/mailman/

listinfo/python-list, or you can send an e-mail containing only the word "subscribe" in the body to python-list-request@python.org. You can also post to the list (even when you are not a subscriber) by mailing your message to python-list@python.org.

comp.lang.python.announce

This low-bandwidth newsgroup is used only for broadcasting announce-ments about Python without promoting discussion. As such, this group is moderated, although anybody can post, provided they have something useful to say.

Again, you can subscribe to a mailing list that duplicates the information on the newsgroup either through the Web page at www.python.org/mailman/listinfo/python-announce-list, or you can send an e-mail con-taining only the word "subscribe" in the body to python-announce-list-request@python.org. You can also post to the list (even though you may not be a subscriber) by mailing your message to python-announce-list@python.org.

python-help@python.org

Also known as help@python.org, this e-mail account is actually handled by a group of Python volunteers who answer questions from users in a closed environment. The postings to this e-mail address are sent to the team of experts, and further communication is handled by e-mail. It's not possible to read the posts or access archives of the messages posted.

tutor@python.org

Similar to the help@python.org address, this e-mail account should be used by people who are trying to learn programming using Python. The differ-ence is that this is a full-discussion e-mail list where people can exchange ideas, within the confines of e-mail, but still effectively in the view of the general public. You can join via the web page www.python.org/mailman/listinfo/tutor.

jpython-interest@python.org

If you are interested in the JPython product then this list will you help you use the package and enable you to discuss problems with other users. More information, and details on how to join, are available at www.python.org/mailman/listinfo/jpython-interest.

ONLINE DOCUMENTATION

The main Python website has a documentation area (www.python.org/doc/) where you can access online all of the Python documentation. The documentation is written and managed by Fred Drake, one of the main developers in the PythonLabs team. You can also download documentation in HTML, PostScript, Acrobat PDF and LaTeX formats. The documentation is split into a number of sections, listed here in Table A.2.

TABLE A.2 Different Python documentation sections

Section	Description
api	Details the C API you can use to extend and/or embed Python
dist	Covers the development of tools for distributing Python modules from the developers point of view
doc	Outlines the methods and tools used for documenting Python and Python programs
ext	Covers the methodologies behind extending and embedding Python – see the **api** document for information on the API itself
inst	Covers the methods for installing third-party Python modules from the end-user point of view
lib	Covers the standard library of modules and extensions supplied with Python
mac	Details the Mac specific extensions and components for using Python
ref	The Python reference manual covers all of the core components of the Python interpreter from the semantics of the language and operators and expressions and statements
tut	A tutorial to learning how to use Python

HTML can be the most practical if you want to create a "home" website with all the documentation on it. Better still, if you have access to a full version of Acrobat (not the Reader) you can use the indexing facility on the PDF version of the documentation to search across all of the individual documents.

PRINT RESOURCES

Python is still a relatively new language, and has not been picked up by many publishers. The list below is almost the entire catalogue of Python books. As the list is currently so small, all of the books are worth having on your shelf for the reference information they provide. (In combination with this book of course!)

Brown, M. C. (1999) *Python Annotated Archives***. Berkeley, CA: Osborne/McGraw-Hill.**
A guide to programming with Python from the point of view of the finished application, rather than the semantics of the language. All of the examples are annotated, line by line, with additional guides and content as required throughout the book.

Harms, D., McDonald, K. (1999) *The Quick Python Book***. Greenwich, CT: Manning Publications.**
A good clear guide to the basics of the Python language, taken from the perspective of existing programmers who don't know the Python syntax.

Beazley, D. (1999) *Python Essential Reference***. Indianapolis, IN: New Riders.**
A combination of tutorial and reference manual – and one of the most concise all round references to the language. This should give you everything you need to start programming effectively with Python.

Lutz, M. (1996) & Ascher, D. (1999) *Learning Python***. Sebastapol, CA: O'Reilly.**
This good teaching guide introduces Python from its initial features and layout, right through to the complexities of using Python as a complete OO environment. It's a good starting point for learning the proper semantics of the Python language.

Lutz, M. (1996) Programming Python. Sebastapol, CA: O'Reilly.
The companion to *Learning Python*, this is the reference guide to the language. It covers everything about the Python language in great detail. There are a few missing components that users of other languages might find frustrating, but on the whole this is the Python bible.

Watters, A., van Rossum, G. & Ahlstrom, J.C. (1996) *Internet Programming with Python.* **New York: M&T Books.**
This good introductory book concentrates on using Python as a language for developing Internet applications. This is not limited to the typical CGI applications to be used with web servers, but also includes using Python for network programming (including some in-depth examples of communication protocols) and how to embed the Python interpreter within other Internet applications.

PERL TO PYTHON QUICK REFERENCE

You can use this guide as a quick reference for converting your existing Perl scripts to Python. Below you will find a list of the major Perl components, their Python equivalent if one exists, or an alternative solution if it's supported. You'll also find the necessary pointers to take you to a chapter with more detailed information.

Perl	Python equivalent	Reference
$!, $ERRNO, $OS_ERROR	Errors and messages are handled through the exception system. If you need to translate error numbers to strings use the **os.strerror()** function. To compare error numbers use the **errno** module	96
$", $LIST_SEPARATOR	Use **string.join()** to manually bond lists together	189
$#, $OFMT	Use the **format % tuple** operator to format a number	68
$$, $PID, $PROCESS_ID	**os.getpid()**	176
$%, $FORMAT_PAGE_NUMBER	N/A	–
$&, $MATCH	You'll need to use a **Match** object returned by the functions in the **re** module to obtain the matches for individual groups	201
$(, $GID, $REAL_GROUP_ID	**os.getgid()**	176
$), $EFFECTIVE_GROUP_ID, $EGID	**os.getegid()**	176

Perl	Python equivalent	Reference
$*, $MULTILINE_MATCHING	Use the **M** flag to the functions in the **re** module to perform multiline matches and substitutions	199
$-, $FORMAT_LINES_LEFT	N/A	–
$', $POSTMATCH	You'll need to use a **Match** object returned by the functions in the **re** module to obtain the matches for individual groups	201
$,, $OFS, $OUTPUT_FIELD _SEPARATOR	You need to explicitly define any output record separator during data output	–
$., $NR, $INPUT_LINE _NUMBER	Use a counter within a loop to get this information	–
$/, $RS, $INPUT_RECORD _SEPARATOR	You'll need to manually read the information and then use **string.split()** on a specific character to emulate this functionality	189
$:, $FORMAT_LINE_BREAK _CHARACTERS	N/A	–
$;, $SUBSCRIPT _SEPARATOR, $SUBSEP	N/A	–
$?, $CHILD_ERROR	You'll need to use the return value from the **wait()** call to determine the child's exit status	191
$@, $EVAL_ERROR	Errors through Python's **exec** statement and **eval()** function are handled through the exception mechanism	147
$[	N/A	–
$\, $ORS, $OUTPUT _RECORD_SEPARATOR	The **print** statement automatically adds the correct line separator for the current platform. To determine the correct value, access the **os.linesep** object. Note that changing the value of this object does not affect the **print** statement	176
$], $OLD_PERL_VERSION	**sys.version[0]**	170
$^, $FORMAT_TOP_NAME	N/A	–
$^A, $ACCUMULATOR	N/A	–
$^C, $COMPILING	N/A	–
$^D, $DEBUGGING	N/A	–
$^E, $EXTENDED_OS_ERROR	N/A	–

Perl	Python equivalent	Reference
$ ^ F, $SYSTEM_FD_MAX	N/A	–
$ ^ H	N/A	–
$ ^ I, $INPLACE_EDIT	N/A	–
$ ^ L, $FORMAT_FORMFEED	N/A	–
$ ^ M	N/A	–
$ ^ O, $OSNAME	**sys.platform()** – alternatively use **os.uname()** under Unix to get a more detailed description	173, 177
$ ^ P, $PERLDB	N/A	–
$ ^ R, $LAST_REGEXP_CODE _RESULT	N/A	–
$ ^ S, $EXCEPTIONS_BEING _CAUGHT	N/A	–
$ ^ T, $BASETIME	N/A	–
$ ^ V, $PERL_VERSION	**sys.version** – actually returns a list, elements zero and one are the major and minor version numbers for the interpreter	170
$ ^ W, $WARNING	N/A	–
$ ^ X, $EXECUTABLE_NAME	**sys.executable()**	–
$_, $ARG	N/A	–
$`, $PREMATCH	You'll need to use a **Match** object returned by the functions in the **re** module to obtain the matches for individual groups	201
${ ^ WARNING_BITS}	N/A	–
${ ^ WIDE_SYSTEM_CALLS}	N/A	–
$|, $AUTOFLUSH, $OUTPUT _AUTOFLUSH	Use **f.flush()** to manually flush output to a file	215
$~, $FORMAT_NAME	N/A	–
$+, $LAST_PAREN_MATCH	You'll need to use a **Match** object returned by the functions in the **re** module to obtain the matches for individual groups	201
$<, $REAL_USER_ID, $UID	**os.getuid()**	–
$=, $FORMAT_LINES_PER _PAGE	N/A	–
$>, $EFFECTIVE_USER_ID, $EUID	**os.geteuid()**	–
$0, $PROGRAM_NAME	**sys.argv[0]**	–

Perl	Python equivalent	Reference
$0..x	You'll need to use a **Match** object returned by the functions in the **re** module to obtain the matches for individual groups. To include a group within a regular expression replacement string use the \\# format	201
$ARGV	N/A	–
%^H	N/A	–
%ENV	**os.environ/os.putenv()** – the **os.environ** object is a mapping object, so changes to the elements within the object are reflected in the environment variables for the current process. This is identical to the **%ENV** hash in Perl	175
%INC	**sys.modules** – the **sys.modules** list includes information about the module names, where they were loaded from, and also their aliaswithin the symbol table	171
%SIG	**signal.getsignal()**, **signal.signal()** – you must use the **signal** module to install or release signal handlers	183
@-	Use the Match object returned by the functions in the **re** module to get individual matches	201
@_, @ARG	Arguments are extracted from a function call by name in the function definition	–
@+	Use the Match object returned by the functions in the **re** module to get individual matches	201
@ARGV	**sys.argv[1:]**	67
@INC	**sys.path**	127, 172
@ISA	Class inheritance is handled on a class by class basis. During class definition you can access the base classes for a class using the __**bases**__ attribute for a given class	135
_ (stat/lstat filehandle cache)	N/A	–
abs()	**abs()**	140
accept()	**s.accept()**	232

Perl	Python equivalent	Reference
alarm()	**signal.alarm()**	183
atan2()	**math.atan2(), cmath.atan2()**	–
bind()	**s.bind()**	231
binmode()	N/A	–
bless()	N/A	–
caller()	**traceback.print_tb()**	–
chdir()	**os.chdir()**	176
chmod()	**os.chmod()**	226
chomp()	**string.strip(), string.rstrip()**	189
chop()	N/A	–
chown()	**os.chown()**	226
chr()	**chr()**	143
chroot()	N/A	–
close()	**f.close(), s.close()**	215, 232
closedir()	Use **glob.glob()** to get a list of files and iterate over the list	–
connect()	**s.connect()**	232
continue	N/A	–
cos()	**math.cos(), cmath.cos()**	–
crypt()	**crypt.crypt()**	187
dbmclose()	N/A	–
dbmopen()	**anydbm.open()**	189
defined()	N/A	–
delete()	del	–
die()	**raise()**	116
do()	**execfile()**	147
dump()	N/A	–
each()	N/A	–
endgrent()	N/A	–
endhostent()	N/A	–
endnetent()	N/A	–

Perl	Python equivalent	Reference
endprotoent()	N/A	–
endpwent()	N/A	–
endservent()	N/A	–
eof()	N/A	–
eval()	**eval(), exec()**	147
exec()	**sys.exec()**	177
exists()	**dict.has_key()**	59
exit()	**sys.exit()**	169
exp()	**math.exp(), cmath.exp()**	–
fcntl()	**fcntl.fcntl()**	–
fileno()	**f.fileno()**	215
flock()	**fcntl.flock()**	–
fork	**os.fork()**	182
format()	N/A	–
formline()	N/A	–
getc()	**f.getc()**	–
getgrent()	**grp.getgrall()**	–
getgrgid()	**grp.getgrgid()**	–
getgrnam()	**grp.getgrnam()**	–
gethostbyaddr()	**socket.gethostbyaddr()**	237
gethostbyname()	**socket.gethostbyname()**	–
gethostent()	N/A	–
getlogin()	N/A	–
getnetbyaddr()	N/A	–
getnetbyname()	N/A	–
getnetent()	N/A	–
getpeername()	**s.getpeername()**	232
getpgrp	**os.getpgrp()**	176
getppid	**os.getppid()**	176
getpriority()	N/A	–
getprotobyname()	**socket.getprotobyname()**	237
getprotobynumber()	N/A	–

Perl	Python equivalent	Reference
getprotoent()	N/A	–
getpwent()	**pwd.getpwall()**	–
getpwnam()	**pwd.pwnam()**	–
getpwuid()	**pwd.pwuid()**	–
getservbyname()	N/A	–
getservbyport()	N/A	–
getservent()	N/A	–
getsockname()	**s.getsockname()**	232
getsockopt()	**s.getsockopt()**	232
glob()	**glob.glob()**	222
gmtime()	**time.gmtime()**	–
goto	N/A	–
grep()	**filter()**	148
hex()	**eval()** will work for strings of the form "Oxffff" – without a leading **0x** this will be interpreted as an identifier and raise an exception	147
import()	**import, from**	120
index()	**string.index(), string.find()**	189
int()	**int()**	151
ioctl()	**fcntl.ioctl()**	–
join()	**string.join()**	189
keys()	**dict.keys()**	59, 206
kill()	**os.kill()**	183
last()	break	81
lc()	**string.lower()**	189
lcfirst()	N/A	–
length()	**len()**	152
link()	**os.link()**	–
listen()	**s.listen()**	232
local	N/A	–
localtime()	**time.localtime()**	–
log()	**math.log(), cmath.log()**	–

Perl	Python equivalent	Reference
lstat()	**os.lstat()**	226
m//	**re.match(), re.findall()**	201, 200
map()	**map()**	153
mkdir()	**os.mkdir()**	223
msgctl()	N/A	–
msgget()	N/A	–
msgrcv()	N/A	–
msgsnd()	N/A	–
my	N/A	–
next()	continue	81
no	N/A	–
oct()	**eval()** will work for strings of the form "0377" – without a leading zero this will be interpreted as a decimal	147
open()	**open(), os.popen(), os.open()**	62, 179
opendir()	Use **glob.glob()** to get a list of files and iterate over the list	222
ord()	**ord()**	157
pack()	**struct.pack()**	–
package	N/A	–
pipe()	**os.pipe()**	–
pop()	**list.pop()**	56
pos()	**m.pos()**	201
print()	print, **f.write(), s.send()**	140, 215, 232
printf()	print format % tuple	68
prototype()	N/A	–
push()	**list.append()**	56
q/STRING/	N/A	–
qq/STRING/	N/A	–
qr//	**re.escape()**	2–5
quotemeta()	**re.compile()**	2–3

Perl	Python equivalent	Reference
qw//	N/A	–
qx//	**os.exec*()**	177
rand()	**whrandom.random()**, **whrandom.randint()**	–
read()	**f.read(), s.recv()**	215, 232
readdir()	N/A	–
readline()	**f.readline()**	215
readlink()	**os.readlink()**	–
readpipe()	**os.read()**	–
recv()	**s.recv()**	232
redo()	N/A	–
ref()	**type()**	162
rename()	**os.rename()**	223
require	N/A	–
reset()	N/A	–
return()	return	89
reverse()	**s.reverse()**	56
rewinddir()	N/A	–
rindex()	**string.rfind(), string.rindex()**	189
rmdir()	**os.rmdir()**	223
s///	**re.sub(), re.subn()**	202, 203
scalar()	N/A	–
seek()	**os.lseek(), f.seek()**	215
seekdir()	Use **glob.glob()** to get a list of files and iterate over the list	222
select (default filehandle selection)	You can redirect the standard output by re-opening **sys.stdout** to point to an alternative file or other filehandle object. Use **sys.__stdout__** to print to the original	168
select() (polling input)	**select.select()**	–
semctl()	N/A	–

Perl	Python equivalent	Reference
semget()	N/A	–
semop()	N/A	–
send()	**s.send()**	232
setgrent()	N/A	–
sethostent()	N/A	–
setnetent()	N/A	–
setpgrp()	**os.setpgrp()**	177
setpriority()	N/A	–
setprotoent()	N/A	–
setpwent()	N/A	–
setservent()	N/A	–
setsockopt()	**s.setsockopt()**	232
shift()	**s.pop(0)**	56
shmctl()	N/A	–
shmget()	N/A	–
shmread()	N/A	–
shmwrite()	N/A	–
shutdown()	**s.shutdown()**	232
sin()	**math.sin()**, **cmath.sin()**	–
sleep()	**time.sleep()**	–
socket()	**socket.socket()**	232
socketpair()	N/A	–
sort()	**s.sort()**	56
splice()	array[x:y] = [a,b]	54
split()	**string.split()**, **re.split()**	189, 193
sprintf()	Use the **format % tuple** operator, which returns a formatted string	68
sqrt()	**math.sqrt()**, **cmath.sqrt()**	–
srand()	**whrandom.seed()**	–
stat()	**os.stat()**	224
STDERR	**sys.stderr** (original version always available in **sys.__stderr__**)	168

Perl	Python equivalent	Reference
STDIN	**sys.stdin** (original version always available in **sys.__stdin__**)	168
STDOUT	**sys.stdout** (original version always available in **sys.__stdout__**)	168
study()	N/A	–
sub	def (for anonymous subroutines use the **lambda** statement)	85, 94
substr()	s[x:y]	50
symlink()	**os.symlink()**	223
syscall()	N/A	–
sysopen()	**sys.open()**	–
sysread()	**f.read()**	215
sysseek()	**f.sysseek()**	–
system()	**os.system()**	178
syswrite()	**f.write()**	215
tell()	**f.tell()**	215
telldir()	N/A	–
tie()	N/A	–
tied()	N/A	–
time()	**time.time()**	–
times()	**os.times()**	–
tr///	**string.maketrans()**, **string.translate()**	189
truncate()	**f.truncate()**	215
uc()	**string.upper()**	189
ucfirst()	**string.captilize()**	189
umask()	**os.umask()**	177
undef	None	–
unlink()	**os.remove()**, **os.unlink()**	223
unpack()	**struct.unpack()**	–
unshift()	**s.insert(0,x)**	54
untie()	N/A	–
use	import	118
utime()	**os.utime()**	–

Perl	Python equivalent	Reference
values()	**dict.values()**	59
vec()	**struct.pack()**	–
wait()	**os.wait()**	182
waitpid()	**os.waitpid()**	182
wantarray()	N/A	–
warn()	N/A	–
write()	**sys.write()**, **f.write()**	215
-X (filetests)	**os.access()**, **os.stat()**	224

INDEX